PROFESSIONAL DIVERS'
LOG BOOK

SPECIAL NOTE: This edition of the Professional Divers' Log
Book includes updating and changes to
conform to the regulations and guidelines as
set forth by the following governments:

Australia	Ireland
Brazil	Mexico
Canada	New Zealand
England	Norway
France	Scotland
Iceland	United States

First Published 1978
Second Printing 1982
Third Printing 1986
Fourth Printing 1991

ISBN 0-941332-01-2 BEST PUBLISHING COMPANY
COPYRIGHT© 1986 BEST PUBLISHING COMPANY

INSTRUCTIONS:

The following matters shall be entered in the diver's log book in respect of each diving operation in which he takes part:

(a) the name and address of the diving contractor;

(b) the date;

(c) the name or other designation and the location of the offshore installation, work site, craft or harbor from which the diving operation was carried on;

(d) the name of the diving supervisor;

(e) the maximum depth reached on each occasion;

(f) the time he left the surface, his bottom time and the time he reached the surface on each occasion;

(g) where the dive includes time spent in a compression chamber, details of any time spent outside the chamber at a different pressure;

(h) the type of breathing apparatus and mixture used by him;

(i) any work done by him on each occasion and the equipment (including tools) used by him in that work;

(j) any decompression schedules followed by him on each occasion;

(k) any decompression sickness or other illness, discomfort or injury suffered by him;

(l) any other factor relevant to his safety or health.

This professional diver's log book is the results of the efforts of the

ASSOCIATION OF COMMERCIAL DIVING EDUCATORS

The objectives of the Association are:

1. To provide lines of communicaiton between and among the schools and the programs within schools which offer diver training in the United States;

2. To operate as liaison between and among government agencies, the Association of Diving Contractors and other representative organizations, and various unions, to the extent that the activities of these agencies affect commercial diving and/or commercial diver education;

3. To research and identify employment opportunities in commercial diving;

4. To work toward the standardization of the classification of diver training programs through the establishment of minimum parameters for curricula, hours, equipment, and other factors relating to excellence of diver training;

5. To identify areas of problem or need which may affect the quality of diver training, the efficiency and safety of divers, or any other aspect related to the objectives of the Association, and to take action in finding solutions as appropriate;

6. To promote commercial diving as a career.

INSTRUCTIONS

1. This Log Book conforms to the requirements of the regulations issued by the following authorities:

   United States Coast Guard

   United States Department of Labor
   Occupational Safety and Health Administration

   United Kingdom's Health and Safety at Work
   (Diving Operators) Regulations

   Director of Shipping, Reykjavic, Iceland

   New Zealand Ministry of Energy

   Western Australian Department of Mines

   Victorian Department of Minerals and Energy

   Canada Government

2. Identification of the person to whom this Log Book refers should be by photograph in the appropriate place; the photograph/page to be overstamped by the issuing diving school or company. The diver's signature also is required in the space provided.

3. Every diver shall present his Log Book to the doctor examining him and a medical examination meeting the requirements of the appropriate authority must be carried out by a registered/licensed medical practitioner qualified in diving medicine. Such examinations must be continuously updated in accordance with the regulations in force.

4. On every day on which he takes part in a diving operation a diver shall record in his Log Book the matters set out on the page "Record of Dive," and he shall sign each entry and it shall be countersigned by the diving supervisor.

5. The Log Book must be available and produced on demand to prospective employers and compliance officers/inspectors of authority.

6. The diver/tender shall maintain a Log Book as a personal record in which he shall enter dive data on every day on which he takes part in a diving operation.

7. All entries shall be made in ink.

8. The Log Book shall be retained by the diver/tender for a minimum of four years from the date of the last entry.

PERSONAL INFORMATION

Surname _____

First Names _____

Date of Birth ___/___/19___   Place of Birth _____

Address _____

City/State/Country _____

_____

Citizenship_____

Passport Number _____

Social Security Number _____

Change of Address: _____

_____

Change of Address: _____

_____

Change of Address: _____

_____

Change of Address: _____

_____

Signature _____

Photograph
(head)
1¾" x 2" min.
(50 x 45mm)

School or Company
Stamp to Be Placed Over
Photograph and Page

RECORD OF MEDICAL INFORMATION

Name _____

Blood Type _____ Rh _____

Sex _____ Race _____ Religion Preference _____

Date of Birth _____ Place of Birth _____

Height _____ Weight _____

Color Hair _____ Color Eyes _____

Abnormalities or Limitations:

Type	Date Identified
_____	/ /19 _____
_____	/ /19 _____
_____	/ /19 _____
_____	/ /19 _____

Allergies/Reactions to Medication:

Medication or Substance	Date of Reaction
_____	/ /19 _____
_____	/ /19 _____
_____	/ /19 _____

Pressure and Oxygen Tolerance Test:

Date ___/___/___   Date ___/___/___   Date ___/___/___

Depth _____   Depth _____   Depth _____

Time _____   Time _____   Time _____

Medical or Religious Objection to Blood Transfusion ☐ Yes   ☐ No

Details of Inoculation and Other Injections:

Date	Type	Date	Type
_____	_____	_____	_____
_____	_____	_____	_____
_____	_____	_____	_____

Person to Be Notified in Case of an Emergency:

_____
(Name)

_____
(Address)

_____
(City/State/Country)

_____
(Telephone)   (Relationship — father, brother, friend, wife, etc.)

RECORD OF MEDICAL EXAMINATION

Name of Person Examined _____

Date of Examination _____

Type of Examination _____

Date of Commencement: _____ Expiration: _____

Duration of Validity of Medical Examination _____

Patient's Employer _____
(Supervisor)

_____
(Company)

Recommendation:
Fit for Diving   ☐
Not Fit for Diving (See Remarks)   ☐
Other (Describe)   ☐

_____

_____

_____

Remarks of Medical Practitioner: _____

_____

_____

_____

X-Ray Record:
    Date   Views/Type

_____   _____

_____   _____

_____   _____

Medical Examination in Accordance with the Requirements:

_____

_____

_____
(Physician's Name)

_____
(Address)

_____
(City/State/Country)

_____
(Telephone Numbers)

Physician's Signature _____

RECORD OF MEDICAL EXAMINATION

Name of Person Examined _____

Date of Examination _____

Type of Examination _____

Date of Commencement: _____ Expiration: _____

Duration of Validity of Medical Examination _____

Patient's Employer _____
(Supervisor)

_____
(Company)

Recommendation:
    Fit for Diving   ☐
    Not Fit for Diving (See Remarks) ☐
    Other (Describe)   ☐

_____

_____

_____

Remarks of Medical Practitioner: _____

_____

_____

_____

X-Ray Record:
    Date   Views/Type

_____   _____

_____   _____

_____   _____

Medical Examination in Accordance with the Requirements:

_____

_____

_____
(Physician's Name)

_____
(Address)

_____
(City/State/Country)

_____
(Telephone Numbers)

Physician's Signature _____

RECORD OF MEDICAL EXAMINATION

Name of Person Examined _____

Date of Examination _____

Type of Examination _____

Date of Commencement: _____ Expiration: _____

Duration of Validity of Medical Examination _____

Patient's Employer _____

                                                    (Supervisor)

_____
                                                    (Company)

Recommendation:
    Fit for Diving   ☐
    Not Fit for Diving (See Remarks) ☐
    Other (Describe)   ☐

_____

_____

_____

Remarks of Medical Practitioner: _____

_____

_____

_____

X-Ray Record:

    Date   Views/Type

_____   _____

_____   _____

_____   _____

Medical Examination in Accordance with the Requirements:

_____

_____

_____
(Physician's Name)

_____
(Address)

_____
(City/State/Country)

_____
(Telephone Numbers)

Physician's Signature _____

RECORD OF MEDICAL EXAMINATION

Name of Person Examined _____

Date of Examination _____

Type of Examination _____

Date of Commencement: _____ Expiration: _____

Duration of Validity of Medical Examination _____

Patient's Employer _____
                                                          (Supervisor)

_____
                                                          (Company)

Recommendation:
    Fit for Diving   ☐
    Not Fit for Diving (See Remarks) ☐
    Other (Describe)   ☐

_____

_____

_____

Remarks of Medical Practitioner: _____

_____

_____

_____

X-Ray Record:
    Date   Views/Type

_____   _____

_____   _____

_____   _____

Medical Examination in Accordance with the Requirements:

_____

_____

_____
(Physician's Name)

_____
(Address)

_____
(City/State/Country)

_____
(Telephone Numbers)

Physician's Signature _____

RECORD OF MEDICAL EXAMINATION

Name of Person Examined _____

Date of Examination _____

Type of Examination _____

Date of Commencement: _____ Expiration: _____

Duration of Validity of Medical Examination _____

Patient's Employer _____

                                                   (Supervisor)

                                                   (Company)

Recommendation:

    Fit for Diving   ☐

    Not Fit for Diving (See Remarks)   ☐

    Other (Describe)   ☐

_____

_____

_____

Remarks of Medical Practitioner: _____

_____

_____

_____

X-Ray Record:

    Date   Views/Type

_____   _____

_____   _____

_____   _____

Medical Examination in Accordance with the Requirements:

_____

_____

_____

(Physician's Name)

_____

(Address)

_____

(City/State/Country)

_____

(Telephone Numbers)

Physician's Signature _____

RECORD OF MEDICAL EXAMINATION

Name of Person Examined _____

Date of Examination _____

Type of Examination _____

Date of Commencement: _____ Expiration: _____

Duration of Validity of Medical Examination _____

Patient's Employer _____

(Supervisor)

_____

(Company)

Recommendation:
    Fit for Diving   ☐
    Not Fit for Diving (See Remarks) ☐
    Other (Describe)   ☐

_____

_____

_____

Remarks of Medical Practitioner: _____

_____

_____

_____

X-Ray Record:

    Date   Views/Type

_____   _____

_____   _____

_____   _____

Medical Examination in Accordance with the Requirements:

_____

_____

_____

(Physician's Name)

_____

(Address)

_____

(City/State/Country)

_____

(Telephone Numbers)

Physician's Signature _____

RECORD OF MEDICAL EXAMINATION

Name of Person Examined _____

Date of Examination _____

Type of Examination _____

Date of Commencement: _____ Expiration: _____

Duration of Validity of Medical Examination _____

Patient's Employer _____
                                                  (Supervisor)

_____
                                                  (Company)

Recommendation:
    Fit for Diving   ☐
    Not Fit for Diving (See Remarks) ☐
    Other (Describe)   ☐

_____

_____

_____

Remarks of Medical Practitioner: _____

_____

_____

_____

X-Ray Record:
    Date   Views/Type

_____   _____

_____   _____

_____   _____

Medical Examination in Accordance with the Requirements:

_____

_____

_____
(Physician's Name)

_____
(Address)

_____
(City/State/Country)

_____
(Telephone Numbers)

Physician's Signature _____

TRAINING RECORD

Name of Course or Training Program	Name of Training School or Company	Date of Enrollment	Date of Completion	Certificate of Training or Qualifications Obtained

Name of Course or Training Program	Name of Training School or Company	Date of Enrollment	Date of Completion	Certificate of Training or Qualifications Obtained

SPECIALIZED TRAINING DOCUMENTATION

SPECIALIZED TRAINING DOCUMENTATION

EMPLOYMENT RECORD

Company Name _____

Company Address _____

Telephone No. (_____) _____

Employed as _____

From _____/____/19 ____ To _____/____/19 ____

Company Name _____

Company Address _____

Telephone No. (_____) _____

Employed as _____

From _____/____/19 ____ To _____/____/19 ____

Company Name _____

Company Address _____

Telephone No. (_____) _____

Employed as _____

From _____/____/19 ____ To _____/____/19 ____

Company Name _____

Company Address _____

Telephone No. (_____) _____

Employed as _____

From _____/____/19 ____ To _____/____/19 ____

Company Name _____

Company Address _____

Telephone No. (_____) _____

Employed as _____

From _____/____/19 ____ To _____/____/19 ____

Company Name _____

Company Address _____

Telephone No. (_____) _____

Employed as _____

From _____/____/19 ____ To _____/____/19 ____

EMPLOYMENT RECORD

Company Name _____

Company Address _____

Telephone No. (_____) _____

Employed as _____

From _____ /____ /19 ____ To _____ /____ /19 ____

Company Name _____

Company Address _____

Telephone No. (_____) _____

Employed as _____

From _____ /____ /19 ____ To _____ /____ /19 ____

Company Name _____

Company Address _____

Telephone No. (_____) _____

Employed as _____

From _____ /____ /19 ____ To _____ /____ /19 ____

Company Name _____

Company Address _____

Telephone No. (_____) _____

Employed as _____

From _____ /____ /19 ____ To _____ /____ /19 ____

Company Name _____

Company Address _____

Telephone No. (_____) _____

Employed as _____

From _____ /____ /19 ____ To _____ /____ /19 ____

Company Name _____

Company Address _____

Telephone No. (_____) _____

Employed as _____

From _____ /____ /19 ____ To _____ /____ /19 ____

RECORD OF DIVE

Date of Dive _____ Diver's Signature _____

BOTTOM CONDITION: (X appropriate blocks)   Geographic Location
☐ Sand ☐ Shell ☐ Gravel ☐ Hard ☐ Soft
_____

SEA STATE:
☐ Calm ☐ Fair ☐ Moderate ☐ Heavy ☐ Gale Sea
_____

BOTTOM TEMPERATURE:
☐ Cold (below 55) ☐ Normal (55 to 75) ☐ Warm (above 75)   Vessel or Platform

BOTTOM VISIBILITY:
☐ Poor (0 to 5') ☐ Moderate (5' to 20') ☐ (Good 20 +)
_____

BOTTOM CURRENT:
☐ Weak (0 to 0.5KT) ☐ Moderate (0.5 to 2) ☐ Strong (2+)
_____

Bell Bounce or Surface Dives:	Dive One	Dive Two	Dive Three
Maximum depth of dive:	☐☐☐ feet	☐☐☐ feet	☐☐☐ feet
Time left surface or started pressurization:	☐☐ H ☐☐ min	☐☐ H ☐☐ min	☐☐ H ☐☐ min
Bottom Time:	☐☐☐ min	☐☐☐ min	☐☐☐ min
Decompression Completed at:	☐☐ H ☐☐ min	☐☐ H ☐☐ min	☐☐ H ☐☐ min
For surface decompression only: Surface interval:	☐☐☐ min	☐☐☐ min	☐☐☐ min
and time spent in chamber:	☐☐ H ☐☐ min	☐☐ H ☐☐ min	☐☐ H ☐☐ min

Saturation Dives:		
Storage depth:	☐☐☐ feet	☐☐☐ feet
Maximum depth of dive:	☐☐☐ feet	☐☐☐ feet
Time leaving storage depth:	☐☐ H ☐☐ min on ☐☐ day	☐☐ H ☐☐ min on ☐☐ day
Time returning to storage depth:	☐☐ H ☐☐ min on ☐☐ day	☐☐ H ☐☐ min on ☐☐ day
Bottom time:	☐☐ H ☐☐ min	☐☐ H ☐☐ min

Breathing Apparatus used: _____

Breathing Mixture used: _____

Work Description, Equipment and Tools Used:
_____
_____

Type of Dive	
Scuba	
Surface	
Wet Bell	
Bell Bounce	
Saturation	
Other	

Name of Decompression Schedules used: _____

Note regarding any   _____
Decompression Sickness   _____
or other Illness or Injury: _____

Any Other Remarks: _____
_____
_____

APPROVED
Name of Diving Contractor: _____

Address of Diving Contractor _____
_____

Name of Diving Supervisor (Print) _____

Signature _____ Date: _____

RECORD OF DIVE

Date of Dive _____ Diver's Signature _____

BOTTOM CONDITION: (X appropriate blocks)
☐ Sand ☐ Shell ☐ Gravel ☐ Hard ☐ Soft

Geographic Location
_____

SEA STATE:
☐ Calm ☐ Fair ☐ Moderate ☐ Heavy ☐ Gale Sea

BOTTOM TEMPERATURE:
☐ Cold (below 55) ☐ Normal (55 to 75) ☐ Warm (above 75)

Vessel or Platform
_____

BOTTOM VISIBILITY:
☐ Poor (0 to 5') ☐ Moderate (5' to 20') ☐ (Good 20 +)

BOTTOM CURRENT:
☐ Weak (0 to 0.5KT) ☐ Moderate (0.5 to 2) ☐ Strong (2+)

_____

Bell Bounce or Surface Dives:	Dive One	Dive Two	Dive Three
Maximum depth of dive:	☐☐☐ feet	☐☐☐ feet	☐☐☐ feet
Time left surface or started pressurization:	☐☐ H ☐☐ min	☐☐ H ☐☐ min	☐☐ H ☐☐ min
Bottom Time:	☐☐☐ min	☐☐☐ min	☐☐☐ min
Decompression Completed at:	☐☐ H ☐☐ min	☐☐ H ☐☐ min	☐☐ H ☐☐ min
For surface decompression only: Surface interval:	☐☐ min	☐☐ min	☐☐ min
and time spent in chamber:	☐☐ H ☐☐ min	☐☐ H ☐☐ min	☐☐ H ☐☐ min

Saturation Dives:		
Storage depth:	☐☐☐ feet	☐☐☐ feet
Maximum depth of dive:	☐☐☐ feet	☐☐☐ feet
Time leaving storage depth:	☐☐ H ☐☐ min on ☐☐ day	☐☐ H ☐☐ min on ☐☐ day
Time returning to storage depth:	☐☐ H ☐☐ min on ☐☐ day	☐☐ H ☐☐ min on ☐☐ day
Bottom time:	☐☐ H ☐☐ min	☐☐ H ☐☐ min

Breathing Apparatus used: _____
_____

Breathing Mixture used: _____
_____

Work Description, Equipment and Tools Used:
_____
_____

Name of Decompression Schedules used: _____

Note regarding any
Decompression Sickness
or other Illness or Injury: _____

Any Other Remarks: _____
_____
_____

Type of Dive	
Scuba	
Surface	
Wet Bell	
Bell Bounce	
Saturation	
Other	

APPROVED

Name of Diving Contractor: _____

Address of Diving Contractor _____
_____

Name of Diving Supervisor (Print) _____

Signature _____ Date: _____

RECORD OF DIVE

Date of Dive _____ Diver's Signature _____

BOTTOM CONDITION: (X appropriate blocks)　　　　　Geographic Location
☐ Sand　☐ Shell　☐ Gravel　☐ Hard　☐ Soft
　　　　　　　　　　　　　　　　　　　　　　　　　　　_____
SEA STATE:
☐ Calm　☐ Fair　☐ Moderate　☐ Heavy　☐ Gale Sea
　　　　　　　　　　　　　　　　　　　　　　　　　　　_____
BOTTOM TEMPERATURE:
☐ Cold (below 55)　☐ Normal (55 to 75)　☐ Warm (above 75)　　Vessel or Platform
BOTTOM VISIBILITY:
☐ Poor (0 to 5')　☐ Moderate (5' to 20')　☐ (Good 20 +)
　　　　　　　　　　　　　　　　　　　　　　　　　　　_____
BOTTOM CURRENT:
☐ Weak (0 to 0.5KT)　☐ Moderate (0.5 to 2)　☐ Strong (2+)
　　　　　　　　　　　　　　　　　　　　　　　　　　　_____

Bell Bounce or Surface Dives:	Dive One	Dive Two	Dive Three
Maximum depth of dive:	☐☐☐ feet	☐☐☐ feet	☐☐☐ feet
Time left surface or started pressurization:	☐☐ H ☐☐ min	☐☐ H ☐☐ min	☐☐ H ☐☐ min
Bottom Time:	☐☐☐ min	☐☐☐ min	☐☐☐ min
Decompression Completed at:	☐☐ H ☐☐ min	☐☐ H ☐☐ min	☐☐ H ☐☐ min
For surface decompression only:			
Surface interval:	☐☐☐ min	☐☐☐ min	☐☐☐ min
and time spent in chamber:	☐☐ H ☐☐ min	☐☐ H ☐☐ min	☐☐ H ☐☐ min

Saturation Dives:		
Storage depth:	☐☐☐ feet	☐☐☐ feet
Maximum depth of dive:	☐☐☐ feet	☐☐☐ feet
Time leaving storage depth:	☐☐ H ☐☐ min on ☐☐ day	☐☐ H ☐☐ min on ☐☐ day
Time returning to storage depth:	☐☐ H ☐☐ min on ☐☐ day	☐☐ H ☐☐ min on ☐☐ day
Bottom time:	☐☐ H ☐☐ min	☐☐ H ☐☐ min

Breathing Apparatus used: _____

Breathing Mixture used: _____

Work Description, Equipment and Tools Used: _____

Name of Decompression Schedules used: _____

Note regarding any
Decompression Sickness　　_____
or other Illness or Injury:

Any Other Remarks: _____

Type of Dive	
Scuba	
Surface	
Wet Bell	
Bell Bounce	
Saturation	
Other	

APPROVED
Name of Diving Contractor: _____

Address of Diving Contractor _____

Name of Diving Supervisor (Print) _____

Signature _____ Date: _____

RECORD OF DIVE

Date of Dive _____ Diver's Signature _____

BOTTOM CONDITION: (X appropriate blocks)
☐ Sand ☐ Shell ☐ Gravel ☐ Hard ☐ Soft

SEA STATE:
☐ Calm ☐ Fair ☐ Moderate ☐ Heavy ☐ Gale Sea

BOTTOM TEMPERATURE:
☐ Cold (below 55) ☐ Normal (55 to 75) ☐ Warm (above 75)

BOTTOM VISIBILITY:
☐ Poor (0 to 5') ☐ Moderate (5' to 20') ☐ (Good 20 +)

BOTTOM CURRENT:
☐ Weak (0 to 0.5KT) ☐ Moderate (0.5 to 2) ☐ Strong (2+)

Geographic Location
_____

_____

Vessel or Platform
_____

_____

Bell Bounce or Surface Dives:

	Dive One	Dive Two	Dive Three
Maximum depth of dive:	☐☐☐ feet	☐☐☐ feet	☐☐☐ feet
Time left surface or started pressurization:	☐☐ H ☐☐ min	☐☐ H ☐☐ min	☐☐ H ☐☐ min
Bottom Time:	☐☐☐ min	☐☐☐ min	☐☐☐ min
Decompression Completed at:	☐☐ H ☐☐ min	☐☐ H ☐☐ min	☐☐ H ☐☐ min
For surface decompression only: Surface interval:	☐☐☐ min	☐☐☐ min	☐☐☐ min
and time spent in chamber:	☐☐ H ☐☐ min	☐☐ H ☐☐ min	☐☐ H ☐☐ min

Saturation Dives:

Storage depth:	☐☐☐ feet		☐☐☐ feet
Maximum depth of dive:	☐☐☐ feet		☐☐☐ feet
Time leaving storage depth:	☐☐ H ☐☐ min on ☐☐ day		☐☐ H ☐☐ min on ☐☐ day
Time returning to storage depth:	☐☐ H ☐☐ min on ☐☐ day		☐☐ H ☐☐ min on ☐☐ day
Bottom time:	☐☐ H ☐☐ min		☐☐ H ☐☐ min

Breathing Apparatus used: _____

Breathing Mixture used: _____

Work Description, Equipment and Tools Used: _____

_____

Name of Decompression Schedules used: _____

Note regarding any _____
Decompression Sickness _____
or other Illness or Injury: _____

Any Other Remarks: _____

_____

_____

Type of Dive
Scuba	☐
Surface	☐
Wet Bell	☐
Bell Bounce	☐
Saturation	☐

Other
_____
_____

APPROVED

Name of Diving Contractor: _____

Address of Diving Contractor _____

_____

Name of Diving Supervisor (Print) _____

Signature _____ Date: _____

RECORD OF DIVE

Date of Dive _____ Diver's Signature _____

BOTTOM CONDITION: (X appropriate blocks)
☐ Sand ☐ Shell ☐ Gravel ☐ Hard ☐ Soft

SEA STATE:
☐ Calm ☐ Fair ☐ Moderate ☐ Heavy ☐ Gale Sea

BOTTOM TEMPERATURE:
☐ Cold (below 55) ☐ Normal (55 to 75) ☐ Warm (above 75)

BOTTOM VISIBILITY:
☐ Poor (0 to 5') ☐ Moderate (5' to 20') ☐ (Good 20 +)

BOTTOM CURRENT:
☐ Weak (0 to 0.5KT) ☐ Moderate (0.5 to 2) ☐ Strong (2+)

Geographic Location
_____

_____

Vessel or Platform

_____

_____

Bell Bounce or Surface Dives:

	Dive One	Dive Two	Dive Three
Maximum depth of dive:	☐☐☐ feet	☐☐☐ feet	☐☐☐ feet
Time left surface or started pressurization:	☐☐ H ☐☐ min	☐☐ H ☐☐ min	☐☐ H ☐☐ min
Bottom Time:	☐☐ min	☐☐ min	☐☐ min
Decompression Completed at:	☐☐ H ☐☐ min	☐☐ H ☐☐ min	☐☐ H ☐☐ min
For surface decompression only: Surface interval:	☐☐ min	☐☐ min	☐☐ min
and time spent in chamber:	☐☐ H ☐☐ min	☐☐ H ☐☐ min	☐☐ H ☐☐ min

Saturation Dives:

Storage depth:	☐☐☐ feet	☐☐☐ feet	
Maximum depth of dive:	☐☐☐ feet	☐☐☐ feet	
Time leaving storage depth:	☐☐ H ☐☐ min on ☐☐ day	☐☐ H ☐☐ min on ☐☐ day	
Time returning to storage depth:	☐☐ H ☐☐ min on ☐☐ day	☐☐ H ☐☐ min on ☐☐ day	
Bottom time:	☐☐ H ☐☐ min	☐☐ H ☐☐ min	

Breathing Apparatus used: _____

Breathing Mixture used: _____

Work Description, Equipment and Tools Used: _____

_____

Name of Decompression Schedules used: _____

Note regarding any Decompression Sickness or other Illness or Injury: _____

Any Other Remarks: _____

_____

_____

Type of Dive	
Scuba	☐
Surface	☐
Wet Bell	☐
Bell Bounce	☐
Saturation	☐
Other	

_____

_____

APPROVED

Name of Diving Contractor: _____

Address of Diving Contractor _____

Name of Diving Supervisor (Print) _____

Signature _____ Date: _____

RECORD OF DIVE

Date of Dive ＿＿＿＿＿＿＿ Diver's Signature ＿＿＿＿＿＿＿＿＿

BOTTOM CONDITION: (X appropriate blocks)
☐ Sand ☐ Shell ☐ Gravel ☐ Hard ☐ Soft

SEA STATE:
☐ Calm ☐ Fair ☐ Moderate ☐ Heavy ☐ Gale Sea

BOTTOM TEMPERATURE:
☐ Cold (below 55) ☐ Normal (55 to 75) ☐ Warm (above 75)

BOTTOM VISIBILITY:
☐ Poor (0 to 5') ☐ Moderate (5' to 20') ☐ (Good 20 +)

BOTTOM CURRENT:
☐ Weak (0 to 0.5KT) ☐ Moderate (0.5 to 2) ☐ Strong (2+)

Geographic Location
＿＿＿＿＿＿＿＿

Vessel or Platform
＿＿＿＿＿＿＿＿

Bell Bounce or Surface Dives:	Dive One	Dive Two	Dive Three
Maximum depth of dive:	☐☐☐ feet	☐☐☐ feet	☐☐☐ feet
Time left surface or started pressurization:	☐☐ H ☐☐ min	☐☐ H ☐☐ min	☐☐ H ☐☐ min
Bottom Time:	☐☐☐ min	☐☐☐ min	☐☐☐ min
Decompression Completed at:	☐☐ H ☐☐ min	☐☐ H ☐☐ min	☐☐ H ☐☐ min
For surface decompression only: Surface interval:	☐☐☐ min	☐☐☐ min	☐☐☐ min
and time spent in chamber:	☐☐ H ☐☐ min	☐☐ H ☐☐ min	☐☐ H ☐☐ min

Saturation Dives:

Storage depth:	☐☐☐☐ feet	☐☐☐☐ feet
Maximum depth of dive:	☐☐☐☐ feet	☐☐☐☐ feet
Time leaving storage depth:	☐☐ H ☐☐ min on ☐☐ day	☐☐ H ☐☐ min on ☐☐ day
Time returning to storage depth:	☐☐ H ☐☐ min on ☐☐ day	☐☐ H ☐☐ min on ☐☐ day
Bottom time:	☐☐ H ☐☐ min	☐☐ H ☐☐ min

Breathing Apparatus used: ＿＿＿＿＿＿＿＿＿＿＿
＿＿＿＿＿＿＿＿＿＿＿＿＿＿＿＿＿＿＿

Breathing Mixture used: ＿＿＿＿＿＿＿＿＿＿＿
＿＿＿＿＿＿＿＿＿＿＿＿＿＿＿＿＿＿＿

Work Description, Equipment and Tools Used:
＿＿＿＿＿＿＿＿＿＿＿＿＿＿＿＿＿＿＿
＿＿＿＿＿＿＿＿＿＿＿＿＿＿＿＿＿＿＿

Name of Decompression Schedules used: ＿＿＿＿＿＿＿

Note regarding any
Decompression Sickness
or other Illness or Injury:

Any Other Remarks: ＿＿＿＿＿＿＿＿＿＿＿＿＿＿＿＿＿＿

Type of Dive	
Scuba	
Surface	
Wet Bell	
Bell Bounce	
Saturation	
Other	

APPROVED

Name of Diving Contractor: ＿＿＿＿＿＿＿＿＿＿＿＿＿＿＿

Address of Diving Contractor ＿＿＿＿＿＿＿＿＿＿＿＿＿＿＿
＿＿＿＿＿＿＿＿＿＿＿＿＿＿＿＿＿＿＿＿＿＿＿＿＿

Name of Diving Supervisor (Print) ＿＿＿＿＿＿＿＿＿＿＿＿＿

Signature ＿＿＿＿＿＿＿＿＿＿＿＿ Date: ＿＿＿＿＿＿

RECORD OF DIVE

Date of Dive _____ Diver's Signature _____

BOTTOM CONDITION: (X appropriate blocks)
□ Sand   □ Shell   □ Gravel   □ Hard   □ Soft

Geographic Location _____

SEA STATE:
□ Calm   □ Fair   □ Moderate   □ Heavy   □ Gale Sea

_____

BOTTOM TEMPERATURE:
□ Cold (below 55)   □ Normal (55 to 75)   □ Warm (above 75)

Vessel or Platform

BOTTOM VISIBILITY:
□ Poor (0 to 5')   □ Moderate (5' to 20')   □ (Good 20 +)

_____

BOTTOM CURRENT:
□ Weak (0 to 0.5KT)   □ Moderate (0.5 to 2)   □ Strong (2+)

_____

Bell Bounce or Surface Dives:	Dive One	Dive Two	Dive Three
Maximum depth of dive:	☐☐☐ feet	☐☐☐ feet	☐☐☐ feet
Time left surface or started pressurization:	☐☐ H ☐☐ min	☐☐ H ☐☐ min	☐☐ H ☐☐ min
Bottom Time:	☐☐☐ min	☐☐☐ min	☐☐☐ min
Decompression Completed at:	☐☐ H ☐☐ min	☐☐ H ☐☐ min	☐☐ H ☐☐ min
For surface decompression only: Surface interval:	☐☐ min	☐☐ min	☐☐ min
and time spent in chamber:	☐☐ H ☐☐ min	☐☐ H ☐☐ min	☐☐ H ☐☐ min

Saturation Dives:		
Storage depth:	☐☐☐ feet	☐☐☐ feet
Maximum depth of dive:	☐☐☐ feet	☐☐☐ feet
Time leaving storage depth:	☐☐ H ☐☐ min on ☐☐ day	☐☐ H ☐☐ min on ☐☐ day
Time returning to storage depth:	☐☐ H ☐☐ min on ☐☐ day	☐☐ H ☐☐ min on ☐☐ day
Bottom time:	☐☐ H ☐☐ min	☐☐ H ☐☐ min

Breathing Apparatus used: _____

Breathing Mixture used: _____

Work Description, Equipment and Tools Used: _____

Name of Decompression Schedules used: _____

Note regarding any Decompression Sickness or other Illness or Injury: _____

Any Other Remarks: _____

Type of Dive	
Scuba	☐
Surface	☐
Wet Bell	☐
Bell Bounce	☐
Saturation	☐
Other	

APPROVED
Name of Diving Contractor: _____

Address of Diving Contractor _____

Name of Diving Supervisor (Print) _____

Signature _____ Date: _____

RECORD OF DIVE

Date of Dive _____ Diver's Signature _____

BOTTOM CONDITION: (X appropriate blocks)
☐ Sand ☐ Shell ☐ Gravel ☐ Hard ☐ Soft

SEA STATE:
☐ Calm ☐ Fair ☐ Moderate ☐ Heavy ☐ Gale Sea

BOTTOM TEMPERATURE:
☐ Cold (below 55) ☐ Normal (55 to 75) ☐ Warm (above 75)

BOTTOM VISIBILITY:
☐ Poor (0 to 5') ☐ Moderate (5' to 20') ☐ (Good 20 +)

BOTTOM CURRENT:
☐ Weak (0 to 0.5KT) ☐ Moderate (0.5 to 2) ☐ Strong (2+)

Geographic Location
_____

_____

Vessel or Platform
_____

_____

Bell Bounce or Surface Dives:	Dive One	Dive Two	Dive Three
Maximum depth of dive:	☐☐ feet	☐☐ feet	☐☐ feet
Time left surface or started pressurization:	☐☐ H ☐☐ min	☐☐ H ☐☐ min	☐☐ H ☐☐ min
Bottom Time:	☐☐ min	☐☐ min	☐☐ min
Decompression Completed at:	☐☐ H ☐☐ min	☐☐ H ☐☐ min	☐☐ H ☐☐ min
For surface decompression only: Surface interval:	☐☐ min	☐☐ min	☐☐ min
and time spent in chamber:	☐☐ H ☐☐ min	☐☐ H ☐☐ min	☐☐ H ☐☐ min

Saturation Dives:		
Storage depth:	☐☐☐ feet	☐☐☐ feet
Maximum depth of dive:	☐☐☐ feet	☐☐☐ feet
Time leaving storage depth:	☐☐ H ☐☐ min on ☐☐ day	☐☐ H ☐☐ min on ☐☐ day
Time returning to storage depth:	☐☐ H ☐☐ min on ☐☐ day	☐☐ H ☐☐ min on ☐☐ day
Bottom time:	☐☐ H ☐☐ min	☐☐ H ☐☐ min

Breathing Apparatus used: _____

Breathing Mixture used: _____
_____

Work Description, Equipment and Tools Used:
_____
_____
_____

Name of Decompression Schedules used: _____

Note regarding any
Decompression Sickness _____
or other Illness or Injury: _____
_____

Type of Dive	
Scuba	
Surface	
Wet Bell	
Bell Bounce	
Saturation	
Other	

Any Other Remarks: _____
_____
_____

APPROVED
Name of Diving Contractor: _____

Address of Diving Contractor _____
_____

Name of Diving Supervisor (Print) _____

Signature _____ Date: _____

RECORD OF DIVE

Date of Dive _____ Diver's Signature _____

BOTTOM CONDITION: (X appropriate blocks)
☐ Sand ☐ Shell ☐ Gravel ☐ Hard ☐ Soft

Geographic Location

_____

SEA STATE:
☐ Calm ☐ Fair ☐ Moderate ☐ Heavy ☐ Gale Sea

_____

BOTTOM TEMPERATURE:
☐ Cold (below 55) ☐ Normal (55 to 75) ☐ Warm (above 75)

Vessel or Platform

BOTTOM VISIBILITY:
☐ Poor (0 to 5') ☐ Moderate (5' to 20') ☐ (Good 20 +)

_____

BOTTOM CURRENT:
☐ Weak (0 to 0.5KT) ☐ Moderate (0.5 to 2) ☐ Strong (2+)

_____

Bell Bounce or Surface Dives:	Dive One	Dive Two	Dive Three
Maximum depth of dive:	☐☐☐ feet	☐☐☐ feet	☐☐☐ feet
Time left surface or started pressurization:	☐☐H☐☐ min	☐☐H☐☐ min	☐☐H☐☐ min
Bottom Time:	☐☐☐ min	☐☐☐ min	☐☐☐ min
Decompression Completed at:	☐☐H☐☐ min	☐☐H☐☐ min	☐☐H☐☐ min
For surface decompression only: Surface interval:	☐☐ min	☐☐ min	☐☐ min
and time spent in chamber:	☐☐H☐☐ min	☐☐H☐☐ min	☐☐H☐☐ min

Saturation Dives:		
Storage depth:	☐☐☐ feet	☐☐☐ feet
Maximum depth of dive:	☐☐☐ feet	☐☐☐ feet
Time leaving storage depth:	☐☐H☐☐ min on ☐☐ day	☐☐H☐☐ min on ☐☐ day
Time returning to storage depth:	☐☐H☐☐ min on ☐☐ day	☐☐H☐☐ min on ☐☐ day
Bottom time:	☐☐H☐☐ min	☐☐H☐☐ min

Breathing Apparatus used: _____

Breathing Mixture used: _____

Work Description, Equipment and Tools Used: _____

Name of Decompression Schedules used: _____

Note regarding any
Decompression Sickness _____
or other Illness or Injury:

Any Other Remarks: _____

Type of Dive	
Scuba	
Surface	
Wet Bell	
Bell Bounce	
Saturation	
Other	
_____	
_____	

APPROVED

Name of Diving Contractor: _____

Address of Diving Contractor _____

Name of Diving Supervisor (Print) _____

Signature _____ Date: _____

RECORD OF DIVE

Date of Dive _____ Diver's Signature _____

BOTTOM CONDITION: (X appropriate blocks)
☐ Sand ☐ Shell ☐ Gravel ☐ Hard ☐ Soft

Geographic Location

SEA STATE:
☐ Calm ☐ Fair ☐ Moderate ☐ Heavy ☐ Gale Sea

_____

BOTTOM TEMPERATURE:
☐ Cold (below 55) ☐ Normal (55 to 75) ☐ Warm (above 75)

_____

Vessel or Platform

BOTTOM VISIBILITY:
☐ Poor (0 to 5') ☐ Moderate (5' to 20') ☐ (Good 20 +)

_____

BOTTOM CURRENT:
☐ Weak (0 to 0.5KT) ☐ Moderate (0.5 to 2) ☐ Strong (2+)

_____

Bell Bounce or Surface Dives:	Dive One	Dive Two	Dive Three
Maximum depth of dive:	☐☐☐ feet	☐☐☐ feet	☐☐☐ feet
Time left surface or started pressurization:	☐☐ H ☐☐ min	☐☐ H ☐☐ min	☐☐ H ☐☐ min
Bottom Time:	☐☐☐ min	☐☐☐ min	☐☐☐ min
Decompression Completed at:	☐☐ H ☐☐ min	☐☐ H ☐☐ min	☐☐ H ☐☐ min
For surface decompression only: Surface interval:	☐☐☐ min	☐☐☐ min	☐☐☐ min
and time spent in chamber:	☐☐ H ☐☐ min	☐☐ H ☐☐ min	☐☐ H ☐☐ min

Saturation Dives:		
Storage depth:	☐☐☐☐ feet	☐☐☐☐ feet
Maximum depth of dive:	☐☐☐☐ feet	☐☐☐☐ feet
Time leaving storage depth:	☐☐ H ☐☐ min on ☐☐ day	☐☐ H ☐☐ min on ☐☐ day
Time returning to storage depth:	☐☐ H ☐☐ min on ☐☐ day	☐☐ H ☐☐ min on ☐☐ day
Bottom time:	☐☐ H ☐☐ min	☐☐ H ☐☐ min

Breathing Apparatus used: _____

Breathing Mixture used: _____

Work Description, Equipment and Tools Used:

_____
_____
_____

Type of Dive	
Scuba	
Surface	
Wet Bell	
Bell Bounce	
Saturation	
Other	

Name of Decompression Schedules used: _____

Note regarding any Decompression Sickness or other Illness or Injury:
_____
_____
_____
_____

_____
_____

Any Other Remarks: _____
_____
_____

APPROVED

Name of Diving Contractor: _____

Address of Diving Contractor _____
_____

Name of Diving Supervisor (Print) _____

Signature _____ Date: _____

RECORD OF DIVE

Date of Dive _____ Diver's Signature _____

BOTTOM CONDITION: (X appropriate blocks)
☐ Sand ☐ Shell ☐ Gravel ☐ Hard ☐ Soft

Geographic Location

_____

SEA STATE:
☐ Calm ☐ Fair ☐ Moderate ☐ Heavy ☐ Gale Sea

_____

BOTTOM TEMPERATURE:
☐ Cold (below 55) ☐ Normal (55 to 75) ☐ Warm (above 75)

Vessel or Platform

BOTTOM VISIBILITY:
☐ Poor (0 to 5') ☐ Moderate (5' to 20') ☐ (Good 20 +)

_____

BOTTOM CURRENT:
☐ Weak (0 to 0.5KT) ☐ Moderate (0.5 to 2) ☐ Strong (2+)

_____

Bell Bounce or Surface Dives:	Dive One	Dive Two	Dive Three
Maximum depth of dive:	☐☐☐ feet	☐☐☐ feet	☐☐☐ feet
Time left surface or started pressurization:	☐☐ H ☐☐ min	☐☐ H ☐☐ min	☐☐ H ☐☐ min
Bottom Time:	☐☐☐ min	☐☐☐ min	☐☐☐ min
Decompression Completed at:	☐☐ H ☐☐ min	☐☐ H ☐☐ min	☐☐ H ☐☐ min
For surface decompression only: Surface interval:	☐☐☐ min	☐☐☐ min	☐☐☐ min
and time spent in chamber:	☐☐ H ☐☐ min	☐☐ H ☐☐ min	☐☐ H ☐☐ min

Saturation Dives:		
Storage depth:	☐☐☐☐ feet	☐☐☐ feet
Maximum depth of dive:	☐☐☐☐ feet	☐☐☐ feet
Time leaving storage depth:	☐☐ H ☐☐ min on ☐☐ day	☐☐ H ☐☐ min on ☐☐ day
Time returning to storage depth:	☐☐ H ☐☐ min on ☐☐ day	☐☐ H ☐☐ min on ☐☐ day
Bottom time:	☐☐ H ☐☐ min	☐☐ H ☐☐ min

Breathing Apparatus used: _____

_____

Breathing Mixture used: _____

_____

Work Description, Equipment and Tools Used: _____

_____

_____

Name of Decompression Schedules used: _____

Note regarding any
Decompression Sickness _____
or other Illness or Injury: _____

Any Other Remarks: _____

_____

_____

Type of Dive	
Scuba	
Surface	
Wet Bell	
Bell Bounce	
Saturation	
Other	
_____	
_____	

APPROVED

Name of Diving Contractor: _____

Address of Diving Contractor _____

_____

Name of Diving Supervisor (Print) _____

Signature _____ Date: _____

RECORD OF DIVE

Date of Dive _____ Diver's Signature _____

BOTTOM CONDITION: (X appropriate blocks)
☐ Sand ☐ Shell ☐ Gravel ☐ Hard ☐ Soft

SEA STATE:
☐ Calm ☐ Fair ☐ Moderate ☐ Heavy ☐ Gale Sea

BOTTOM TEMPERATURE:
☐ Cold (below 55) ☐ Normal (55 to 75) ☐ Warm (above 75)

BOTTOM VISIBILITY:
☐ Poor (0 to 5') ☐ Moderate (5' to 20') ☐ (Good 20 +)

BOTTOM CURRENT:
☐ Weak (0 to 0.5KT) ☐ Moderate (0.5 to 2) ☐ Strong (2+)

Geographic Location
_____

_____

Vessel or Platform
_____

_____

Bell Bounce or Surface Dives:	Dive One	Dive Two	Dive Three
Maximum depth of dive:	☐☐☐ feet	☐☐☐ feet	☐☐☐ feet
Time left surface or started pressurization:	☐☐ H ☐☐ min	☐☐ H ☐☐ min	☐☐ H ☐☐ min
Bottom Time:	☐☐☐ min	☐☐☐ min	☐☐☐ min
Decompression Completed at:	☐☐ H ☐☐ min	☐☐ H ☐☐ min	☐☐ H ☐☐ min
For surface decompression only: Surface interval:	☐☐ min	☐☐ min	☐☐ min
and time spent in chamber:	☐☐ H ☐☐ min	☐☐ H ☐☐ min	☐☐ H ☐☐ min

Saturation Dives:		
Storage depth:	☐☐☐ feet	☐☐☐ feet
Maximum depth of dive:	☐☐☐ feet	☐☐☐ feet
Time leaving storage depth:	☐☐ H ☐☐ min on ☐☐ day	☐☐ H ☐☐ min on ☐☐ day
Time returning to storage depth:	☐☐ H ☐☐ min on ☐☐ day	☐☐ H ☐☐ min on ☐☐ day
Bottom time:	☐☐ H ☐☐ min	☐☐ H ☐☐ min

Breathing Apparatus used: _____

_____

Breathing Mixture used: _____

_____

Work Description, Equipment and Tools Used: _____

_____

_____

Name of Decompression Schedules used: _____

Note regarding any
Decompression Sickness
or other Illness or Injury: _____

Any Other Remarks: _____

_____

_____

Type of Dive	
Scuba	
Surface	
Wet Bell	
Bell Bounce	
Saturation	
Other	
_____	
_____	

APPROVED

Name of Diving Contractor: _____

Address of Diving Contractor _____

_____

Name of Diving Supervisor (Print) _____

Signature _____ Date: _____

RECORD OF DIVE

Date of Dive _____ Diver's Signature _____

BOTTOM CONDITION: (X appropriate blocks)
☐ Sand   ☐ Shell   ☐ Gravel   ☐ Hard   ☐ Soft

SEA STATE:
☐ Calm   ☐ Fair   ☐ Moderate   ☐ Heavy   ☐ Gale Sea

BOTTOM TEMPERATURE:
☐ Cold (below 55)   ☐ Normal (55 to 75)   ☐ Warm (above 75)

BOTTOM VISIBILITY:
☐ Poor (0 to 5')   ☐ Moderate (5' to 20')   ☐ (Good 20 +)

BOTTOM CURRENT:
☐ Weak (0 to 0.5KT)   ☐ Moderate (0.5 to 2)   ☐ Strong (2+)

Geographic Location
_____

_____

Vessel or Platform

_____

_____

Bell Bounce or Surface Dives:	Dive One	Dive Two	Dive Three
Maximum depth of dive:	☐☐☐ feet	☐☐☐ feet	☐☐☐ feet
Time left surface or started pressurization:	☐☐ H ☐☐ min	☐☐ H ☐☐ min	☐☐ H ☐☐ min
Bottom Time:	☐☐☐ min	☐☐☐ min	☐☐☐ min
Decompression Completed at:	☐☐ H ☐☐ min	☐☐ H ☐☐ min	☐☐ H ☐☐ min
For surface decompression only: Surface interval:	☐☐☐ min	☐☐☐ min	☐☐☐ min
and time spent in chamber:	☐☐ H ☐☐ min	☐☐ H ☐☐ min	☐☐ H ☐☐ min

Saturation Dives:		
Storage depth:	☐☐☐☐ feet	☐☐☐ feet
Maximum depth of dive:	☐☐☐☐ feet	☐☐☐ feet
Time leaving storage depth:	☐☐ H ☐☐ min on ☐☐ day	☐☐ H ☐☐ min on ☐☐ day
Time returning to storage depth:	☐☐ H ☐☐ min on ☐☐ day	☐☐ H ☐☐ min on ☐☐ day
Bottom time:	☐☐ H ☐☐ min	☐☐ H ☐☐ min

Breathing Apparatus used: _____

_____

Breathing Mixture used: _____

_____

Work Description, Equipment and Tools Used:

_____

_____

Name of Decompression Schedules used: _____

Note regarding any
Decompression Sickness
or other Illness or Injury: _____

Any Other Remarks: _____

_____

_____

Type of Dive	
Scuba	
Surface	
Wet Bell	
Bell Bounce	
Saturation	
Other	

_____

_____

APPROVED
Name of Diving Contractor: _____

Address of Diving Contractor _____

_____

Name of Diving Supervisor (Print) _____

Signature _____ Date: _____

RECORD OF DIVE

Date of Dive _____ Diver's Signature _____

BOTTOM CONDITION: (X appropriate blocks)　　　　　Geographic Location
☐ Sand ☐ Shell ☐ Gravel ☐ Hard ☐ Soft
SEA STATE:　　　　　　　　　　　　　　　　　　_____
☐ Calm ☐ Fair ☐ Moderate ☐ Heavy ☐ Gale Sea
BOTTOM TEMPERATURE:
☐ Cold (below 55) ☐ Normal (55 to 75) ☐ Warm (above 75)　　Vessel or Platform
BOTTOM VISIBILITY:
☐ Poor (0 to 5') ☐ Moderate (5' to 20') ☐ (Good 20 +)　　_____
BOTTOM CURRENT:
☐ Weak (0 to 0.5KT) ☐ Moderate (0.5 to 2) ☐ Strong (2+)

Bell Bounce or Surface Dives:	Dive One	Dive Two	Dive Three
Maximum depth of dive:	☐☐☐ feet	☐☐☐ feet	☐☐☐ feet
Time left surface or started pressurization:	☐☐ H ☐☐ min	☐☐ H ☐☐ min	☐☐ H ☐☐ min
Bottom Time:	☐☐ min	☐☐ min	☐☐ min
Decompression Completed at:	☐☐ H ☐☐ min	☐☐ H ☐☐ min	☐☐ H ☐☐ min
For surface decompression only: Surface interval:	☐☐ min	☐☐ min	☐☐ min
and time spent in chamber:	☐☐ H ☐☐ min	☐☐ H ☐☐ min	☐☐ H ☐☐ min

Saturation Dives:		
Storage depth:	☐☐☐ feet	☐☐☐ feet
Maximum depth of dive:	☐☐☐ feet	☐☐☐ feet
Time leaving storage depth:	☐☐ H ☐☐ min on ☐☐ day	☐☐ H ☐☐ min on ☐☐ day
Time returning to storage depth:	☐☐ H ☐☐ min on ☐☐ day	☐☐ H ☐☐ min on ☐☐ day
Bottom time:	☐☐ H ☐☐ min	☐☐ H ☐☐ min

Breathing Apparatus used: _____

Breathing Mixture used: _____

Work Description, Equipment and Tools Used: _____

Name of Decompression Schedules used: _____

Note regarding any　　　　　_____
Decompression Sickness　　_____
or other Illness or Injury:　　_____

Any Other Remarks: _____

Type of Dive	
Scuba	☐
Surface	☐
Wet Bell	☐
Bell Bounce	☐
Saturation	☐
Other	

APPROVED
Name of Diving Contractor: _____
Address of Diving Contractor _____

Name of Diving Supervisor (Print) _____
Signature _____ Date: _____

RECORD OF DIVE

Date of Dive _____ Diver's Signature _____

BOTTOM CONDITION: (X appropriate blocks)
☐ Sand ☐ Shell ☐ Gravel ☐ Hard ☐ Soft

SEA STATE:
☐ Calm ☐ Fair ☐ Moderate ☐ Heavy ☐ Gale Sea

BOTTOM TEMPERATURE:
☐ Cold (below 55) ☐ Normal (55 to 75) ☐ Warm (above 75)

BOTTOM VISIBILITY:
☐ Poor (0 to 5') ☐ Moderate (5' to 20') ☐ (Good 20 +)

BOTTOM CURRENT:
☐ Weak (0 to 0.5KT) ☐ Moderate (0.5 to 2) ☐ Strong (2+)

Geographic Location
_____

_____

Vessel or Platform
_____

_____

Bell Bounce or Surface Dives:	Dive One	Dive Two	Dive Three
Maximum depth of dive:	☐☐☐ feet	☐☐☐ feet	☐☐☐ feet
Time left surface or started pressurization:	☐☐ H ☐☐ min	☐☐ H ☐☐ min	☐☐ H ☐☐ min
Bottom Time:	☐☐☐ min	☐☐☐ min	☐☐☐ min
Decompression Completed at:	☐☐ H ☐☐ min	☐☐ H ☐☐ min	☐☐ H ☐☐ min
For surface decompression only: Surface interval:	☐☐ min	☐☐ min	☐☐ min
and time spent in chamber:	☐☐ H ☐☐ min	☐☐ H ☐☐ min	☐☐ H ☐☐ min

Saturation Dives:		
Storage depth:	☐☐☐ feet	☐☐☐ feet
Maximum depth of dive:	☐☐☐ feet	☐☐☐ feet
Time leaving storage depth:	☐☐ H ☐☐ min on ☐☐ day	☐☐ H ☐☐ min on ☐☐ day
Time returning to storage depth:	☐☐ H ☐☐ min on ☐☐ day	☐☐ H ☐☐ min on ☐☐ day
Bottom time:	☐☐ H ☐☐ min	☐☐ H ☐☐ min

Breathing Apparatus used: _____
_____

Breathing Mixture used: _____
_____

Work Description, Equipment and Tools Used:
_____
_____
_____

Type of Dive	
Scuba	☐
Surface	☐
Wet Bell	☐
Bell Bounce	☐
Saturation	☐
Other	

Name of Decompression Schedules used: _____

Note regarding any
Decompression Sickness
or other Illness or Injury:
_____
_____
_____

Any Other Remarks: _____
_____
_____

APPROVED
Name of Diving Contractor: _____

Address of Diving Contractor _____
_____

Name of Diving Supervisor (Print) _____

Signature _____ Date: _____

RECORD OF DIVE

Date of Dive _____ Diver's Signature _____

BOTTOM CONDITION: (X appropriate blocks)   Geographic Location
☐ Sand   ☐ Shell   ☐ Gravel   ☐ Hard   ☐ Soft
SEA STATE: _____
☐ Calm   ☐ Fair   ☐ Moderate   ☐ Heavy   ☐ Gale Sea
BOTTOM TEMPERATURE:
☐ Cold (below 55)   ☐ Normal (55 to 75)   ☐ Warm (above 75)   Vessel or Platform
BOTTOM VISIBILITY:
☐ Poor (0 to 5')   ☐ Moderate (5' to 20')   ☐ (Good 20 +)   _____
BOTTOM CURRENT:
☐ Weak (0 to 0.5KT)   ☐ Moderate (0.5 to 2)   ☐ Strong (2+)   _____

Bell Bounce or Surface Dives:	Dive One	Dive Two	Dive Three
Maximum depth of dive:	☐☐☐ feet	☐☐☐ feet	☐☐☐ feet
Time left surface or started pressurization:	☐☐ H ☐☐ min	☐☐ H ☐☐ min	☐☐ H ☐☐ min
Bottom Time:	☐☐ min	☐☐ min	☐☐ min
Decompression Completed at:	☐☐ H ☐☐ min	☐☐ H ☐☐ min	☐☐ H ☐☐ min
For surface decompression only: Surface interval:	☐☐ min	☐☐ min	☐☐ min
and time spent in chamber:	☐☐ H ☐☐ min	☐☐ H ☐☐ min	☐☐ H ☐☐ min

Saturation Dives:		
Storage depth:	☐☐☐ feet	☐☐☐ feet
Maximum depth of dive:	☐☐☐ feet	☐☐☐ feet
Time leaving storage depth:	☐☐ H ☐☐ min on ☐☐ day	☐☐ H ☐☐ min on ☐☐ day
Time returning to storage depth:	☐☐ H ☐☐ min on ☐☐ day	☐☐ H ☐☐ min on ☐☐ day
Bottom time:	☐☐ H ☐☐ min	☐☐ H ☐☐ min

Breathing Apparatus used: _____

Breathing Mixture used: _____

Work Description, Equipment and Tools Used: _____

Type of Dive	
Scuba	
Surface	
Wet Bell	
Bell Bounce	
Saturation	
Other	

Name of Decompression Schedules used: _____

Note regarding any   _____
Decompression Sickness   _____
or other Illness or Injury: _____

Any Other Remarks: _____

_____

APPROVED
Name of Diving Contractor: _____

Address of Diving Contractor _____

_____

Name of Diving Supervisor (Print) _____

Signature _____ Date: _____

RECORD OF DIVE

Date of Dive _____ Diver's Signature _____

BOTTOM CONDITION: (X appropriate blocks)
☐ Sand ☐ Shell ☐ Gravel ☐ Hard ☐ Soft

Geographic Location
_____

SEA STATE:
☐ Calm ☐ Fair ☐ Moderate ☐ Heavy ☐ Gale Sea

_____

BOTTOM TEMPERATURE:
☐ Cold (below 55) ☐ Normal (55 to 75) ☐ Warm (above 75)

Vessel or Platform

BOTTOM VISIBILITY:
☐ Poor (0 to 5') ☐ Moderate (5' to 20') ☐ (Good 20 +)

_____

BOTTOM CURRENT:
☐ Weak (0 to 0.5KT) ☐ Moderate (0.5 to 2) ☐ Strong (2+)

Bell Bounce or Surface Dives:	Dive One	Dive Two	Dive Three
Maximum depth of dive:	☐☐☐ feet	☐☐☐ feet	☐☐☐ feet
Time left surface or started pressurization:	☐☐ H ☐☐ min	☐☐ H ☐☐ min	☐☐ H ☐☐ min
Bottom Time:	☐☐☐ min	☐☐☐ min	☐☐☐ min
Decompression Completed at:	☐☐ H ☐☐ min	☐☐ H ☐☐ min	☐☐ H ☐☐ min
For surface decompression only: Surface interval:	☐☐☐ min	☐☐☐ min	☐☐☐ min
and time spent in chamber:	☐☐ H ☐☐ min	☐☐ H ☐☐ min	☐☐ H ☐☐ min

Saturation Dives:		
Storage depth:	☐☐☐ feet	☐☐☐ feet
Maximum depth of dive:	☐☐☐ feet	☐☐☐ feet
Time leaving storage depth:	☐☐ H ☐☐ min on ☐☐ day	☐☐ H ☐☐ min on ☐☐ day
Time returning to storage depth:	☐☐ H ☐☐ min on ☐☐ day	☐☐ H ☐☐ min on ☐☐ day
Bottom time:	☐☐ H ☐☐ min	☐☐ H ☐☐ min

Breathing Apparatus used: _____

Breathing Mixture used: _____

Work Description, Equipment and Tools Used: _____
_____
_____

Name of Decompression Schedules used: _____

Note regarding any
Decompression Sickness
or other Illness or Injury:
_____

Any Other Remarks: _____
_____
_____

Type of Dive

Scuba	☐
Surface	☐
Wet Bell	☐
Bell Bounce	☐
Saturation	☐
Other	

_____
_____

APPROVED
Name of Diving Contractor: _____

Address of Diving Contractor _____

Name of Diving Supervisor (Print) _____

Signature _____ Date: _____

RECORD OF DIVE

Date of Dive _____ Diver's Signature _____

BOTTOM CONDITION: (X appropriate blocks)   Geographic Location
☐ Sand ☐ Shell ☐ Gravel ☐ Hard ☐ Soft
SEA STATE: _____
☐ Calm ☐ Fair ☐ Moderate ☐ Heavy ☐ Gale Sea
BOTTOM TEMPERATURE: _____
☐ Cold (below 55) ☐ Normal (55 to 75) ☐ Warm (above 75)   Vessel or Platform
BOTTOM VISIBILITY:
☐ Poor (0 to 5') ☐ Moderate (5' to 20') ☐ (Good 20 +)   _____
BOTTOM CURRENT:
☐ Weak (0 to 0.5KT) ☐ Moderate (0.5 to 2) ☐ Strong (2+)   _____

Bell Bounce or Surface Dives:	Dive One	Dive Two	Dive Three
Maximum depth of dive:	☐☐☐ feet	☐☐☐ feet	☐☐☐ feet
Time left surface or started pressurization:	☐☐ H ☐☐ min	☐☐ H ☐☐ min	☐☐ H ☐☐ min
Bottom Time:	☐☐☐ min	☐☐☐ min	☐☐☐ min
Decompression Completed at:	☐☐ H ☐☐ min	☐☐ H ☐☐ min	☐☐ H ☐☐ min
For surface decompression only:			
Surface interval:	☐☐☐ min	☐☐☐ min	☐☐☐ min
and time spent in chamber:	☐☐ H ☐☐ min	☐☐ H ☐☐ min	☐☐ H ☐☐ min

Saturation Dives:		
Storage depth:	☐☐☐ feet	☐☐☐ feet
Maximum depth of dive:	☐☐☐ feet	☐☐☐ feet
Time leaving storage depth:	☐☐ H ☐☐ min on ☐☐ day	☐☐ H ☐☐ min on ☐☐ day
Time returning to storage depth:	☐☐ H ☐☐ min on ☐☐ day	☐☐ H ☐☐ min on ☐☐ day
Bottom time:	☐☐ H ☐☐ min	☐☐ H ☐☐ min

Breathing Apparatus used: _____

Breathing Mixture used: _____

Work Description, Equipment and Tools Used: _____

_____

Name of Decompression Schedules used: _____

Note regarding any
Decompression Sickness   _____
or other Illness or Injury: _____

Any Other Remarks: _____

_____

Type of Dive	
Scuba	☐
Surface	☐
Wet Bell	☐
Bell Bounce	☐
Saturation	☐
Other	
	_____
	_____

APPROVED
Name of Diving Contractor: _____

Address of Diving Contractor _____

_____

Name of Diving Supervisor (Print) _____

Signature _____ Date: _____

RECORD OF DIVE

Date of Dive _____ Diver's Signature _____

BOTTOM CONDITION: (X appropriate blocks)　　　　Geographic Location
☐ Sand ☐ Shell ☐ Gravel ☐ Hard ☐ Soft
_____

SEA STATE:
☐ Calm ☐ Fair ☐ Moderate ☐ Heavy ☐ Gale Sea
_____

BOTTOM TEMPERATURE:
☐ Cold (below 55) ☐ Normal (55 to 75) ☐ Warm (above 75)　　Vessel or Platform

BOTTOM VISIBILITY:
☐ Poor (0 to 5') ☐ Moderate (5' to 20') ☐ (Good 20 +)
_____

BOTTOM CURRENT:
☐ Weak (0 to 0.5KT) ☐ Moderate (0.5 to 2) ☐ Strong (2+)
_____

Bell Bounce or Surface Dives:

	Dive One	Dive Two	Dive Three
Maximum depth of dive:	☐☐☐ feet	☐☐☐ feet	☐☐☐ feet
Time left surface or started pressurization:	☐☐ H ☐☐ min	☐☐ H ☐☐ min	☐☐ H ☐☐ min
Bottom Time:	☐☐ min	☐☐ min	☐☐ min
Decompression Completed at:	☐☐ H ☐☐ min	☐☐ H ☐☐ min	☐☐ H ☐☐ min
For surface decompression only: Surface interval:	☐☐ min	☐☐ min	☐☐ min
and time spent in chamber:	☐☐ H ☐☐ min	☐☐ H ☐☐ min	☐☐ H ☐☐ min

Saturation Dives:

Storage depth:	☐☐☐ feet	☐☐☐ feet
Maximum depth of dive:	☐☐☐ feet	☐☐☐ feet
Time leaving storage depth:	☐☐ H ☐☐ min on ☐☐ day	☐☐ H ☐☐ min on ☐☐ day
Time returning to storage depth:	☐☐ H ☐☐ min on ☐☐ day	☐☐ H ☐☐ min on ☐☐ day
Bottom time:	☐☐ H ☐☐ min	☐☐ H ☐☐ min

Breathing Apparatus used: _____

_____

Breathing Mixture used: _____

_____

Work Description, Equipment and Tools Used: _____

_____

_____

Name of Decompression Schedules used: _____

Note regarding any　　　　　_____
Decompression Sickness　　　_____
or other Illness or Injury:　　_____

Any Other Remarks: _____

_____

_____

Type of Dive	
Scuba	
Surface	
Wet Bell	
Bell Bounce	
Saturation	
Other	

APPROVED

Name of Diving Contractor: _____

Address of Diving Contractor _____

_____

Name of Diving Supervisor (Print) _____

Signature _____ Date: _____

RECORD OF DIVE

Date of Dive _____ Diver's Signature _____

BOTTOM CONDITION: (X appropriate blocks)　　　　　Geographic Location
☐ Sand　☐ Shell　☐ Gravel　☐ Hard　☐ Soft
SEA STATE:　　　　　　　　　　　　　　　　　　　　_____
☐ Calm　☐ Fair　☐ Moderate　☐ Heavy　☐ Gale Sea
BOTTOM TEMPERATURE:
☐ Cold (below 55)　☐ Normal (55 to 75)　☐ Warm (above 75)　　Vessel or Platform
BOTTOM VISIBILITY:
☐ Poor (0 to 5')　☐ Moderate (5' to 20')　☐ (Good 20 +)　　_____
BOTTOM CURRENT:
☐ Weak (0 to 0.5KT)　☐ Moderate (0.5 to 2)　☐ Strong (2+)　_____

Bell Bounce or Surface Dives:	Dive One	Dive Two	Dive Three
Maximum depth of dive:	☐☐☐ feet	☐☐☐ feet	☐☐☐ feet
Time left surface or started pressurization:	☐☐ H ☐☐ min	☐☐ H ☐☐ min	☐☐ H ☐☐ min
Bottom Time:	☐☐ min	☐☐ min	☐☐ min
Decompression Completed at:	☐☐ H ☐☐ min	☐☐ H ☐☐ min	☐☐ H ☐☐ min
For surface decompression only:			
Surface interval:	☐☐ min	☐☐ min	☐☐ min
and time spent in chamber:	☐☐ H ☐☐ min	☐☐ H ☐☐ min	☐☐ H ☐☐ min

Saturation Dives:		
Storage depth:	☐☐☐ feet	☐☐☐ feet
Maximum depth of dive:	☐☐☐ feet	☐☐☐ feet
Time leaving storage depth:	☐☐ H ☐☐ min on ☐☐ day	☐☐ H ☐☐ min on ☐☐ day
Time returning to storage depth:	☐☐ H ☐☐ min on ☐☐ day	☐☐ H ☐☐ min on ☐☐ day
Bottom time:	☐☐ H ☐☐ min	☐☐ H ☐☐ min

Breathing Apparatus used: _____

Breathing Mixture used: _____

Work Description, Equipment and Tools Used: _____

_____

Name of Decompression Schedules used: _____

Note regarding any　　　　_____
Decompression Sickness　_____
or other Illness or Injury:　_____

Any Other Remarks: _____
_____
_____

Type of Dive	
Scuba	
Surface	
Wet Bell	
Bell Bounce	
Saturation	
Other	

_____
_____

APPROVED
Name of Diving Contractor: _____

Address of Diving Contractor _____

Name of Diving Supervisor (Print) _____

Signature _____ Date: _____

RECORD OF DIVE

Date of Dive _____ Diver's Signature _____

BOTTOM CONDITION: (X appropriate blocks)
☐ Sand ☐ Shell ☐ Gravel ☐ Hard ☐ Soft

SEA STATE:
☐ Calm ☐ Fair ☐ Moderate ☐ Heavy ☐ Gale Sea

BOTTOM TEMPERATURE:
☐ Cold (below 55) ☐ Normal (55 to 75) ☐ Warm (above 75)

BOTTOM VISIBILITY:
☐ Poor (0 to 5') ☐ Moderate (5' to 20') ☐ (Good 20 +)

BOTTOM CURRENT:
☐ Weak (0 to 0.5KT) ☐ Moderate (0.5 to 2) ☐ Strong (2+)

Geographic Location
_____

_____

Vessel or Platform
_____

_____

Bell Bounce or Surface Dives:	Dive One	Dive Two	Dive Three
Maximum depth of dive:	☐☐☐ feet	☐☐☐ feet	☐☐ feet
Time left surface or started pressurization:	☐☐ H ☐☐ min	☐☐ H ☐☐ min	☐☐ H ☐☐ min
Bottom Time:	☐☐ min	☐☐ min	☐☐ min
Decompression Completed at:	☐☐ H ☐☐ min	☐☐ H ☐☐ min	☐☐ H ☐☐ min
For surface decompression only: Surface interval:	☐☐ min	☐☐ min	☐☐ min
and time spent in chamber:	☐☐ H ☐☐ min	☐☐ H ☐☐ min	☐☐ H ☐☐ min

Saturation Dives:

Storage depth:	☐☐☐ feet	☐☐☐ feet
Maximum depth of dive:	☐☐☐ feet	☐☐☐ feet
Time leaving storage depth:	☐☐ H ☐☐ min on ☐☐ day	☐☐ H ☐☐ min on ☐☐ day
Time returning to storage depth:	☐☐ H ☐☐ min on ☐☐ day	☐☐ H ☐☐ min on ☐☐ day
Bottom time:	☐☐ H ☐☐ min	☐☐ H ☐☐ min

Breathing Apparatus used: _____

_____

Breathing Mixture used: _____

_____

Work Description, Equipment and Tools Used:

_____

_____

Name of Decompression Schedules used: _____

Note regarding any
Decompression Sickness _____
or other Illness or Injury: _____

Any Other Remarks: _____

_____

_____

Type of Dive	
Scuba	☐
Surface	☐
Wet Bell	☐
Bell Bounce	☐
Saturation	☐
Other	

_____

_____

APPROVED

Name of Diving Contractor: _____

Address of Diving Contractor _____

_____

Name of Diving Supervisor (Print) _____

Signature _____ Date: _____

RECORD OF DIVE

Date of Dive _____ Diver's Signature _____

BOTTOM CONDITION: (X appropriate blocks)
□ Sand □ Shell □ Gravel □ Hard □ Soft

Geographic Location

SEA STATE:
□ Calm □ Fair □ Moderate □ Heavy □ Gale Sea

_____

BOTTOM TEMPERATURE:
□ Cold (below 55) □ Normal (55 to 75) □ Warm (above 75)

Vessel or Platform

BOTTOM VISIBILITY:
□ Poor (0 to 5') □ Moderate (5' to 20') □ (Good 20 +)

_____

BOTTOM CURRENT:
□ Weak (0 to 0.5KT) □ Moderate (0.5 to 2) □ Strong (2+)

Bell Bounce or Surface Dives:

	Dive One	Dive Two	Dive Three
Maximum depth of dive:	☐☐☐ feet	☐☐☐ feet	☐☐☐ feet
Time left surface or started pressurization:	☐☐ H ☐☐ min	☐☐ H ☐☐ min	☐☐ H ☐☐ min
Bottom Time:	☐☐☐ min	☐☐☐ min	☐☐☐ min
Decompression Completed at:	☐☐ H ☐☐ min	☐☐ H ☐☐ min	☐☐ H ☐☐ min
For surface decompression only:			
Surface interval:	☐☐☐ min	☐☐☐ min	☐☐☐ min
and time spent in chamber:	☐☐ H ☐☐ min	☐☐ H ☐☐ min	☐☐ H ☐☐ min

Saturation Dives:

Storage depth:	☐☐☐ feet	☐☐☐ feet
Maximum depth of dive:	☐☐☐ feet	☐☐☐ feet
Time leaving storage depth:	☐☐ H ☐☐ min on ☐☐ day	☐☐ H ☐☐ min on ☐☐ day
Time returning to storage depth:	☐☐ H ☐☐ min on ☐☐ day	☐☐ H ☐☐ min on ☐☐ day
Bottom time:	☐☐ H ☐☐ min	☐☐ H ☐☐ min

Breathing Apparatus used: _____

Breathing Mixture used: _____

Work Description, Equipment and Tools Used:
_____
_____

Name of Decompression Schedules used: _____

Note regarding any
Decompression Sickness _____
or other Illness or Injury: _____

Any Other Remarks: _____
_____
_____

Type of Dive

Scuba	
Surface	
Wet Bell	
Bell Bounce	
Saturation	

Other
_____
_____

APPROVED
Name of Diving Contractor: _____

Address of Diving Contractor _____
_____

Name of Diving Supervisor (Print) _____

Signature _____ Date: _____

RECORD OF DIVE

Date of Dive _____ Diver's Signature _____

BOTTOM CONDITION: (X appropriate blocks)   Geographic Location
☐ Sand ☐ Shell ☐ Gravel ☐ Hard ☐ Soft
SEA STATE: _____
☐ Calm ☐ Fair ☐ Moderate ☐ Heavy ☐ Gale Sea
BOTTOM TEMPERATURE: _____
☐ Cold (below 55) ☐ Normal (55 to 75) ☐ Warm (above 75)   Vessel or Platform
BOTTOM VISIBILITY:
☐ Poor (0 to 5') ☐ Moderate (5' to 20') ☐ (Good 20 +)   _____
BOTTOM CURRENT:
☐ Weak (0 to 0.5KT) ☐ Moderate (0.5 to 2) ☐ Strong (2+)   _____

Bell Bounce or Surface Dives:	Dive One	Dive Two	Dive Three
Maximum depth of dive:	☐☐☐ feet	☐☐☐ feet	☐☐☐ feet
Time left surface or started pressurization:	☐☐ H ☐☐ min	☐☐ H ☐☐ min	☐☐ H ☐☐ min
Bottom Time:	☐☐☐ min	☐☐☐ min	☐☐☐ min
Decompression Completed at:	☐☐ H ☐☐ min	☐☐ H ☐☐ min	☐☐ H ☐☐ min
For surface decompression only: Surface interval:	☐☐ min	☐☐ min	☐☐ min
and time spent in chamber:	☐☐ H ☐☐ min	☐☐ H ☐☐ min	☐☐ H ☐☐ min

Saturation Dives:		
Storage depth:	☐☐☐ feet	☐☐☐ feet
Maximum depth of dive:	☐☐☐ feet	☐☐☐ feet
Time leaving storage depth:	☐☐ H ☐☐ min on ☐☐ day	☐☐ H ☐☐ min on ☐☐ day
Time returning to storage depth:	☐☐ H ☐☐ min on ☐☐ day	☐☐ H ☐☐ min on ☐☐ day
Bottom time:	☐☐ H ☐☐ min	☐☐ H ☐☐ min

Breathing Apparatus used: _____

Breathing Mixture used: _____

Work Description, Equipment and Tools Used: _____
_____
_____

Name of Decompression Schedules used: _____

Note regarding any   _____
Decompression Sickness   _____
or other Illness or Injury: _____

Any Other Remarks: _____
_____
_____

Type of Dive	
Scuba	
Surface	
Wet Bell	
Bell Bounce	
Saturation	
Other	

_____
_____

APPROVED
Name of Diving Contractor: _____

Address of Diving Contractor _____
_____

Name of Diving Supervisor (Print) _____

Signature _____ Date: _____

RECORD OF DIVE

Date of Dive _____ Diver's Signature _____

BOTTOM CONDITION: (X appropriate blocks)

☐ Sand ☐ Shell ☐ Gravel ☐ Hard ☐ Soft

SEA STATE:

☐ Calm ☐ Fair ☐ Moderate ☐ Heavy ☐ Gale Sea

BOTTOM TEMPERATURE:

☐ Cold (below 55) ☐ Normal (55 to 75) ☐ Warm (above 75)

BOTTOM VISIBILITY:

☐ Poor (0 to 5') ☐ Moderate (5' to 20') ☐ (Good 20 +)

BOTTOM CURRENT:

☐ Weak (0 to 0.5KT) ☐ Moderate (0.5 to 2) ☐ Strong (2+)

Geographic Location

_____

_____

Vessel or Platform

_____

_____

Bell Bounce or Surface Dives:	Dive One	Dive Two	Dive Three
Maximum depth of dive:	☐☐☐ feet	☐☐☐ feet	☐☐☐ feet
Time left surface or started pressurization:	☐☐ H ☐☐ min	☐☐ H ☐☐ min	☐☐ H ☐☐ min
Bottom Time:	☐☐ min	☐☐ min	☐☐ min
Decompression Completed at:	☐☐ H ☐☐ min	☐☐ H ☐☐ min	☐☐ H ☐☐ min
For surface decompression only: Surface interval:	☐☐ min	☐☐ min	☐☐ min
and time spent in chamber:	☐☐ H ☐☐ min	☐☐ H ☐☐ min	☐☐ H ☐☐ min

Saturation Dives:		
Storage depth:	☐☐☐☐ feet	☐☐☐☐ feet
Maximum depth of dive:	☐☐☐☐ feet	☐☐☐☐ feet
Time leaving storage depth:	☐☐ H ☐☐ min on ☐☐ day	☐☐ H ☐☐ min on ☐☐ day
Time returning to storage depth:	☐☐ H ☐☐ min on ☐☐ day	☐☐ H ☐☐ min on ☐☐ day
Bottom time:	☐☐ H ☐☐ min	☐☐ H ☐☐ min

Breathing Apparatus used: _____

_____

Breathing Mixture used: _____

_____

Work Description, Equipment and Tools Used: _____

_____

_____

Name of Decompression Schedules used: _____

Note regarding any
Decompression Sickness _____
or other Illness or Injury: _____

Any Other Remarks: _____

_____

_____

Type of Dive	
Scuba	
Surface	
Wet Bell	
Bell Bounce	
Saturation	
Other	

_____

_____

APPROVED

Name of Diving Contractor: _____

Address of Diving Contractor _____

_____

Name of Diving Supervisor (Print) _____

Signature _____ Date: _____

RECORD OF DIVE

Date of Dive _____ Diver's Signature _____

BOTTOM CONDITION: (X appropriate blocks)
☐ Sand ☐ Shell ☐ Gravel ☐ Hard ☐ Soft

Geographic Location

SEA STATE:
☐ Calm ☐ Fair ☐ Moderate ☐ Heavy ☐ Gale Sea

_____

BOTTOM TEMPERATURE:
☐ Cold (below 55) ☐ Normal (55 to 75) ☐ Warm (above 75)

_____

Vessel or Platform

BOTTOM VISIBILITY:
☐ Poor (0 to 5') ☐ Moderate (5' to 20') ☐ (Good 20 +)

_____

BOTTOM CURRENT:
☐ Weak (0 to 0.5KT) ☐ Moderate (0.5 to 2) ☐ Strong (2+)

_____

Bell Bounce or Surface Dives:	Dive One	Dive Two	Dive Three
Maximum depth of dive:	☐☐☐ feet	☐☐☐ feet	☐☐☐ feet
Time left surface or started pressurization:	☐☐ H ☐☐ min	☐☐ H ☐☐ min	☐☐ H ☐☐ min
Bottom Time:	☐☐☐ min	☐☐☐ min	☐☐☐ min
Decompression Completed at:	☐☐ H ☐☐ min	☐☐ H ☐☐ min	☐☐ H ☐☐ min
For surface decompression only: Surface interval:	☐☐☐ min	☐☐☐ min	☐☐☐ min
and time spent in chamber:	☐☐ H ☐☐ min	☐☐ H ☐☐ min	☐☐ H ☐☐ min

Saturation Dives:			
Storage depth:	☐☐☐☐ feet		☐☐☐☐ feet
Maximum depth of dive:	☐☐☐☐ feet		☐☐☐☐ feet
Time leaving storage depth:	☐☐ H ☐☐ min on ☐☐ day		☐☐ H ☐☐ min on ☐☐ day
Time returning to storage depth:	☐☐ H ☐☐ min on ☐☐ day		☐☐ H ☐☐ min on ☐☐ day
Bottom time:	☐☐ H ☐☐ min		☐☐ H ☐☐ min

Breathing Apparatus used: _____
_____

Breathing Mixture used: _____
_____

Work Description, Equipment and Tools Used: _____
_____
_____

Name of Decompression Schedules used: _____

Note regarding any
Decompression Sickness _____
or other Illness or Injury: _____
_____

Any Other Remarks: _____
_____
_____

Type of Dive	
Scuba	☐
Surface	☐
Wet Bell	☐
Bell Bounce	☐
Saturation	☐
Other	

_____
_____

APPROVED

Name of Diving Contractor: _____

Address of Diving Contractor _____
_____

Name of Diving Supervisor (Print) _____

Signature _____ Date: _____

RECORD OF DIVE

Date of Dive _____ Diver's Signature _____

BOTTOM CONDITION: (X appropriate blocks)   Geographic Location
☐ Sand ☐ Shell ☐ Gravel ☐ Hard ☐ Soft
SEA STATE: _____
☐ Calm ☐ Fair ☐ Moderate ☐ Heavy ☐ Gale Sea
BOTTOM TEMPERATURE:
☐ Cold (below 55) ☐ Normal (55 to 75) ☐ Warm (above 75)   Vessel or Platform
BOTTOM VISIBILITY:
☐ Poor (0 to 5') ☐ Moderate (5' to 20') ☐ (Good 20 +)   _____
BOTTOM CURRENT:
☐ Weak (0 to 0.5KT) ☐ Moderate (0.5 to 2) ☐ Strong (2+)   _____

Bell Bounce or Surface Dives:	Dive One	Dive Two	Dive Three
Maximum depth of dive:	☐☐☐ feet	☐☐☐ feet	☐☐☐ feet
Time left surface or started pressurization:	☐☐H ☐☐ min	☐☐H ☐☐ min	☐☐H ☐☐ min
Bottom Time:	☐☐ min	☐☐ min	☐☐ min
Decompression Completed at:	☐☐H ☐☐ min	☐☐H ☐☐ min	☐☐H ☐☐ min
For surface decompression only:			
Surface interval:	☐☐ min	☐☐ min	☐☐ min
and time spent in chamber:	☐☐H ☐☐ min	☐☐H ☐☐ min	☐☐H ☐☐ min

Saturation Dives:		
Storage depth:	☐☐☐ feet	☐☐☐ feet
Maximum depth of dive:	☐☐☐ feet	☐☐☐ feet
Time leaving storage depth:	☐☐H ☐☐ min on ☐☐ day	☐☐H ☐☐ min on ☐☐ day
Time returning to storage depth:	☐☐H ☐☐ min on ☐☐ day	☐☐H ☐☐ min on ☐☐ day
Bottom time:	☐☐H ☐☐ min	☐☐H ☐☐ min

Breathing Apparatus used: _____

Breathing Mixture used: _____

Work Description, Equipment and Tools Used: _____

_____

Type of Dive	
Scuba	
Surface	
Wet Bell	
Bell Bounce	
Saturation	
Other	

Name of Decompression Schedules used: _____

Note regarding any   _____
Decompression Sickness   _____
or other Illness or Injury: _____

Any Other Remarks: _____

_____
_____

APPROVED
Name of Diving Contractor: _____

Address of Diving Contractor _____

_____

Name of Diving Supervisor (Print) _____

Signature _____ Date: _____

RECORD OF DIVE

Date of Dive _____ Diver's Signature _____

BOTTOM CONDITION: (X appropriate blocks)   Geographic Location
☐ Sand ☐ Shell ☐ Gravel ☐ Hard ☐ Soft
SEA STATE: _____
☐ Calm ☐ Fair ☐ Moderate ☐ Heavy ☐ Gale Sea
BOTTOM TEMPERATURE: _____
☐ Cold (below 55) ☐ Normal (55 to 75) ☐ Warm (above 75)   Vessel or Platform
BOTTOM VISIBILITY:
☐ Poor (0 to 5') ☐ Moderate (5' to 20') ☐ (Good 20 +)   _____
BOTTOM CURRENT:
☐ Weak (0 to 0.5KT) ☐ Moderate (0.5 to 2) ☐ Strong (2+)   _____

Bell Bounce or Surface Dives:	Dive One	Dive Two	Dive Three
Maximum depth of dive:	☐☐☐ feet	☐☐☐ feet	☐☐☐ feet
Time left surface or started pressurization:	☐☐ H ☐☐ min	☐☐ H ☐☐ min	☐☐ H ☐☐ min
Bottom Time:	☐☐ min	☐☐ min	☐☐ min
Decompression Completed at:	☐☐ H ☐☐ min	☐☐ H ☐☐ min	☐☐ H ☐☐ min
For surface decompression only: Surface interval:	☐☐ min	☐☐ min	☐☐ min
and time spent in chamber:	☐☐ H ☐☐ min	☐☐ H ☐☐ min	☐☐ H ☐☐ min

Saturation Dives:		
Storage depth:	☐☐☐ feet	☐☐☐ feet
Maximum depth of dive:	☐☐☐ feet	☐☐☐ feet
Time leaving storage depth:	☐☐ H ☐☐ min on ☐☐ day	☐☐ H ☐☐ min on ☐☐ day
Time returning to storage depth:	☐☐ H ☐☐ min on ☐☐ day	☐☐ H ☐☐ min on ☐☐ day
Bottom time:	☐☐ H ☐☐ min	☐☐ H ☐☐ min

Breathing Apparatus used: _____
_____

Breathing Mixture used: _____

Work Description, Equipment and Tools Used: _____
_____
_____

Name of Decompression Schedules used: _____

Note regarding any   _____
Decompression Sickness   _____
or other Illness or Injury: _____

Any Other Remarks: _____
_____
_____

Type of Dive

Scuba	☐
Surface	☐
Wet Bell	☐
Bell Bounce	☐
Saturation	☐
Other	
_____	
_____	

APPROVED
Name of Diving Contractor: _____

Address of Diving Contractor _____
_____

Name of Diving Supervisor (Print) _____

Signature _____ Date: _____

RECORD OF DIVE

Date of Dive _____ Diver's Signature _____

BOTTOM CONDITION: (X appropriate blocks)
☐ Sand ☐ Shell ☐ Gravel ☐ Hard ☐ Soft

Geographic Location
_____

SEA STATE:
☐ Calm ☐ Fair ☐ Moderate ☐ Heavy ☐ Gale Sea

_____

BOTTOM TEMPERATURE:
☐ Cold (below 55) ☐ Normal (55 to 75) ☐ Warm (above 75)

Vessel or Platform

BOTTOM VISIBILITY:
☐ Poor (0 to 5') ☐ Moderate (5' to 20') ☐ (Good 20 +)

_____

BOTTOM CURRENT:
☐ Weak (0 to 0.5KT) ☐ Moderate (0.5 to 2) ☐ Strong (2+)

_____

Bell Bounce or Surface Dives:	Dive One	Dive Two	Dive Three
Maximum depth of dive:	☐☐☐ feet	☐☐☐ feet	☐☐☐ feet
Time left surface or started pressurization:	☐☐ H ☐☐ min	☐☐ H ☐☐ min	☐☐ H ☐☐ min
Bottom Time:	☐☐☐ min	☐☐☐ min	☐☐☐ min
Decompression Completed at:	☐☐ H ☐☐ min	☐☐ H ☐☐ min	☐☐ H ☐☐ min
For surface decompression only: Surface interval:	☐☐☐ min	☐☐☐ min	☐☐☐ min
and time spent in chamber:	☐☐ H ☐☐ min	☐☐ H ☐☐ min	☐☐ H ☐☐ min

Saturation Dives:		
Storage depth:	☐☐☐☐ feet	☐☐☐☐ feet
Maximum depth of dive:	☐☐☐☐ feet	☐☐☐☐ feet
Time leaving storage depth:	☐☐ H ☐☐ min on ☐☐ day	☐☐ H ☐☐ min on ☐☐ day
Time returning to storage depth:	☐☐ H ☐☐ min on ☐☐ day	☐☐ H ☐☐ min on ☐☐ day
Bottom time:	☐☐ H ☐☐ min	☐☐ H ☐☐ min

Breathing Apparatus used: _____

Breathing Mixture used: _____

Work Description, Equipment and Tools Used:
_____
_____

Name of Decompression Schedules used: _____

Note regarding any
Decompression Sickness
or other Illness or Injury:
_____
_____
_____

Any Other Remarks: _____
_____
_____

Type of Dive	
Scuba	☐
Surface	☐
Wet Bell	☐
Bell Bounce	☐
Saturation	☐
Other	
_____	
_____	

APPROVED
Name of Diving Contractor: _____

Address of Diving Contractor _____
_____

Name of Diving Supervisor (Print) _____

Signature _____ Date: _____

RECORD OF DIVE

Date of Dive _____ Diver's Signature _____

BOTTOM CONDITION: (X appropriate blocks)
☐ Sand ☐ Shell ☐ Gravel ☐ Hard ☐ Soft

Geographic Location
_____

SEA STATE:
☐ Calm ☐ Fair ☐ Moderate ☐ Heavy ☐ Gale Sea
_____

BOTTOM TEMPERATURE:
☐ Cold (below 55) ☐ Normal (55 to 75) ☐ Warm (above 75)

Vessel or Platform

BOTTOM VISIBILITY:
☐ Poor (0 to 5') ☐ Moderate (5' to 20') ☐ (Good 20 +)
_____

BOTTOM CURRENT:
☐ Weak (0 to 0.5KT) ☐ Moderate (0.5 to 2) ☐ Strong (2+)
_____

Bell Bounce or Surface Dives:	Dive One	Dive Two	Dive Three
Maximum depth of dive:	☐☐☐ feet	☐☐☐ feet	☐☐☐ feet
Time left surface or started pressurization:	☐☐ H ☐☐ min	☐☐ H ☐☐ min	☐☐ H ☐☐ min
Bottom Time:	☐☐ min	☐☐ min	☐☐ min
Decompression Completed at:	☐☐ H ☐☐ min	☐☐ H ☐☐ min	☐☐ H ☐☐ min
For surface decompression only: Surface interval:	☐☐ min	☐☐ min	☐☐ min
and time spent in chamber:	☐☐ H ☐☐ min	☐☐ H ☐☐ min	☐☐ H ☐☐ min

Saturation Dives:		
Storage depth:	☐☐☐ feet	☐☐☐ feet
Maximum depth of dive:	☐☐☐ feet	☐☐☐ feet
Time leaving storage depth:	☐☐ H ☐☐ min on ☐☐ day	☐☐ H ☐☐ min on ☐☐ day
Time returning to storage depth:	☐☐ H ☐☐ min on ☐☐ day	☐☐ H ☐☐ min on ☐☐ day
Bottom time:	☐☐ H ☐☐ min	☐☐ H ☐☐ min

Breathing Apparatus used: _____
_____

Breathing Mixture used: _____

Work Description, Equipment and Tools Used:
_____
_____
_____

Name of Decompression Schedules used: _____

Note regarding any
Decompression Sickness   _____
or other Illness or Injury: _____
_____

Any Other Remarks: _____
_____
_____

Type of Dive	
Scuba	☐
Surface	☐
Wet Bell	☐
Bell Bounce	☐
Saturation	☐
Other	
_____	
_____	

APPROVED

Name of Diving Contractor: _____

Address of Diving Contractor _____

Name of Diving Supervisor (Print) _____

Signature _____ Date: _____

RECORD OF DIVE

Date of Dive _____ Diver's Signature _____

BOTTOM CONDITION: (X appropriate blocks)
☐ Sand ☐ Shell ☐ Gravel ☐ Hard ☐ Soft

Geographic Location

SEA STATE:
☐ Calm ☐ Fair ☐ Moderate ☐ Heavy ☐ Gale Sea

_____

BOTTOM TEMPERATURE:
☐ Cold (below 55) ☐ Normal (55 to 75) ☐ Warm (above 75)

Vessel or Platform

BOTTOM VISIBILITY:
☐ Poor (0 to 5') ☐ Moderate (5' to 20') ☐ (Good 20 +)

_____

BOTTOM CURRENT:
☐ Weak (0 to 0.5KT) ☐ Moderate (0.5 to 2) ☐ Strong (2+)

_____

Bell Bounce or Surface Dives:	Dive One	Dive Two	Dive Three
Maximum depth of dive:	☐☐☐ feet	☐☐☐ feet	☐☐☐ feet
Time left surface or started pressurization:	☐☐ H ☐☐ min	☐☐ H ☐☐ min	☐☐ H ☐☐ min
Bottom Time:	☐☐☐ min	☐☐☐ min	☐☐☐ min
Decompression Completed at:	☐☐ H ☐☐ min	☐☐ H ☐☐ min	☐☐ H ☐☐ min
For surface decompression only: Surface interval:	☐☐☐ min	☐☐☐ min	☐☐☐ min
and time spent in chamber:	☐☐ H ☐☐ min	☐☐ H ☐☐ min	☐☐ H ☐☐ min

Saturation Dives:		
Storage depth:	☐☐☐ feet	☐☐☐ feet
Maximum depth of dive:	☐☐☐ feet	☐☐☐ feet
Time leaving storage depth:	☐☐ H ☐☐ min on ☐☐ day	☐☐ H ☐☐ min on ☐☐ day
Time returning to storage depth:	☐☐ H ☐☐ min on ☐☐ day	☐☐ H ☐☐ min on ☐☐ day
Bottom time:	☐☐ H ☐☐ min	☐☐ H ☐☐ min

Breathing Apparatus used: _____

Breathing Mixture used: _____

Work Description, Equipment and Tools Used: _____

Name of Decompression Schedules used: _____

Note regarding any
Decompression Sickness _____
or other Illness or Injury: _____

Any Other Remarks: _____

Type of Dive	
Scuba	☐
Surface	☐
Wet Bell	☐
Bell Bounce	☐
Saturation	☐
Other	

APPROVED
Name of Diving Contractor: _____

Address of Diving Contractor _____

Name of Diving Supervisor (Print) _____

Signature _____ Date: _____

RECORD OF DIVE

Date of Dive _____ Diver's Signature _____

BOTTOM CONDITION: (X appropriate blocks)
☐ Sand ☐ Shell ☐ Gravel ☐ Hard ☐ Soft

Geographic Location

_____

SEA STATE:
☐ Calm ☐ Fair ☐ Moderate ☐ Heavy ☐ Gale Sea

_____

BOTTOM TEMPERATURE:
☐ Cold (below 55) ☐ Normal (55 to 75) ☐ Warm (above 75)

Vessel or Platform

BOTTOM VISIBILITY:
☐ Poor (0 to 5') ☐ Moderate (5' to 20') ☐ (Good 20 +)

_____

BOTTOM CURRENT:
☐ Weak (0 to 0.5KT) ☐ Moderate (0.5 to 2) ☐ Strong (2+)

Bell Bounce or Surface Dives:	Dive One	Dive Two	Dive Three
Maximum depth of dive:	☐☐☐ feet	☐☐☐ feet	☐☐☐ feet
Time left surface or started pressurization:	☐☐ H ☐☐ min	☐☐ H ☐☐ min	☐☐ H ☐☐ min
Bottom Time:	☐☐☐ min	☐☐☐ min	☐☐☐ min
Decompression Completed at:	☐☐ H ☐☐ min	☐☐ H ☐☐ min	☐☐ H ☐☐ min
For surface decompression only: Surface interval:	☐☐☐ min	☐☐☐ min	☐☐☐ min
and time spent in chamber:	☐☐ H ☐☐ min	☐☐ H ☐☐ min	☐☐ H ☐☐ min

Saturation Dives:		
Storage depth:	☐☐☐ feet	☐☐☐ feet
Maximum depth of dive:	☐☐☐ feet	☐☐☐ feet
Time leaving storage depth:	☐☐ H ☐☐ min on ☐☐ day	☐☐ H ☐☐ min on ☐☐ day
Time returning to storage depth:	☐☐ H ☐☐ min on ☐☐ day	☐☐ H ☐☐ min on ☐☐ day
Bottom time:	☐☐ H ☐☐ min	☐☐ H ☐☐ min

Breathing Apparatus used: _____

Breathing Mixture used: _____

Work Description, Equipment and Tools Used: _____

Name of Decompression Schedules used: _____

Note regarding any
Decompression Sickness
or other Illness or Injury: _____

Any Other Remarks: _____

Type of Dive	
Scuba	
Surface	
Wet Bell	
Bell Bounce	
Saturation	
Other	

APPROVED
Name of Diving Contractor: _____

Address of Diving Contractor _____

Name of Diving Supervisor (Print) _____

Signature _____ Date: _____

RECORD OF DIVE

Date of Dive _____ Diver's Signature _____

BOTTOM CONDITION: (X appropriate blocks)
☐ Sand ☐ Shell ☐ Gravel ☐ Hard ☐ Soft

Geographic Location
_____

SEA STATE:
☐ Calm ☐ Fair ☐ Moderate ☐ Heavy ☐ Gale Sea
_____

BOTTOM TEMPERATURE:
☐ Cold (below 55) ☐ Normal (55 to 75) ☐ Warm (above 75)

Vessel or Platform

BOTTOM VISIBILITY:
☐ Poor (0 to 5′) ☐ Moderate (5′ to 20′) ☐ (Good 20 +)
_____

BOTTOM CURRENT:
☐ Weak (0 to 0.5KT) ☐ Moderate (0.5 to 2) ☐ Strong (2+)
_____

Bell Bounce or Surface Dives:

	Dive One	Dive Two	Dive Three
Maximum depth of dive:	☐☐☐ feet	☐☐☐ feet	☐☐☐ feet
Time left surface or started pressurization:	☐☐ H ☐☐ min	☐☐ H ☐☐ min	☐☐ H ☐☐ min
Bottom Time:	☐☐ min	☐☐ min	☐☐ min
Decompression Completed at:	☐☐ H ☐☐ min	☐☐ H ☐☐ min	☐☐ H ☐☐ min
For surface decompression only: Surface interval:	☐☐ min	☐☐ min	☐☐ min
and time spent in chamber:	☐☐ H ☐☐ min	☐☐ H ☐☐ min	☐☐ H ☐☐ min

Saturation Dives:

Storage depth:	☐☐☐ feet	☐☐☐ feet
Maximum depth of dive:	☐☐☐ feet	☐☐☐ feet
Time leaving storage depth:	☐☐ H ☐☐ min on ☐☐ day	☐☐ H ☐☐ min on ☐☐ day
Time returning to storage depth:	☐☐ H ☐☐ min on ☐☐ day	☐☐ H ☐☐ min on ☐☐ day
Bottom time:	☐☐ H ☐☐ min	☐☐ H ☐☐ min

Breathing Apparatus used: _____
_____

Breathing Mixture used: _____
_____

Work Description, Equipment and Tools Used: _____
_____
_____

Name of Decompression Schedules used: _____

Note regarding any
Decompression Sickness
or other Illness or Injury: _____

Any Other Remarks: _____
_____
_____

Type of Dive	
Scuba	☐
Surface	☐
Wet Bell	☐
Bell Bounce	☐
Saturation	☐
Other	

APPROVED

Name of Diving Contractor: _____

Address of Diving Contractor _____
_____

Name of Diving Supervisor (Print) _____

Signature _____ Date: _____

RECORD OF DIVE

Date of Dive _____ Diver's Signature _____

BOTTOM CONDITION: (X appropriate blocks)
□ Sand □ Shell □ Gravel □ Hard □ Soft

SEA STATE:
□ Calm □ Fair □ Moderate □ Heavy □ Gale Sea

BOTTOM TEMPERATURE:
□ Cold (below 55) □ Normal (55 to 75) □ Warm (above 75)

BOTTOM VISIBILITY:
□ Poor (0 to 5') □ Moderate (5' to 20') □ (Good 20 +)

BOTTOM CURRENT:
□ Weak (0 to 0.5KT) □ Moderate (0.5 to 2) □ Strong (2+)

Geographic Location

_____

_____

Vessel or Platform

_____

_____

Bell Bounce or Surface Dives:

	Dive One	Dive Two	Dive Three
Maximum depth of dive:	☐☐☐ feet	☐☐☐ feet	☐☐☐ feet
Time left surface or started pressurization:	☐☐ H ☐☐ min	☐☐ H ☐☐ min	☐☐ H ☐☐ min
Bottom Time:	☐☐☐ min	☐☐☐ min	☐☐☐ min
Decompression Completed at:	☐☐ H ☐☐ min	☐☐ H ☐☐ min	☐☐ H ☐☐ min
For surface decompression only: Surface interval:	☐☐☐ min	☐☐☐ min	☐☐☐ min
and time spent in chamber:	☐☐ H ☐☐ min	☐☐ H ☐☐ min	☐☐ H ☐☐ min

Saturation Dives:

Storage depth:	☐☐☐ feet	☐☐☐ feet
Maximum depth of dive:	☐☐☐ feet	☐☐☐ feet
Time leaving storage depth:	☐☐ H ☐☐ min on ☐☐ day	☐☐ H ☐☐ min on ☐☐ day
Time returning to storage depth:	☐☐ H ☐☐ min on ☐☐ day	☐☐ H ☐☐ min on ☐☐ day
Bottom time:	☐☐ H ☐☐ min	☐☐ H ☐☐ min

Breathing Apparatus used: _____

_____

Breathing Mixture used: _____

_____

Work Description, Equipment and Tools Used:

_____

_____

Name of Decompression Schedules used: _____

Note regarding any
Decompression Sickness   _____
or other Illness or Injury: _____

Any Other Remarks: _____

_____

_____

Type of Dive

Scuba	
Surface	
Wet Bell	
Bell Bounce	
Saturation	

Other

_____

_____

APPROVED
Name of Diving Contractor: _____

Address of Diving Contractor _____

_____

Name of Diving Supervisor (Print) _____

Signature _____ Date: _____

RECORD OF DIVE

Date of Dive _____ Diver's Signature _____

BOTTOM CONDITION: (X appropriate blocks)   Geographic Location
☐ Sand ☐ Shell ☐ Gravel ☐ Hard ☐ Soft
SEA STATE: _____
☐ Calm ☐ Fair ☐ Moderate ☐ Heavy ☐ Gale Sea
BOTTOM TEMPERATURE:
☐ Cold (below 55) ☐ Normal (55 to 75) ☐ Warm (above 75)   Vessel or Platform
BOTTOM VISIBILITY:
☐ Poor (0 to 5') ☐ Moderate (5' to 20') ☐ (Good 20 +)   _____
BOTTOM CURRENT:
☐ Weak (0 to 0.5KT) ☐ Moderate (0.5 to 2) ☐ Strong (2+)

Bell Bounce or Surface Dives:	Dive One	Dive Two	Dive Three
Maximum depth of dive:	☐☐☐ feet	☐☐☐ feet	☐☐☐ feet
Time left surface or started pressurization:	☐☐ H ☐☐ min	☐☐ H ☐☐ min	☐☐ H ☐☐ min
Bottom Time:	☐☐ min	☐☐ min	☐☐ min
Decompression Completed at:	☐☐ H ☐☐ min	☐☐ H ☐☐ min	☐☐ H ☐☐ min
For surface decompression only: Surface interval:	☐☐ min	☐☐ min	☐☐ min
and time spent in chamber:	☐☐ H ☐☐ min	☐☐ H ☐☐ min	☐☐ H ☐☐ min

Saturation Dives:		
Storage depth:	☐☐☐ feet	☐☐☐ feet
Maximum depth of dive:	☐☐☐ feet	☐☐☐ feet
Time leaving storage depth:	☐☐ H ☐☐ min on ☐☐ day	☐☐ H ☐☐ min on ☐☐ day
Time returning to storage depth:	☐☐ H ☐☐ min on ☐☐ day	☐☐ H ☐☐ min on ☐☐ day
Bottom time:	☐☐ H ☐☐ min	☐☐ H ☐☐ min

Breathing Apparatus used: _____

Breathing Mixture used: _____

Work Description, Equipment and Tools Used: _____
_____
_____

Name of Decompression Schedules used: _____

Note regarding any   _____
Decompression Sickness   _____
or other Illness or Injury: _____

Any Other Remarks: _____
_____
_____

Type of Dive	
Scuba	
Surface	
Wet Bell	
Bell Bounce	
Saturation	
Other	

APPROVED
Name of Diving Contractor: _____

Address of Diving Contractor _____
_____

Name of Diving Supervisor (Print) _____

Signature _____ Date: _____

RECORD OF DIVE

Date of Dive _____ Diver's Signature _____

BOTTOM CONDITION: (X appropriate blocks)
□ Sand   □ Shell   □ Gravel   □ Hard   □ Soft

SEA STATE:
□ Calm   □ Fair   □ Moderate   □ Heavy   □ Gale Sea

BOTTOM TEMPERATURE:
□ Cold (below 55)   □ Normal (55 to 75)   □ Warm (above 75)

BOTTOM VISIBILITY:
□ Poor (0 to 5')   □ Moderate (5' to 20')   □ (Good 20 +)

BOTTOM CURRENT:
□ Weak (0 to 0.5KT)   □ Moderate (0.5 to 2)   □ Strong (2+)

Geographic Location
_____

_____

Vessel or Platform
_____

_____

Bell Bounce or Surface Dives:	Dive One	Dive Two	Dive Three
Maximum depth of dive:	☐☐☐ feet	☐☐☐ feet	☐☐☐ feet
Time left surface or started pressurization:	☐☐ H ☐☐ min	☐☐ H ☐☐ min	☐☐ H ☐☐ min
Bottom Time:	☐☐ min	☐☐ min	☐☐ min
Decompression Completed at:	☐☐ H ☐☐ min	☐☐ H ☐☐ min	☐☐ H ☐☐ min
For surface decompression only: Surface interval:	☐☐ min	☐☐ min	☐☐ min
and time spent in chamber:	☐☐ H ☐☐ min	☐☐ H ☐☐ min	☐☐ H ☐☐ min

Saturation Dives:		
Storage depth:	☐☐☐☐ feet	☐☐☐ feet
Maximum depth of dive:	☐☐☐☐ feet	☐☐☐ feet
Time leaving storage depth:	☐☐ H ☐☐ min on ☐☐ day	☐☐ H ☐☐ min on ☐☐ day
Time returning to storage depth:	☐☐ H ☐☐ min on ☐☐ day	☐☐ H ☐☐ min on ☐☐ day
Bottom time:	☐☐ H ☐☐ min	☐☐ H ☐☐ min

Breathing Apparatus used: _____

Breathing Mixture used: _____

Work Description, Equipment and Tools Used: _____
_____

Name of Decompression Schedules used: _____

Note regarding any Decompression Sickness or other Illness or Injury: _____

Any Other Remarks: _____
_____
_____

Type of Dive	
Scuba	
Surface	
Wet Bell	
Bell Bounce	
Saturation	
Other	

_____
_____

APPROVED
Name of Diving Contractor: _____
Address of Diving Contractor _____
_____

Name of Diving Supervisor (Print) _____
Signature _____ Date: _____

RECORD OF DIVE

Date of Dive _____ Diver's Signature _____

BOTTOM CONDITION: (X appropriate blocks)
☐ Sand ☐ Shell ☐ Gravel ☐ Hard ☐ Soft

Geographic Location

SEA STATE:
☐ Calm ☐ Fair ☐ Moderate ☐ Heavy ☐ Gale Sea

_____

BOTTOM TEMPERATURE:
☐ Cold (below 55) ☐ Normal (55 to 75) ☐ Warm (above 75)

Vessel or Platform

BOTTOM VISIBILITY:
☐ Poor (0 to 5') ☐ Moderate (5' to 20') ☐ (Good 20 +)

_____

BOTTOM CURRENT:
☐ Weak (0 to 0.5KT) ☐ Moderate (0.5 to 2) ☐ Strong (2+)

Bell Bounce or Surface Dives:	Dive One	Dive Two	Dive Three
Maximum depth of dive:	☐☐☐ feet	☐☐☐ feet	☐☐☐ feet
Time left surface or started pressurization:	☐☐ H ☐☐ min	☐☐ H ☐☐ min	☐☐ H ☐☐ min
Bottom Time:	☐☐☐ min	☐☐☐ min	☐☐☐ min
Decompression Completed at:	☐☐ H ☐☐ min	☐☐ H ☐☐ min	☐☐ H ☐☐ min
For surface decompression only:			
Surface interval:	☐☐☐ min	☐☐☐ min	☐☐☐ min
and time spent in chamber:	☐☐ H ☐☐ min	☐☐ H ☐☐ min	☐☐ H ☐☐ min

Saturation Dives:		
Storage depth:	☐☐☐ feet	☐☐☐ feet
Maximum depth of dive:	☐☐☐ feet	☐☐☐ feet
Time leaving storage depth:	☐☐ H ☐☐ min on ☐☐ day	☐☐ H ☐☐ min on ☐☐ day
Time returning to storage depth:	☐☐ H ☐☐ min on ☐☐ day	☐☐ H ☐☐ min on ☐☐ day
Bottom time:	☐☐ H ☐☐ min	☐☐ H ☐☐ min

Breathing Apparatus used: _____

_____

Breathing Mixture used: _____

_____

Work Description, Equipment and Tools Used:

_____

_____

Name of Decompression Schedules used: _____

Note regarding any
Decompression Sickness
or other Illness or Injury: _____

Any Other Remarks: _____

_____

_____

Type of Dive	
Scuba	
Surface	
Wet Bell	
Bell Bounce	
Saturation	
Other	

_____

_____

APPROVED

Name of Diving Contractor: _____

Address of Diving Contractor _____

_____

Name of Diving Supervisor (Print) _____

Signature _____ Date: _____

RECORD OF DIVE

Date of Dive _____ Diver's Signature _____

BOTTOM CONDITION: (X appropriate blocks)
☐ Sand ☐ Shell ☐ Gravel ☐ Hard ☐ Soft

SEA STATE:
☐ Calm ☐ Fair ☐ Moderate ☐ Heavy ☐ Gale Sea

BOTTOM TEMPERATURE:
☐ Cold (below 55) ☐ Normal (55 to 75) ☐ Warm (above 75)

BOTTOM VISIBILITY:
☐ Poor (0 to 5') ☐ Moderate (5' to 20') ☐ (Good 20 +)

BOTTOM CURRENT:
☐ Weak (0 to 0.5KT) ☐ Moderate (0.5 to 2) ☐ Strong (2+)

Geographic Location

_____

_____

Vessel or Platform

_____

_____

Bell Bounce or Surface Dives:	Dive One	Dive Two	Dive Three
Maximum depth of dive:	☐☐☐ feet	☐☐☐ feet	☐☐☐ feet
Time left surface or started pressurization:	☐☐ H ☐☐ min	☐☐ H ☐☐ min	☐☐ H ☐☐ min
Bottom Time:	☐☐☐ min	☐☐☐ min	☐☐☐ min
Decompression Completed at:	☐☐ H ☐☐ min	☐☐ H ☐☐ min	☐☐ H ☐☐ min
For surface decompression only: Surface interval:	☐☐☐ min	☐☐☐ min	☐☐☐ min
and time spent in chamber:	☐☐ H ☐☐ min	☐☐ H ☐☐ min	☐☐ H ☐☐ min

Saturation Dives:		
Storage depth:	☐☐☐☐ feet	☐☐☐☐ feet
Maximum depth of dive:	☐☐☐☐ feet	☐☐☐☐ feet
Time leaving storage depth:	☐☐ H ☐☐ min on ☐☐ day	☐☐ H ☐☐ min on ☐☐ day
Time returning to storage depth:	☐☐ H ☐☐ min on ☐☐ day	☐☐ H ☐☐ min on ☐☐ day
Bottom time:	☐☐ H ☐☐ min	☐☐ H ☐☐ min

Breathing Apparatus used: _____

_____

Breathing Mixture used: _____

Work Description, Equipment and Tools Used:

_____

_____

Name of Decompression Schedules used: _____

Note regarding any
Decompression Sickness _____
or other Illness or Injury: _____

Any Other Remarks: _____

_____

_____

Type of Dive	
Scuba	☐
Surface	☐
Wet Bell	☐
Bell Bounce	☐
Saturation	☐
Other	

_____

_____

APPROVED
Name of Diving Contractor: _____

Address of Diving Contractor _____

_____

Name of Diving Supervisor (Print) _____

Signature _____ Date: _____

RECORD OF DIVE

Date of Dive _____ Diver's Signature _____

BOTTOM CONDITION: (X appropriate blocks)
☐ Sand ☐ Shell ☐ Gravel ☐ Hard ☐ Soft

SEA STATE:
☐ Calm ☐ Fair ☐ Moderate ☐ Heavy ☐ Gale Sea

BOTTOM TEMPERATURE:
☐ Cold (below 55) ☐ Normal (55 to 75) ☐ Warm (above 75)

BOTTOM VISIBILITY:
☐ Poor (0 to 5') ☐ Moderate (5' to 20') ☐ (Good 20 +)

BOTTOM CURRENT:
☐ Weak (0 to 0.5KT) ☐ Moderate (0.5 to 2) ☐ Strong (2+)

Geographic Location

_____

Vessel or Platform

_____

Bell Bounce or Surface Dives:

	Dive One	Dive Two	Dive Three
Maximum depth of dive:	☐☐☐ feet	☐☐☐ feet	☐☐☐ feet
Time left surface or started pressurization:	☐☐ H ☐☐ min	☐☐ H ☐☐ min	☐☐ H ☐☐ min
Bottom Time:	☐☐☐ min	☐☐☐ min	☐☐☐ min
Decompression Completed at:	☐☐ H ☐☐ min	☐☐ H ☐☐ min	☐☐ H ☐☐ min
For surface decompression only: Surface interval:	☐☐☐ min	☐☐☐ min	☐☐☐ min
and time spent in chamber:	☐☐ H ☐☐ min	☐☐ H ☐☐ min	☐☐ H ☐☐ min

Saturation Dives:

Storage depth:	☐☐☐ feet	☐☐☐ feet
Maximum depth of dive:	☐☐☐ feet	☐☐☐ feet
Time leaving storage depth:	☐☐ H ☐☐ min on ☐☐ day	☐☐ H ☐☐ min on ☐☐ day
Time returning to storage depth:	☐☐ H ☐☐ min on ☐☐ day	☐☐ H ☐☐ min on ☐☐ day
Bottom time:	☐☐ H ☐☐ min	☐☐ H ☐☐ min

Breathing Apparatus used: _____

Breathing Mixture used: _____

Work Description, Equipment and Tools Used: _____

Type of Dive	
Scuba	
Surface	
Wet Bell	
Bell Bounce	
Saturation	
Other	

_____

_____

Name of Decompression Schedules used: _____

Note regarding any
Decompression Sickness
or other Illness or Injury: _____

Any Other Remarks: _____

APPROVED
Name of Diving Contractor: _____

Address of Diving Contractor _____

Name of Diving Supervisor (Print) _____

Signature _____ Date: _____

RECORD OF DIVE

Date of Dive _____ Diver's Signature _____

BOTTOM CONDITION: (X appropriate blocks)
☐ Sand ☐ Shell ☐ Gravel ☐ Hard ☐ Soft

SEA STATE:
☐ Calm ☐ Fair ☐ Moderate ☐ Heavy ☐ Gale Sea

BOTTOM TEMPERATURE:
☐ Cold (below 55) ☐ Normal (55 to 75) ☐ Warm (above 75)

BOTTOM VISIBILITY:
☐ Poor (0 to 5′) ☐ Moderate (5′ to 20′) ☐ (Good 20 +)

BOTTOM CURRENT:
☐ Weak (0 to 0.5KT) ☐ Moderate (0.5 to 2) ☐ Strong (2+)

Geographic Location

_____

_____

Vessel or Platform

_____

_____

Bell Bounce or Surface Dives:

	Dive One	Dive Two	Dive Three
Maximum depth of dive:	☐☐☐ feet	☐☐☐ feet	☐☐☐ feet
Time left surface or started pressurization:	☐☐ H ☐☐ min	☐☐ H ☐☐ min	☐☐ H ☐☐ min
Bottom Time:	☐☐☐ min	☐☐☐ min	☐☐☐ min
Decompression Completed at:	☐☐ H ☐☐ min	☐☐ H ☐☐ min	☐☐ H ☐☐ min
For surface decompression only: Surface interval:	☐☐☐ min	☐☐☐ min	☐☐☐ min
and time spent in chamber:	☐☐ H ☐☐ min	☐☐ H ☐☐ min	☐☐ H ☐☐ min

Saturation Dives:

Storage depth:	☐☐☐ feet	☐☐☐ feet
Maximum depth of dive:	☐☐☐ feet	☐☐☐ feet
Time leaving storage depth:	☐☐ H ☐☐ min on ☐☐ day	☐☐ H ☐☐ min on ☐☐ day
Time returning to storage depth:	☐☐ H ☐☐ min on ☐☐ day	☐☐ H ☐☐ min on ☐☐ day
Bottom time:	☐☐ H ☐☐ min	☐☐ H ☐☐ min

Breathing Apparatus used: _____

Breathing Mixture used: _____

Work Description, Equipment and Tools Used: _____

_____

Name of Decompression Schedules used: _____

Note regarding any Decompression Sickness or other Illness or Injury: _____

Any Other Remarks: _____

_____

Type of Dive	
Scuba	
Surface	
Wet Bell	
Bell Bounce	
Saturation	
Other	

_____

_____

APPROVED

Name of Diving Contractor: _____

Address of Diving Contractor _____

_____

Name of Diving Supervisor (Print) _____

Signature _____ Date: _____

RECORD OF DIVE

Date of Dive _____ Diver's Signature _____

BOTTOM CONDITION: (X appropriate blocks)
☐ Sand ☐ Shell ☐ Gravel ☐ Hard ☐ Soft

SEA STATE:
☐ Calm ☐ Fair ☐ Moderate ☐ Heavy ☐ Gale Sea

BOTTOM TEMPERATURE:
☐ Cold (below 55) ☐ Normal (55 to 75) ☐ Warm (above 75)

BOTTOM VISIBILITY:
☐ Poor (0 to 5') ☐ Moderate (5' to 20') ☐ (Good 20 +)

BOTTOM CURRENT:
☐ Weak (0 to 0.5KT) ☐ Moderate (0.5 to 2) ☐ Strong (2+)

Geographic Location
_____
_____
_____

Vessel or Platform
_____
_____
_____

Bell Bounce or Surface Dives:

	Dive One	Dive Two	Dive Three
Maximum depth of dive:	☐☐☐ feet	☐☐☐ feet	☐☐☐ feet
Time left surface or started pressurization:	☐☐ H ☐☐ min	☐☐ H ☐☐ min	☐☐ H ☐☐ min
Bottom Time:	☐☐ min	☐☐ min	☐☐ min
Decompression Completed at:	☐☐ H ☐☐ min	☐☐ H ☐☐ min	☐☐ H ☐☐ min
For surface decompression only: Surface interval:	☐☐ min	☐☐ min	☐☐ min
and time spent in chamber:	☐☐ H ☐☐ min	☐☐ H ☐☐ min	☐☐ H ☐☐ min

Saturation Dives:

Storage depth:	☐☐☐ feet	☐☐☐ feet
Maximum depth of dive:	☐☐☐ feet	☐☐☐ feet
Time leaving storage depth:	☐☐ H ☐☐ min on ☐☐ day	☐☐ H ☐☐ min on ☐☐ day
Time returning to storage depth:	☐☐ H ☐☐ min on ☐☐ day	☐☐ H ☐☐ min on ☐☐ day
Bottom time:	☐☐ H ☐☐ min	☐☐ H ☐☐ min

Breathing Apparatus used: _____

_____

Breathing Mixture used: _____

_____

Work Description, Equipment and Tools Used:

_____

_____

_____

Name of Decompression Schedules used: _____

Note regarding any
Decompression Sickness _____
or other Illness or Injury: _____

Any Other Remarks: _____
_____
_____

Type of Dive	
Scuba	☐
Surface	☐
Wet Bell	☐
Bell Bounce	☐
Saturation	☐
Other	

_____

_____

APPROVED

Name of Diving Contractor: _____

Address of Diving Contractor _____

_____

Name of Diving Supervisor (Print) _____

Signature _____ Date: _____

RECORD OF DIVE

Date of Dive _____ Diver's Signature _____

BOTTOM CONDITION: (X appropriate blocks)
☐ Sand ☐ Shell ☐ Gravel ☐ Hard ☐ Soft

Geographic Location

_____

SEA STATE:
☐ Calm ☐ Fair ☐ Moderate ☐ Heavy ☐ Gale Sea

_____

BOTTOM TEMPERATURE:
☐ Cold (below 55) ☐ Normal (55 to 75) ☐ Warm (above 75)

Vessel or Platform

BOTTOM VISIBILITY:
☐ Poor (0 to 5') ☐ Moderate (5' to 20') ☐ (Good 20 +)

_____

BOTTOM CURRENT:
☐ Weak (0 to 0.5KT) ☐ Moderate (0.5 to 2) ☐ Strong (2+)

_____

Bell Bounce or Surface Dives:	Dive One	Dive Two	Dive Three
Maximum depth of dive:	☐☐☐ feet	☐☐☐ feet	☐☐☐ feet
Time left surface or started pressurization:	☐☐ H ☐☐ min	☐☐ H ☐☐ min	☐☐ H ☐☐ min
Bottom Time:	☐☐☐ min	☐☐☐ min	☐☐☐ min
Decompression Completed at:	☐☐ H ☐☐ min	☐☐ H ☐☐ min	☐☐ H ☐☐ min
For surface decompression only:			
Surface interval:	☐☐ min	☐☐ min	☐☐ min
and time spent in chamber:	☐☐ H ☐☐ min	☐☐ H ☐☐ min	☐☐ H ☐☐ min

Saturation Dives:

Storage depth:	☐☐☐ feet		☐☐☐ feet
Maximum depth of dive:	☐☐☐ feet		☐☐☐ feet
Time leaving storage depth:	☐☐ H ☐☐ min on ☐☐ day		☐☐ H ☐☐ min on ☐☐ day
Time returning to storage depth:	☐☐ H ☐☐ min on ☐☐ day		☐☐ H ☐☐ min on ☐☐ day
Bottom time:	☐☐ H ☐☐ min		☐☐ H ☐☐ min

Breathing Apparatus used: _____

Breathing Mixture used: _____

Work Description, Equipment and Tools Used: _____

Type of Dive	
Scuba	☐
Surface	☐
Wet Bell	☐
Bell Bounce	☐
Saturation	☐
Other	

Name of Decompression Schedules used: _____

Note regarding any Decompression Sickness or other Illness or Injury: _____

Any Other Remarks: _____

APPROVED
Name of Diving Contractor: _____

Address of Diving Contractor _____

Name of Diving Supervisor (Print) _____

Signature _____ Date: _____

RECORD OF DIVE

Date of Dive _____ Diver's Signature _____

BOTTOM CONDITION: (X appropriate blocks)   Geographic Location
☐ Sand ☐ Shell ☐ Gravel ☐ Hard ☐ Soft

SEA STATE: _____
☐ Calm ☐ Fair ☐ Moderate ☐ Heavy ☐ Gale Sea

BOTTOM TEMPERATURE:
☐ Cold (below 55) ☐ Normal (55 to 75) ☐ Warm (above 75)   Vessel or Platform

BOTTOM VISIBILITY:
☐ Poor (0 to 5') ☐ Moderate (5' to 20') ☐ (Good 20 +)   _____

BOTTOM CURRENT:
☐ Weak (0 to 0.5KT) ☐ Moderate (0.5 to 2) ☐ Strong (2+)   _____

Bell Bounce or Surface Dives:	Dive One	Dive Two	Dive Three
Maximum depth of dive:	☐☐☐ feet	☐☐☐ feet	☐☐☐ feet
Time left surface or started pressurization:	☐☐ H ☐☐ min	☐☐ H ☐☐ min	☐☐ H ☐☐ min
Bottom Time:	☐☐ min	☐☐ min	☐☐ min
Decompression Completed at:	☐☐ H ☐☐ min	☐☐ H ☐☐ min	☐☐ H ☐☐ min
For surface decompression only: Surface interval:	☐☐ min	☐☐ min	☐☐ min
and time spent in chamber:	☐☐ H ☐☐ min	☐☐ H ☐☐ min	☐☐ H ☐☐ min

Saturation Dives:		
Storage depth:	☐☐☐ feet	☐☐☐ feet
Maximum depth of dive:	☐☐☐ feet	☐☐☐ feet
Time leaving storage depth:	☐☐ H ☐☐ min on ☐☐ day	☐☐ H ☐☐ min on ☐☐ day
Time returning to storage depth:	☐☐ H ☐☐ min on ☐☐ day	☐☐ H ☐☐ min on ☐☐ day
Bottom time:	☐☐ H ☐☐ min	☐☐ H ☐☐ min

Breathing Apparatus used: _____

Breathing Mixture used: _____

Work Description, Equipment and Tools Used: _____
_____
_____

Name of Decompression Schedules used: _____

Note regarding any   _____
Decompression Sickness   _____
or other Illness or Injury: _____

Any Other Remarks: _____
_____
_____

Type of Dive	
Scuba	☐
Surface	☐
Wet Bell	☐
Bell Bounce	☐
Saturation	☐
Other	

APPROVED
Name of Diving Contractor: _____

Address of Diving Contractor _____
_____

Name of Diving Supervisor (Print) _____

Signature _____ Date: _____

RECORD OF DIVE

Date of Dive _____ Diver's Signature _____

BOTTOM CONDITION: (X appropriate blocks)
☐ Sand ☐ Shell ☐ Gravel ☐ Hard ☐ Soft

Geographic Location
_____

SEA STATE:
☐ Calm ☐ Fair ☐ Moderate ☐ Heavy ☐ Gale Sea
_____

BOTTOM TEMPERATURE:
☐ Cold (below 55) ☐ Normal (55 to 75) ☐ Warm (above 75)

Vessel or Platform

BOTTOM VISIBILITY:
☐ Poor (0 to 5') ☐ Moderate (5' to 20') ☐ (Good 20 +)
_____

BOTTOM CURRENT:
☐ Weak (0 to 0.5KT) ☐ Moderate (0.5 to 2) ☐ Strong (2+)
_____

Bell Bounce or Surface Dives:	Dive One	Dive Two	Dive Three
Maximum depth of dive:	☐☐☐ feet	☐☐☐ feet	☐☐☐ feet
Time left surface or started pressurization:	☐☐ H ☐☐ min	☐☐ H ☐☐ min	☐☐ H ☐☐ min
Bottom Time:	☐☐ min	☐☐ min	☐☐ min
Decompression Completed at:	☐☐ H ☐☐ min	☐☐ H ☐☐ min	☐☐ H ☐☐ min
For surface decompression only: Surface interval:	☐☐ min	☐☐ min	☐☐ min
and time spent in chamber:	☐☐ H ☐☐ min	☐☐ H ☐☐ min	☐☐ H ☐☐ min

Saturation Dives:		
Storage depth:	☐☐☐ feet	☐☐☐ feet
Maximum depth of dive:	☐☐☐ feet	☐☐☐ feet
Time leaving storage depth:	☐☐ H ☐☐ min on ☐☐ day	☐☐ H ☐☐ min on ☐☐ day
Time returning to storage depth:	☐☐ H ☐☐ min on ☐☐ day	☐☐ H ☐☐ min on ☐☐ day
Bottom time:	☐☐ H ☐☐ min	☐☐ H ☐☐ min

Breathing Apparatus used: _____

Breathing Mixture used: _____

Work Description, Equipment and Tools Used: _____

_____

Name of Decompression Schedules used: _____

Note regarding any
Decompression Sickness
or other Illness or Injury:

Any Other Remarks: _____

_____

Type of Dive	
Scuba	☐
Surface	☐
Wet Bell	☐
Bell Bounce	☐
Saturation	☐
Other	

APPROVED
Name of Diving Contractor: _____

Address of Diving Contractor _____

Name of Diving Supervisor (Print) _____

Signature _____ Date: _____

RECORD OF DIVE

Date of Dive _____ Diver's Signature _____

BOTTOM CONDITION: (X appropriate blocks)
☐ Sand ☐ Shell ☐ Gravel ☐ Hard ☐ Soft

Geographic Location
_____

SEA STATE:
☐ Calm ☐ Fair ☐ Moderate ☐ Heavy ☐ Gale Sea
_____

BOTTOM TEMPERATURE:
☐ Cold (below 55) ☐ Normal (55 to 75) ☐ Warm (above 75)

Vessel or Platform

BOTTOM VISIBILITY:
☐ Poor (0 to 5') ☐ Moderate (5' to 20') ☐ (Good 20 +)
_____

BOTTOM CURRENT:
☐ Weak (0 to 0.5KT) ☐ Moderate (0.5 to 2) ☐ Strong (2+)
_____

Bell Bounce or Surface Dives:	Dive One	Dive Two	Dive Three
Maximum depth of dive:	☐☐☐ feet	☐☐☐ feet	☐☐☐ feet
Time left surface or started pressurization:	☐☐H ☐☐ min	☐☐H ☐☐ min	☐☐H ☐☐ min
Bottom Time:	☐☐ min	☐☐ min	☐☐ min
Decompression Completed at:	☐☐H ☐☐ min	☐☐H ☐☐ min	☐☐H ☐☐ min
For surface decompression only: Surface interval:	☐☐ min	☐☐ min	☐☐ min
and time spent in chamber:	☐☐H ☐☐ min	☐☐H ☐☐ min	☐☐H ☐☐ min

Saturation Dives:		
Storage depth:	☐☐☐ feet	☐☐☐ feet
Maximum depth of dive:	☐☐☐ feet	☐☐☐ feet
Time leaving storage depth:	☐☐H ☐☐ min on ☐☐ day	☐☐H ☐☐ min on ☐☐ day
Time returning to storage depth:	☐☐H ☐☐ min on ☐☐ day	☐☐H ☐☐ min on ☐☐ day
Bottom time:	☐☐H ☐☐ min	☐☐H ☐☐ min

Breathing Apparatus used: _____

Breathing Mixture used: _____

Work Description, Equipment and Tools Used: _____

_____

Name of Decompression Schedules used: _____

Note regarding any
Decompression Sickness   _____
or other Illness or Injury: _____

Any Other Remarks: _____

_____

Type of Dive	
Scuba	
Surface	
Wet Bell	
Bell Bounce	
Saturation	
Other	

_____

APPROVED
Name of Diving Contractor: _____

Address of Diving Contractor _____

Name of Diving Supervisor (Print) _____

Signature _____ Date: _____

RECORD OF DIVE

Date of Dive _____ Diver's Signature _____

BOTTOM CONDITION: (X appropriate blocks)   Geographic Location
☐ Sand   ☐ Shell   ☐ Gravel   ☐ Hard   ☐ Soft

SEA STATE: _____
☐ Calm   ☐ Fair   ☐ Moderate   ☐ Heavy   ☐ Gale Sea

BOTTOM TEMPERATURE: _____
☐ Cold (below 55)   ☐ Normal (55 to 75)   ☐ Warm (above 75)   Vessel or Platform

BOTTOM VISIBILITY:
☐ Poor (0 to 5')   ☐ Moderate (5' to 20')   ☐ (Good 20 +)   _____

BOTTOM CURRENT:
☐ Weak (0 to 0.5KT)   ☐ Moderate (0.5 to 2)   ☐ Strong (2+)   _____

Bell Bounce or Surface Dives:	Dive One	Dive Two	Dive Three
Maximum depth of dive:	☐☐☐ feet	☐☐☐ feet	☐☐☐ feet
Time left surface or started pressurization:	☐☐ H ☐☐ min	☐☐ H ☐☐ min	☐☐ H ☐☐ min
Bottom Time:	☐☐ min	☐☐ min	☐☐ min
Decompression Completed at:	☐☐ H ☐☐ min	☐☐ H ☐☐ min	☐☐ H ☐☐ min
For surface decompression only: Surface interval:	☐☐ min	☐☐ min	☐☐ min
and time spent in chamber:	☐☐ H ☐☐ min	☐☐ H ☐☐ min	☐☐ H ☐☐ min

Saturation Dives:		
Storage depth:	☐☐☐ feet	☐☐☐ feet
Maximum depth of dive:	☐☐☐ feet	☐☐☐ feet
Time leaving storage depth:	☐☐ H ☐☐ min on ☐☐ day	☐☐ H ☐☐ min on ☐☐ day
Time returning to storage depth:	☐☐ H ☐☐ min on ☐☐ day	☐☐ H ☐☐ min on ☐☐ day
Bottom time:	☐☐ H ☐☐ min	☐☐ H ☐☐ min

Breathing Apparatus used: _____

Breathing Mixture used: _____

Work Description, Equipment and Tools Used:
_____
_____

Name of Decompression Schedules used: _____

Note regarding any   _____
Decompression Sickness   _____
or other Illness or Injury: _____

Any Other Remarks: _____
_____
_____

Type of Dive	
Scuba	☐
Surface	☐
Wet Bell	☐
Bell Bounce	☐
Saturation	☐
Other	
_____	
_____	

APPROVED
Name of Diving Contractor: _____

Address of Diving Contractor _____
_____

Name of Diving Supervisor (Print) _____

Signature _____ Date: _____

RECORD OF DIVE

Date of Dive _____ Diver's Signature _____

BOTTOM CONDITION: (X appropriate blocks)
□ Sand   □ Shell   □ Gravel   □ Hard   □ Soft

SEA STATE:
□ Calm   □ Fair   □ Moderate   □ Heavy   □ Gale Sea

BOTTOM TEMPERATURE:
□ Cold (below 55)   □ Normal (55 to 75)   □ Warm (above 75)

BOTTOM VISIBILITY:
□ Poor (0 to 5')   □ Moderate (5' to 20')   □ (Good 20 +)

BOTTOM CURRENT:
□ Weak (0 to 0.5KT)   □ Moderate (0.5 to 2)   □ Strong (2+)

Geographic Location
_____

_____

Vessel or Platform
_____

_____

Bell Bounce or Surface Dives:	Dive One	Dive Two	Dive Three
Maximum depth of dive:	□□□ feet	□□□ feet	□□□ feet
Time left surface or started pressurization:	□□ H □□ min	□□ H □□ min	□□ H □□ min
Bottom Time:	□□ min	□□ min	□□ min
Decompression Completed at:	□□ H □□ min	□□ H □□ min	□□ H □□ min
For surface decompression only: Surface interval:	□□ min	□□ min	□□ min
and time spent in chamber:	□□ H □□ min	□□ H □□ min	□□ H □□ min

Saturation Dives:		
Storage depth:	□□□ feet	□□□ feet
Maximum depth of dive:	□□□ feet	□□□ feet
Time leaving storage depth:	□□ H □□ min on □□ day	□□ H □□ min on □□ day
Time returning to storage depth:	□□ H □□ min on □□ day	□□ H □□ min on □□ day
Bottom time:	□□ H □□ min	□□ H □□ min

Breathing Apparatus used: _____

_____

Breathing Mixture used: _____

_____

Work Description, Equipment and Tools Used: _____

_____

Name of Decompression Schedules used: _____

Note regarding any
Decompression Sickness
or other Illness or Injury: _____

Any Other Remarks: _____

_____

_____

Type of Dive	
Scuba	
Surface	
Wet Bell	
Bell Bounce	
Saturation	
Other	

_____

_____

APPROVED

Name of Diving Contractor: _____

Address of Diving Contractor _____

_____

Name of Diving Supervisor (Print) _____

Signature _____ Date: _____

RECORD OF DIVE

Date of Dive ＿＿＿＿＿＿＿ Diver's Signature ＿＿＿＿＿＿＿＿＿＿＿＿＿

BOTTOM CONDITION: (X appropriate blocks)
☐ Sand ☐ Shell ☐ Gravel ☐ Hard ☐ Soft

Geographic Location
＿＿＿＿＿＿＿＿＿＿

SEA STATE:
☐ Calm ☐ Fair ☐ Moderate ☐ Heavy ☐ Gale Sea
＿＿＿＿＿＿＿＿＿＿

BOTTOM TEMPERATURE:
☐ Cold (below 55) ☐ Normal (55 to 75) ☐ Warm (above 75)

Vessel or Platform
＿＿＿＿＿＿＿＿＿＿

BOTTOM VISIBILITY:
☐ Poor (0 to 5') ☐ Moderate (5' to 20') ☐ (Good 20 +)
＿＿＿＿＿＿＿＿＿＿

BOTTOM CURRENT:
☐ Weak (0 to 0.5KT) ☐ Moderate (0.5 to 2) ☐ Strong (2+)
＿＿＿＿＿＿＿＿＿＿

Bell Bounce or Surface Dives:	Dive One	Dive Two	Dive Three
Maximum depth of dive:	☐☐☐ feet	☐☐☐ feet	☐☐☐ feet
Time left surface or started pressurization:	☐☐ H ☐☐ min	☐☐ H ☐☐ min	☐☐ H ☐☐ min
Bottom Time:	☐☐ min	☐☐ min	☐☐ min
Decompression Completed at:	☐☐ H ☐☐ min	☐☐ H ☐☐ min	☐☐ H ☐☐ min
For surface decompression only: Surface interval:	☐☐ min	☐☐ min	☐☐ min
and time spent in chamber:	☐☐ H ☐☐ min	☐☐ H ☐☐ min	☐☐ H ☐☐ min

Saturation Dives:		
Storage depth:	☐☐☐ feet	☐☐☐ feet
Maximum depth of dive:	☐☐☐ feet	☐☐☐ feet
Time leaving storage depth:	☐☐ H ☐☐ min on ☐☐ day	☐☐ H ☐☐ min on ☐☐ day
Time returning to storage depth:	☐☐ H ☐☐ min on ☐☐ day	☐☐ H ☐☐ min on ☐☐ day
Bottom time:	☐☐ H ☐☐ min	☐☐ H ☐☐ min

Breathing Apparatus used: ＿＿＿＿＿＿＿＿＿＿＿＿＿＿＿＿

Breathing Mixture used: ＿＿＿＿＿＿＿＿＿＿＿＿＿＿＿＿

Work Description, Equipment and Tools Used: ＿＿＿＿＿＿＿＿＿＿＿＿＿＿＿＿＿＿＿＿＿＿＿＿＿＿＿＿＿＿＿

Name of Decompression Schedules used: ＿＿＿＿＿＿＿＿＿＿

Note regarding any ＿＿＿＿＿＿＿＿＿＿＿＿
Decompression Sickness ＿＿＿＿＿＿＿＿＿＿＿＿
or other Illness or Injury: ＿＿＿＿＿＿＿＿＿＿＿＿

Any Other Remarks: ＿＿＿＿＿＿＿＿＿＿＿＿＿＿＿＿＿＿＿＿＿＿＿＿

Type of Dive	
Scuba	☐
Surface	☐
Wet Bell	☐
Bell Bounce	☐
Saturation	☐
Other	

APPROVED
Name of Diving Contractor: ＿＿＿＿＿＿＿＿＿＿＿＿＿＿＿＿＿＿＿＿＿＿＿＿

Address of Diving Contractor ＿＿＿＿＿＿＿＿＿＿＿＿＿＿＿＿＿＿＿＿＿＿＿＿

Name of Diving Supervisor (Print) ＿＿＿＿＿＿＿＿＿＿＿＿＿＿＿＿＿＿＿

Signature ＿＿＿＿＿＿＿＿＿＿＿＿＿＿＿＿＿ Date: ＿＿＿＿＿＿＿＿

RECORD OF DIVE

Date of Dive _____ Diver's Signature _____

BOTTOM CONDITION: (X appropriate blocks)
□ Sand □ Shell □ Gravel □ Hard □ Soft

Geographic Location

SEA STATE:
□ Calm □ Fair □ Moderate □ Heavy □ Gale Sea

_____

BOTTOM TEMPERATURE:
□ Cold (below 55) □ Normal (55 to 75) □ Warm (above 75)

Vessel or Platform

BOTTOM VISIBILITY:
□ Poor (0 to 5') □ Moderate (5' to 20') □ (Good 20 +)

_____

BOTTOM CURRENT:
□ Weak (0 to 0.5KT) □ Moderate (0.5 to 2) □ Strong (2+)

_____

Bell Bounce or Surface Dives:

	Dive One	Dive Two	Dive Three
Maximum depth of dive:	☐☐☐ feet	☐☐☐ feet	☐☐☐ feet
Time left surface or started pressurization:	☐☐ H ☐☐ min	☐☐ H ☐☐ min	☐☐ H ☐☐ min
Bottom Time:	☐☐☐ min	☐☐☐ min	☐☐☐ min
Decompression Completed at:	☐☐ H ☐☐ min	☐☐ H ☐☐ min	☐☐ H ☐☐ min
For surface decompression only:			
Surface interval:	☐☐☐ min	☐☐☐ min	☐☐☐ min
and time spent in chamber:	☐☐ H ☐☐ min	☐☐ H ☐☐ min	☐☐ H ☐☐ min

Saturation Dives:

Storage depth:	☐☐☐ feet	☐☐☐ feet
Maximum depth of dive:	☐☐☐ feet	☐☐☐ feet
Time leaving storage depth:	☐☐ H ☐☐ min on ☐☐ day	☐☐ H ☐☐ min on ☐☐ day
Time returning to storage depth:	☐☐ H ☐☐ min on ☐☐ day	☐☐ H ☐☐ min on ☐☐ day
Bottom time:	☐☐ H ☐☐ min	☐☐ H ☐☐ min

Breathing Apparatus used: _____

Breathing Mixture used: _____

Work Description, Equipment and Tools Used: _____

Name of Decompression Schedules used: _____

Note regarding any Decompression Sickness or other Illness or Injury: _____

Any Other Remarks: _____

Type of Dive	
Scuba	☐
Surface	☐
Wet Bell	☐
Bell Bounce	☐
Saturation	☐
Other	

APPROVED

Name of Diving Contractor: _____

Address of Diving Contractor _____

Name of Diving Supervisor (Print) _____

Signature _____ Date: _____

RECORD OF DIVE

Date of Dive _____ Diver's Signature _____

BOTTOM CONDITION: (X appropriate blocks)
☐ Sand ☐ Shell ☐ Gravel ☐ Hard ☐ Soft

SEA STATE:
☐ Calm ☐ Fair ☐ Moderate ☐ Heavy ☐ Gale Sea

BOTTOM TEMPERATURE:
☐ Cold (below 55) ☐ Normal (55 to 75) ☐ Warm (above 75)

BOTTOM VISIBILITY:
☐ Poor (0 to 5') ☐ Moderate (5' to 20') ☐ (Good 20 +)

BOTTOM CURRENT:
☐ Weak (0 to 0.5KT) ☐ Moderate (0.5 to 2) ☐ Strong (2+)

Geographic Location
_____

_____

Vessel or Platform
_____

_____

Bell Bounce or Surface Dives:	Dive One	Dive Two	Dive Three
Maximum depth of dive:	☐☐☐ feet	☐☐☐ feet	☐☐☐ feet
Time left surface or started pressurization:	☐☐ H ☐☐ min	☐☐ H ☐☐ min	☐☐ H ☐☐ min
Bottom Time:	☐☐☐ min	☐☐☐ min	☐☐☐ min
Decompression Completed at:	☐☐ H ☐☐ min	☐☐ H ☐☐ min	☐☐ H ☐☐ min
For surface decompression only: Surface interval:	☐☐☐ min	☐☐☐ min	☐☐☐ min
and time spent in chamber:	☐☐ H ☐☐ min	☐☐ H ☐☐ min	☐☐ H ☐☐ min

Saturation Dives:		
Storage depth:	☐☐☐ feet	☐☐☐ feet
Maximum depth of dive:	☐☐☐ feet	☐☐☐ feet
Time leaving storage depth:	☐☐ H ☐☐ min on ☐☐ day	☐☐ H ☐☐ min on ☐☐ day
Time returning to storage depth:	☐☐ H ☐☐ min on ☐☐ day	☐☐ H ☐☐ min on ☐☐ day
Bottom time:	☐☐ H ☐☐ min	☐☐ H ☐☐ min

Breathing Apparatus used: _____

Breathing Mixture used: _____

Work Description, Equipment and Tools Used: _____
_____

Name of Decompression Schedules used: _____

Note regarding any Decompression Sickness or other Illness or Injury: _____
_____

Any Other Remarks: _____
_____
_____

Type of Dive	
Scuba	☐
Surface	☐
Wet Bell	☐
Bell Bounce	☐
Saturation	☐
Other	
_____	
_____	

APPROVED
Name of Diving Contractor: _____

Address of Diving Contractor _____

Name of Diving Supervisor (Print) _____

Signature _____ Date: _____

RECORD OF DIVE

Date of Dive _____ Diver's Signature _____

BOTTOM CONDITION: (X appropriate blocks)
☐ Sand ☐ Shell ☐ Gravel ☐ Hard ☐ Soft

Geographic Location

_____

SEA STATE:
☐ Calm ☐ Fair ☐ Moderate ☐ Heavy ☐ Gale Sea

_____

BOTTOM TEMPERATURE:
☐ Cold (below 55) ☐ Normal (55 to 75) ☐ Warm (above 75)

Vessel or Platform

BOTTOM VISIBILITY:
☐ Poor (0 to 5') ☐ Moderate (5' to 20') ☐ (Good 20 +)

_____

BOTTOM CURRENT:
☐ Weak (0 to 0.5KT) ☐ Moderate (0.5 to 2) ☐ Strong (2+)

_____

Bell Bounce or Surface Dives:	Dive One	Dive Two	Dive Three
Maximum depth of dive:	☐☐☐ feet	☐☐☐ feet	☐☐☐ feet
Time left surface or started pressurization:	☐☐ H ☐☐ min	☐☐ H ☐☐ min	☐☐ H ☐☐ min
Bottom Time:	☐☐ min	☐☐ min	☐☐ min
Decompression Completed at:	☐☐ H ☐☐ min	☐☐ H ☐☐ min	☐☐ H ☐☐ min
For surface decompression only:			
Surface interval:	☐☐ min	☐☐ min	☐☐ min
and time spent in chamber:	☐☐ H ☐☐ min	☐☐ H ☐☐ min	☐☐ H ☐☐ min

Saturation Dives:		
Storage depth:	☐☐☐ feet	☐☐☐ feet
Maximum depth of dive:	☐☐☐ feet	☐☐☐ feet
Time leaving storage depth:	☐☐ H ☐☐ min on ☐☐ day	☐☐ H ☐☐ min on ☐☐ day
Time returning to storage depth:	☐☐ H ☐☐ min on ☐☐ day	☐☐ H ☐☐ min on ☐☐ day
Bottom time:	☐☐ H ☐☐ min	☐☐ H ☐☐ min

Breathing Apparatus used: _____

_____

Breathing Mixture used: _____

_____

Work Description, Equipment and Tools Used:

_____

_____

Name of Decompression Schedules used: _____

Note regarding any
Decompression Sickness
or other Illness or Injury: _____

Any Other Remarks: _____

_____

Type of Dive	
Scuba	
Surface	
Wet Bell	
Bell Bounce	
Saturation	
Other	

_____

_____

APPROVED

Name of Diving Contractor: _____

Address of Diving Contractor _____

_____

Name of Diving Supervisor (Print) _____

Signature _____ Date: _____

RECORD OF DIVE

Date of Dive _____ Diver's Signature _____

BOTTOM CONDITION: (X appropriate blocks)   Geographic Location
☐ Sand ☐ Shell ☐ Gravel ☐ Hard ☐ Soft

SEA STATE: _____
☐ Calm ☐ Fair ☐ Moderate ☐ Heavy ☐ Gale Sea

BOTTOM TEMPERATURE: _____
☐ Cold (below 55) ☐ Normal (55 to 75) ☐ Warm (above 75)   Vessel or Platform

BOTTOM VISIBILITY:
☐ Poor (0 to 5') ☐ Moderate (5' to 20') ☐ (Good 20 +)   _____

BOTTOM CURRENT:
☐ Weak (0 to 0.5KT) ☐ Moderate (0.5 to 2) ☐ Strong (2+)   _____

Bell Bounce or Surface Dives:	Dive One	Dive Two	Dive Three
Maximum depth of dive:	☐☐☐ feet	☐☐☐ feet	☐☐☐ feet
Time left surface or started pressurization:	☐☐ H ☐☐ min	☐☐ H ☐☐ min	☐☐ H ☐☐ min
Bottom Time:	☐☐ min	☐☐ min	☐☐ min
Decompression Completed at:	☐☐ H ☐☐ min	☐☐ H ☐☐ min	☐☐ H ☐☐ min
For surface decompression only: Surface interval:	☐☐ min	☐☐ min	☐☐ min
and time spent in chamber:	☐☐ H ☐☐ min	☐☐ H ☐☐ min	☐☐ H ☐☐ min

Saturation Dives:		
Storage depth:	☐☐☐ feet	☐☐☐ feet
Maximum depth of dive:	☐☐☐ feet	☐☐☐ feet
Time leaving storage depth:	☐☐ H ☐☐ min on ☐☐ day	☐☐ H ☐☐ min on ☐☐ day
Time returning to storage depth:	☐☐ H ☐☐ min on ☐☐ day	☐☐ H ☐☐ min on ☐☐ day
Bottom time:	☐☐ H ☐☐ min	☐☐ H ☐☐ min

Breathing Apparatus used: _____

Breathing Mixture used: _____

Work Description, Equipment and Tools Used: _____
_____

Name of Decompression Schedules used: _____

Note regarding any
Decompression Sickness   _____
or other Illness or Injury: _____

Any Other Remarks: _____
_____
_____

Type of Dive	
Scuba	☐
Surface	☐
Wet Bell	☐
Bell Bounce	☐
Saturation	☐
Other	

APPROVED
Name of Diving Contractor: _____

Address of Diving Contractor _____
_____

Name of Diving Supervisor (Print) _____

Signature _____ Date: _____

RECORD OF DIVE

Date of Dive _____ Diver's Signature _____

BOTTOM CONDITION: (X appropriate blocks)
☐ Sand ☐ Shell ☐ Gravel ☐ Hard ☐ Soft

Geographic Location

SEA STATE:
☐ Calm ☐ Fair ☐ Moderate ☐ Heavy ☐ Gale Sea
_____

BOTTOM TEMPERATURE:
☐ Cold (below 55) ☐ Normal (55 to 75) ☐ Warm (above 75)

Vessel or Platform

BOTTOM VISIBILITY:
☐ Poor (0 to 5') ☐ Moderate (5' to 20') ☐ (Good 20 +)
_____

BOTTOM CURRENT:
☐ Weak (0 to 0.5KT) ☐ Moderate (0.5 to 2) ☐ Strong (2+)
_____

Bell Bounce or Surface Dives:	Dive One	Dive Two	Dive Three
Maximum depth of dive:	☐☐☐ feet	☐☐☐ feet	☐☐☐ feet
Time left surface or started pressurization:	☐☐ H ☐☐ min	☐☐ H ☐☐ min	☐☐ H ☐☐ min
Bottom Time:	☐☐☐ min	☐☐☐ min	☐☐☐ min
Decompression Completed at:	☐☐ H ☐☐ min	☐☐ H ☐☐ min	☐☐ H ☐☐ min
For surface decompression only: Surface interval:	☐☐☐ min	☐☐☐ min	☐☐☐ min
and time spent in chamber:	☐☐ H ☐☐ min	☐☐ H ☐☐ min	☐☐ H ☐☐ min

Saturation Dives:		
Storage depth:	☐☐☐ feet	☐☐☐ feet
Maximum depth of dive:	☐☐☐ feet	☐☐☐ feet
Time leaving storage depth:	☐☐ H ☐☐ min on ☐☐ day	☐☐ H ☐☐ min on ☐☐ day
Time returning to storage depth:	☐☐ H ☐☐ min on ☐☐ day	☐☐ H ☐☐ min on ☐☐ day
Bottom time:	☐☐ H ☐☐ min	☐☐ H ☐☐ min

Breathing Apparatus used: _____

Breathing Mixture used: _____

Work Description, Equipment and Tools Used:
_____
_____

Type of Dive	
Scuba	
Surface	
Wet Bell	
Bell Bounce	
Saturation	
Other	

Name of Decompression Schedules used: _____

Note regarding any
Decompression Sickness
or other Illness or Injury: _____

Any Other Remarks: _____
_____
_____

APPROVED
Name of Diving Contractor: _____

Address of Diving Contractor _____
_____

Name of Diving Supervisor (Print) _____

Signature _____ Date: _____

RECORD OF DIVE

Date of Dive _____ Diver's Signature _____

BOTTOM CONDITION: (X appropriate blocks)
☐ Sand ☐ Shell ☐ Gravel ☐ Hard ☐ Soft

Geographic Location
_____

SEA STATE:
☐ Calm ☐ Fair ☐ Moderate ☐ Heavy ☐ Gale Sea

_____

BOTTOM TEMPERATURE:
☐ Cold (below 55) ☐ Normal (55 to 75) ☐ Warm (above 75)

Vessel or Platform

BOTTOM VISIBILITY:
☐ Poor (0 to 5') ☐ Moderate (5' to 20') ☐ (Good 20 +)

_____

BOTTOM CURRENT:
☐ Weak (0 to 0.5KT) ☐ Moderate (0.5 to 2) ☐ Strong (2+)

_____

Bell Bounce or Surface Dives:	Dive One	Dive Two	Dive Three
Maximum depth of dive:	☐☐☐ feet	☐☐☐ feet	☐☐☐ feet
Time left surface or started pressurization:	☐☐ H ☐☐ min	☐☐ H ☐☐ min	☐☐ H ☐☐ min
Bottom Time:	☐☐☐ min	☐☐☐ min	☐☐☐ min
Decompression Completed at:	☐☐ H ☐☐ min	☐☐ H ☐☐ min	☐☐ H ☐☐ min
For surface decompression only: Surface interval:	☐☐☐ min	☐☐☐ min	☐☐☐ min
and time spent in chamber:	☐☐ H ☐☐ min	☐☐ H ☐☐ min	☐☐ H ☐☐ min

Saturation Dives:		
Storage depth:	☐☐☐☐ feet	☐☐☐☐ feet
Maximum depth of dive:	☐☐☐☐ feet	☐☐☐☐ feet
Time leaving storage depth:	☐☐ H ☐☐ min on ☐☐ day	☐☐ H ☐☐ min on ☐☐ day
Time returning to storage depth:	☐☐ H ☐☐ min on ☐☐ day	☐☐ H ☐☐ min on ☐☐ day
Bottom time:	☐☐ H ☐☐ min	☐☐ H ☐☐ min

Breathing Apparatus used: _____

Breathing Mixture used: _____

Work Description, Equipment and Tools Used:
_____
_____

Name of Decompression Schedules used: _____

Note regarding any
Decompression Sickness
or other Illness or Injury: _____

Any Other Remarks: _____
_____
_____

Type of Dive	
Scuba	☐
Surface	☐
Wet Bell	☐
Bell Bounce	☐
Saturation	☐
Other	

_____
_____

APPROVED
Name of Diving Contractor: _____

Address of Diving Contractor _____
_____

Name of Diving Supervisor (Print) _____

Signature _____ Date: _____

RECORD OF DIVE

Date of Dive _____ Diver's Signature _____

BOTTOM CONDITION: (X appropriate blocks)
☐ Sand ☐ Shell ☐ Gravel ☐ Hard ☐ Soft

Geographic Location

SEA STATE:
☐ Calm ☐ Fair ☐ Moderate ☐ Heavy ☐ Gale Sea

_____

BOTTOM TEMPERATURE:
☐ Cold (below 55) ☐ Normal (55 to 75) ☐ Warm (above 75)

Vessel or Platform

BOTTOM VISIBILITY:
☐ Poor (0 to 5') ☐ Moderate (5' to 20') ☐ (Good 20 +)

_____

BOTTOM CURRENT:
☐ Weak (0 to 0.5KT) ☐ Moderate (0.5 to 2) ☐ Strong (2+)

_____

Bell Bounce or Surface Dives:

	Dive One	Dive Two	Dive Three
Maximum depth of dive:	☐☐☐ feet	☐☐☐ feet	☐☐☐ feet
Time left surface or started pressurization:	☐☐ H ☐☐ min	☐☐ H ☐☐ min	☐☐ H ☐☐ min
Bottom Time:	☐☐ min	☐☐ min	☐☐ min
Decompression Completed at:	☐☐ H ☐☐ min	☐☐ H ☐☐ min	☐☐ H ☐☐ min
For surface decompression only: Surface interval:	☐☐ min	☐☐ min	☐☐ min
and time spent in chamber:	☐☐ H ☐☐ min	☐☐ H ☐☐ min	☐☐ H ☐☐ min

Saturation Dives:

Storage depth:	☐☐☐ feet	☐☐☐ feet
Maximum depth of dive:	☐☐☐ feet	☐☐☐ feet
Time leaving storage depth:	☐☐ H ☐☐ min on ☐☐ day	☐☐ H ☐☐ min on ☐☐ day
Time returning to storage depth:	☐☐ H ☐☐ min on ☐☐ day	☐☐ H ☐☐ min on ☐☐ day
Bottom time:	☐☐ H ☐☐ min	☐☐ H ☐☐ min

Breathing Apparatus used: _____

Breathing Mixture used: _____

Work Description, Equipment and Tools Used: _____

Name of Decompression Schedules used: _____

Note regarding any
Decompression Sickness
or other Illness or Injury: _____

Any Other Remarks: _____

Type of Dive	
Scuba	
Surface	
Wet Bell	
Bell Bounce	
Saturation	
Other	

APPROVED

Name of Diving Contractor: _____

Address of Diving Contractor _____

Name of Diving Supervisor (Print) _____

Signature _____ Date: _____

RECORD OF DIVE

Date of Dive _____ Diver's Signature _____

BOTTOM CONDITION: (X appropriate blocks)
□ Sand □ Shell □ Gravel □ Hard □ Soft

Geographic Location
_____

SEA STATE:
□ Calm □ Fair □ Moderate □ Heavy □ Gale Sea
_____

BOTTOM TEMPERATURE:
□ Cold (below 55) □ Normal (55 to 75) □ Warm (above 75)

Vessel or Platform

BOTTOM VISIBILITY:
□ Poor (0 to 5') □ Moderate (5' to 20') □ (Good 20 +)
_____

BOTTOM CURRENT:
□ Weak (0 to 0.5KT) □ Moderate (0.5 to 2) □ Strong (2+)
_____

Bell Bounce or Surface Dives:

	Dive One	Dive Two	Dive Three
Maximum depth of dive:	☐☐☐ feet	☐☐☐ feet	☐☐☐ feet
Time left surface or started pressurization:	☐☐ H ☐☐ min	☐☐ H ☐☐ min	☐☐ H ☐☐ min
Bottom Time:	☐☐ min	☐☐ min	☐☐ min
Decompression Completed at:	☐☐ H ☐☐ min	☐☐ H ☐☐ min	☐☐ H ☐☐ min
For surface decompression only: Surface interval:	☐☐ min	☐☐ min	☐☐ min
and time spent in chamber:	☐☐ H ☐☐ min	☐☐ H ☐☐ min	☐☐ H ☐☐ min

Saturation Dives:

Storage depth:	☐☐☐ feet	☐☐☐ feet
Maximum depth of dive:	☐☐☐ feet	☐☐☐ feet
Time leaving storage depth:	☐☐ H ☐☐ min on ☐☐ day	☐☐ H ☐☐ min on ☐☐ day
Time returning to storage depth:	☐☐ H ☐☐ min on ☐☐ day	☐☐ H ☐☐ min on ☐☐ day
Bottom time:	☐☐ H ☐☐ min	☐☐ H ☐☐ min

Breathing Apparatus used: _____

Breathing Mixture used: _____

Work Description, Equipment and Tools Used: _____

Name of Decompression Schedules used: _____

Note regarding any
Decompression Sickness
or other Illness or Injury: _____

Any Other Remarks: _____

Type of Dive

Scuba	
Surface	
Wet Bell	
Bell Bounce	
Saturation	

Other
_____
_____

APPROVED
Name of Diving Contractor: _____

Address of Diving Contractor _____
_____

Name of Diving Supervisor (Print) _____

Signature _____ Date: _____

RECORD OF DIVE

Date of Dive _____ Diver's Signature _____

BOTTOM CONDITION: (X appropriate blocks)   Geographic Location
☐ Sand ☐ Shell ☐ Gravel ☐ Hard ☐ Soft   _____

SEA STATE:
☐ Calm ☐ Fair ☐ Moderate ☐ Heavy ☐ Gale Sea   _____

BOTTOM TEMPERATURE:
☐ Cold (below 55) ☐ Normal (55 to 75) ☐ Warm (above 75)   Vessel or Platform

BOTTOM VISIBILITY:
☐ Poor (0 to 5') ☐ Moderate (5' to 20') ☐ (Good 20 +)   _____

BOTTOM CURRENT:
☐ Weak (0 to 0.5KT) ☐ Moderate (0.5 to 2) ☐ Strong (2+)   _____

Bell Bounce or Surface Dives:	Dive One	Dive Two	Dive Three
Maximum depth of dive:	☐☐☐ feet	☐☐☐ feet	☐☐☐ feet
Time left surface or started pressurization:	☐☐ H ☐☐ min	☐☐ H ☐☐ min	☐☐ H ☐☐ min
Bottom Time:	☐☐☐ min	☐☐☐ min	☐☐☐ min
Decompression Completed at:	☐☐ H ☐☐ min	☐☐ H ☐☐ min	☐☐ H ☐☐ min
For surface decompression only: Surface interval:	☐☐☐ min	☐☐☐ min	☐☐☐ min
and time spent in chamber:	☐☐ H ☐☐ min	☐☐ H ☐☐ min	☐☐ H ☐☐ min

Saturation Dives:		
Storage depth:	☐☐☐ feet	☐☐☐ feet
Maximum depth of dive:	☐☐☐ feet	☐☐☐ feet
Time leaving storage depth:	☐☐ H ☐☐ min on ☐☐ day	☐☐ H ☐☐ min on ☐☐ day
Time returning to storage depth:	☐☐ H ☐☐ min on ☐☐ day	☐☐ H ☐☐ min on ☐☐ day
Bottom time:	☐☐ H ☐☐ min	☐☐ H ☐☐ min

Breathing Apparatus used: _____

Breathing Mixture used: _____

Work Description, Equipment and Tools Used: _____
_____
_____

Name of Decompression Schedules used: _____

Note regarding any
Decompression Sickness _____
or other Illness or Injury: _____

Any Other Remarks: _____
_____
_____

Type of Dive	
Scuba	☐
Surface	☐
Wet Bell	☐
Bell Bounce	☐
Saturation	☐
Other	

APPROVED
Name of Diving Contractor: _____

Address of Diving Contractor _____
_____

Name of Diving Supervisor (Print) _____

Signature _____ Date: _____

RECORD OF DIVE

Date of Dive _____ Diver's Signature _____

BOTTOM CONDITION: (X appropriate blocks)
☐ Sand ☐ Shell ☐ Gravel ☐ Hard ☐ Soft

Geographic Location
_____

SEA STATE:
☐ Calm ☐ Fair ☐ Moderate ☐ Heavy ☐ Gale Sea
_____

BOTTOM TEMPERATURE:
☐ Cold (below 55) ☐ Normal (55 to 75) ☐ Warm (above 75)

Vessel or Platform

BOTTOM VISIBILITY:
☐ Poor (0 to 5') ☐ Moderate (5' to 20') ☐ (Good 20 +)
_____

BOTTOM CURRENT:
☐ Weak (0 to 0.5KT) ☐ Moderate (0.5 to 2) ☐ Strong (2+)
_____

Bell Bounce or Surface Dives:	Dive One	Dive Two	Dive Three
Maximum depth of dive:	☐☐☐ feet	☐☐☐ feet	☐☐☐ feet
Time left surface or started pressurization:	☐☐ H ☐☐ min	☐☐ H ☐☐ min	☐☐ H ☐☐ min
Bottom Time:	☐☐☐ min	☐☐☐ min	☐☐☐ min
Decompression Completed at:	☐☐ H ☐☐ min	☐☐ H ☐☐ min	☐☐ H ☐☐ min
For surface decompression only: Surface interval:	☐☐☐ min	☐☐☐ min	☐☐☐ min
and time spent in chamber:	☐☐ H ☐☐ min	☐☐ H ☐☐ min	☐☐ H ☐☐ min

Saturation Dives:		
Storage depth:	☐☐☐ feet	☐☐☐ feet
Maximum depth of dive:	☐☐☐ feet	☐☐☐ feet
Time leaving storage depth:	☐☐ H ☐☐ min on ☐☐ day	☐☐ H ☐☐ min on ☐☐ day
Time returning to storage depth:	☐☐ H ☐☐ min on ☐☐ day	☐☐ H ☐☐ min on ☐☐ day
Bottom time:	☐☐ H ☐☐ min	☐☐ H ☐☐ min

Breathing Apparatus used: _____

Breathing Mixture used: _____

Work Description, Equipment and Tools Used: _____

_____

Name of Decompression Schedules used: _____

Note regarding any
Decompression Sickness _____
or other Illness or Injury: _____

Any Other Remarks: _____

_____

Type of Dive	
Scuba	☐
Surface	☐
Wet Bell	☐
Bell Bounce	☐
Saturation	☐
Other	

APPROVED

Name of Diving Contractor: _____

Address of Diving Contractor _____

_____

Name of Diving Supervisor (Print) _____

Signature _____ Date: _____

RECORD OF DIVE

Date of Dive _____ Diver's Signature _____

BOTTOM CONDITION: (X appropriate blocks)
☐ Sand ☐ Shell ☐ Gravel ☐ Hard ☐ Soft

Geographic Location
_____

SEA STATE:
☐ Calm ☐ Fair ☐ Moderate ☐ Heavy ☐ Gale Sea
_____

BOTTOM TEMPERATURE:
☐ Cold (below 55) ☐ Normal (55 to 75) ☐ Warm (above 75)

Vessel or Platform

BOTTOM VISIBILITY:
☐ Poor (0 to 5') ☐ Moderate (5' to 20') ☐ (Good 20 +)
_____

BOTTOM CURRENT:
☐ Weak (0 to 0.5KT) ☐ Moderate (0.5 to 2) ☐ Strong (2+)

Bell Bounce or Surface Dives:	Dive One	Dive Two	Dive Three
Maximum depth of dive:	☐☐☐ feet	☐☐☐ feet	☐☐☐ feet
Time left surface or started pressurization:	☐☐H☐☐ min	☐☐H☐☐ min	☐☐H☐☐ min
Bottom Time:	☐☐☐ min	☐☐☐ min	☐☐☐ min
Decompression Completed at:	☐☐H☐☐ min	☐☐H☐☐ min	☐☐H☐☐ min
For surface decompression only: Surface interval:	☐☐☐ min	☐☐☐ min	☐☐☐ min
and time spent in chamber:	☐☐H☐☐ min	☐☐H☐☐ min	☐☐H☐☐ min

Saturation Dives:		
Storage depth:	☐☐☐☐ feet	☐☐☐☐ feet
Maximum depth of dive:	☐☐☐☐ feet	☐☐☐☐ feet
Time leaving storage depth:	☐☐H☐☐ min on ☐☐ day	☐☐H☐☐ min on ☐☐ day
Time returning to storage depth:	☐☐H☐☐ min on ☐☐ day	☐☐H☐☐ min on ☐☐ day
Bottom time:	☐☐H☐☐ min	☐☐H☐☐ min

Breathing Apparatus used: _____

Breathing Mixture used: _____

Work Description, Equipment and Tools Used: _____
_____
_____

Name of Decompression Schedules used: _____

Note regarding any
Decompression Sickness
or other Illness or Injury: _____

Any Other Remarks: _____
_____
_____

Type of Dive	
Scuba	
Surface	
Wet Bell	
Bell Bounce	
Saturation	
Other	

APPROVED
Name of Diving Contractor: _____

Address of Diving Contractor _____
_____

Name of Diving Supervisor (Print) _____

Signature _____ Date: _____

RECORD OF DIVE

Date of Dive _____ Diver's Signature _____

BOTTOM CONDITION: (X appropriate blocks)
□ Sand □ Shell □ Gravel □ Hard □ Soft

SEA STATE:
□ Calm □ Fair □ Moderate □ Heavy □ Gale Sea

BOTTOM TEMPERATURE:
□ Cold (below 55) □ Normal (55 to 75) □ Warm (above 75)

BOTTOM VISIBILITY:
□ Poor (0 to 5') □ Moderate (5' to 20') □ (Good 20 +)

BOTTOM CURRENT:
□ Weak (0 to 0.5KT) □ Moderate (0.5 to 2) □ Strong (2+)

Geographic Location

_____

_____

Vessel or Platform

_____

_____

Bell Bounce or Surface Dives:

	Dive One	Dive Two	Dive Three
Maximum depth of dive:	☐☐☐ feet	☐☐☐ feet	☐☐☐ feet
Time left surface or started pressurization:	☐☐ H ☐☐ min	☐☐ H ☐☐ min	☐☐ H ☐☐ min
Bottom Time:	☐☐ min	☐☐ min	☐☐ min
Decompression Completed at:	☐☐ H ☐☐ min	☐☐ H ☐☐ min	☐☐ H ☐☐ min
For surface decompression only: Surface interval:	☐☐ min	☐☐ min	☐☐ min
and time spent in chamber:	☐☐ H ☐☐ min	☐☐ H ☐☐ min	☐☐ H ☐☐ min

Saturation Dives:

Storage depth:	☐☐☐ feet	☐☐☐ feet
Maximum depth of dive:	☐☐☐ feet	☐☐☐ feet
Time leaving storage depth:	☐☐ H ☐☐ min on ☐☐ day	☐☐ H ☐☐ min on ☐☐ day
Time returning to storage depth:	☐☐ H ☐☐ min on ☐☐ day	☐☐ H ☐☐ min on ☐☐ day
Bottom time:	☐☐ H ☐☐ min	☐☐ H ☐☐ min

Breathing Apparatus used: _____

Breathing Mixture used: _____

Work Description, Equipment and Tools Used:
_____
_____

Name of Decompression Schedules used: _____

Note regarding any Decompression Sickness or other Illness or Injury:
_____
_____
_____

Any Other Remarks: _____
_____
_____

Type of Dive	
Scuba	☐
Surface	☐
Wet Bell	☐
Bell Bounce	☐
Saturation	☐
Other	

_____

_____

APPROVED
Name of Diving Contractor: _____

Address of Diving Contractor _____
_____

Name of Diving Supervisor (Print) _____

Signature _____ Date: _____

RECORD OF DIVE

Date of Dive _____ Diver's Signature _____

BOTTOM CONDITION: (X appropriate blocks)   Geographic Location
☐ Sand ☐ Shell ☐ Gravel ☐ Hard ☐ Soft   _____

SEA STATE:
☐ Calm ☐ Fair ☐ Moderate ☐ Heavy ☐ Gale Sea   _____

BOTTOM TEMPERATURE:
☐ Cold (below 55) ☐ Normal (55 to 75) ☐ Warm (above 75)   Vessel or Platform

BOTTOM VISIBILITY:
☐ Poor (0 to 5') ☐ Moderate (5' to 20') ☐ (Good 20 +)   _____

BOTTOM CURRENT:
☐ Weak (0 to 0.5KT) ☐ Moderate (0.5 to 2) ☐ Strong (2+)   _____

Bell Bounce or Surface Dives:	Dive One	Dive Two	Dive Three
Maximum depth of dive:	☐☐☐ feet	☐☐☐ feet	☐☐☐ feet
Time left surface or started pressurization:	☐☐H ☐☐ min	☐☐H ☐☐ min	☐☐H ☐☐ min
Bottom Time:	☐☐ min	☐☐ min	☐☐ min
Decompression Completed at:	☐☐H ☐☐ min	☐☐H ☐☐ min	☐☐H ☐☐ min
For surface decompression only: Surface interval:	☐☐ min	☐☐ min	☐☐ min
and time spent in chamber:	☐☐H ☐☐ min	☐☐H ☐☐ min	☐☐H ☐☐ min

Saturation Dives:		
Storage depth:	☐☐☐ feet	☐☐☐ feet
Maximum depth of dive:	☐☐☐ feet	☐☐☐ feet
Time leaving storage depth:	☐☐H ☐☐ min on ☐☐ day	☐☐H ☐☐ min on ☐☐ day
Time returning to storage depth:	☐☐H ☐☐ min on ☐☐ day	☐☐H ☐☐ min on ☐☐ day
Bottom time:	☐☐H ☐☐ min	☐☐H ☐☐ min

Breathing Apparatus used: _____

Breathing Mixture used: _____

Work Description, Equipment and Tools Used: _____
_____
_____

Name of Decompression Schedules used: _____

Note regarding any
Decompression Sickness
or other Illness or Injury: _____

Any Other Remarks: _____
_____
_____

Type of Dive	
Scuba	
Surface	
Wet Bell	
Bell Bounce	
Saturation	
Other	

APPROVED
Name of Diving Contractor: _____

Address of Diving Contractor _____
_____

Name of Diving Supervisor (Print) _____

Signature _____ Date: _____

RECORD OF DIVE

Date of Dive _____ Diver's Signature _____

BOTTOM CONDITION: (X appropriate blocks)
☐ Sand ☐ Shell ☐ Gravel ☐ Hard ☐ Soft

Geographic Location
_____

SEA STATE:
☐ Calm ☐ Fair ☐ Moderate ☐ Heavy ☐ Gale Sea

_____

BOTTOM TEMPERATURE:
☐ Cold (below 55) ☐ Normal (55 to 75) ☐ Warm (above 75)

Vessel or Platform

BOTTOM VISIBILITY:
☐ Poor (0 to 5′) ☐ Moderate (5′ to 20′) ☐ (Good 20 +)

_____

BOTTOM CURRENT:
☐ Weak (0 to 0.5KT) ☐ Moderate (0.5 to 2) ☐ Strong (2+)

_____

Bell Bounce or Surface Dives:	Dive One	Dive Two	Dive Three
Maximum depth of dive:	☐☐☐ feet	☐☐☐ feet	☐☐☐ feet
Time left surface or started pressurization:	☐☐ H ☐☐ min	☐☐ H ☐☐ min	☐☐ H ☐☐ min
Bottom Time:	☐☐ min	☐☐ min	☐☐ min
Decompression Completed at:	☐☐ H ☐☐ min	☐☐ H ☐☐ min	☐☐ H ☐☐ min
For surface decompression only:			
Surface interval:	☐☐ min	☐☐ min	☐☐ min
and time spent in chamber:	☐☐ H ☐☐ min	☐☐ H ☐☐ min	☐☐ H ☐☐ min

Saturation Dives:

Storage depth:	☐☐☐ feet	☐☐☐ feet
Maximum depth of dive:	☐☐☐ feet	☐☐☐ feet
Time leaving storage depth:	☐☐ H ☐☐ min on ☐☐ day	☐☐ H ☐☐ min on ☐☐ day
Time returning to storage depth:	☐☐ H ☐☐ min on ☐☐ day	☐☐ H ☐☐ min on ☐☐ day
Bottom time:	☐☐ H ☐☐ min	☐☐ H ☐☐ min

Breathing Apparatus used: _____

Breathing Mixture used: _____

Work Description, Equipment and Tools Used: _____

Name of Decompression Schedules used: _____

Note regarding any Decompression Sickness or other Illness or Injury: _____

Any Other Remarks: _____

Type of Dive	
Scuba	
Surface	
Wet Bell	
Bell Bounce	
Saturation	
Other	

APPROVED
Name of Diving Contractor: _____

Address of Diving Contractor _____

Name of Diving Supervisor (Print) _____

Signature _____ Date: _____

RECORD OF DIVE

Date of Dive _____ Diver's Signature _____

BOTTOM CONDITION: (X appropriate blocks)
☐ Sand ☐ Shell ☐ Gravel ☐ Hard ☐ Soft

SEA STATE:
☐ Calm ☐ Fair ☐ Moderate ☐ Heavy ☐ Gale Sea

BOTTOM TEMPERATURE:
☐ Cold (below 55) ☐ Normal (55 to 75) ☐ Warm (above 75)

BOTTOM VISIBILITY:
☐ Poor (0 to 5') ☐ Moderate (5' to 20') ☐ (Good 20 +)

BOTTOM CURRENT:
☐ Weak (0 to 0.5KT) ☐ Moderate (0.5 to 2) ☐ Strong (2+)

Geographic Location
_____

_____

Vessel or Platform
_____

_____

Bell Bounce or Surface Dives:	Dive One	Dive Two	Dive Three
Maximum depth of dive:	☐☐☐ feet	☐☐☐ feet	☐☐☐ feet
Time left surface or started pressurization:	☐☐ H ☐☐ min	☐☐ H ☐☐ min	☐☐ H ☐☐ min
Bottom Time:	☐☐ min	☐☐ min	☐☐ min
Decompression Completed at:	☐☐ H ☐☐ min	☐☐ H ☐☐ min	☐☐ H ☐☐ min
For surface decompression only: Surface interval:	☐☐ min	☐☐ min	☐☐ min
and time spent in chamber:	☐☐ H ☐☐ min	☐☐ H ☐☐ min	☐☐ H ☐☐ min

Saturation Dives:		
Storage depth:	☐☐☐ feet	☐☐☐ feet
Maximum depth of dive:	☐☐☐ feet	☐☐☐ feet
Time leaving storage depth:	☐☐ H ☐☐ min on ☐☐ day	☐☐ H ☐☐ min on ☐☐ day
Time returning to storage depth:	☐☐ H ☐☐ min on ☐☐ day	☐☐ H ☐☐ min on ☐☐ day
Bottom time:	☐☐ H ☐☐ min	☐☐ H ☐☐ min

Breathing Apparatus used: _____

Breathing Mixture used: _____

Work Description, Equipment and Tools Used: _____

_____

Name of Decompression Schedules used: _____

Note regarding any
Decompression Sickness
or other Illness or Injury: _____

Any Other Remarks: _____

_____

_____

Type of Dive	
Scuba	
Surface	
Wet Bell	
Bell Bounce	
Saturation	
Other	

APPROVED

Name of Diving Contractor: _____

Address of Diving Contractor _____

_____

Name of Diving Supervisor (Print) _____

Signature _____ Date: _____

RECORD OF DIVE

Date of Dive _____ Diver's Signature _____

BOTTOM CONDITION: (X appropriate blocks)
☐ Sand ☐ Shell ☐ Gravel ☐ Hard ☐ Soft

SEA STATE:
☐ Calm ☐ Fair ☐ Moderate ☐ Heavy ☐ Gale Sea

BOTTOM TEMPERATURE:
☐ Cold (below 55) ☐ Normal (55 to 75) ☐ Warm (above 75)

BOTTOM VISIBILITY:
☐ Poor (0 to 5') ☐ Moderate (5' to 20') ☐ (Good 20 +)

BOTTOM CURRENT:
☐ Weak (0 to 0.5KT) ☐ Moderate (0.5 to 2) ☐ Strong (2+)

Geographic Location
_____

Vessel or Platform
_____
_____

Bell Bounce or Surface Dives:	Dive One	Dive Two	Dive Three
Maximum depth of dive:	☐☐☐ feet	☐☐☐ feet	☐☐☐ feet
Time left surface or started pressurization:	☐☐ H ☐☐ min	☐☐ H ☐☐ min	☐☐ H ☐☐ min
Bottom Time:	☐☐ min	☐☐ min	☐☐ min
Decompression Completed at:	☐☐ H ☐☐ min	☐☐ H ☐☐ min	☐☐ H ☐☐ min
For surface decompression only: Surface interval:	☐☐ min	☐☐ min	☐☐ min
and time spent in chamber:	☐☐ H ☐☐ min	☐☐ H ☐☐ min	☐☐ H ☐☐ min

Saturation Dives:		
Storage depth:	☐☐☐ feet	☐☐☐ feet
Maximum depth of dive:	☐☐☐ feet	☐☐☐ feet
Time leaving storage depth:	☐☐ H ☐☐ min on ☐☐ day	☐☐ H ☐☐ min on ☐☐ day
Time returning to storage depth:	☐☐ H ☐☐ min on ☐☐ day	☐☐ H ☐☐ min on ☐☐ day
Bottom time:	☐☐ H ☐☐ min	☐☐ H ☐☐ min

Breathing Apparatus used: _____

Breathing Mixture used: _____

Work Description, Equipment and Tools Used:
_____
_____

Name of Decompression Schedules used: _____

Note regarding any _____
Decompression Sickness _____
or other Illness or Injury: _____

Any Other Remarks: _____
_____
_____

Type of Dive	
Scuba	☐
Surface	☐
Wet Bell	☐
Bell Bounce	☐
Saturation	☐
Other	
_____	
_____	

APPROVED
Name of Diving Contractor: _____

Address of Diving Contractor _____
_____

Name of Diving Supervisor (Print) _____

Signature _____ Date: _____

RECORD OF DIVE

Date of Dive _____ Diver's Signature _____

BOTTOM CONDITION: (X appropriate blocks)
☐ Sand ☐ Shell ☐ Gravel ☐ Hard ☐ Soft

SEA STATE:
☐ Calm ☐ Fair ☐ Moderate ☐ Heavy ☐ Gale Sea

BOTTOM TEMPERATURE:
☐ Cold (below 55) ☐ Normal (55 to 75) ☐ Warm (above 75)

BOTTOM VISIBILITY:
☐ Poor (0 to 5') ☐ Moderate (5' to 20') ☐ (Good 20 +)

BOTTOM CURRENT:
☐ Weak (0 to 0.5KT) ☐ Moderate (0.5 to 2) ☐ Strong (2+)

Geographic Location

_____

_____

Vessel or Platform

_____

_____

Bell Bounce or Surface Dives:	Dive One	Dive Two	Dive Three
Maximum depth of dive:	☐☐☐ feet	☐☐☐ feet	☐☐☐ feet
Time left surface or started pressurization:	☐☐H ☐☐ min	☐☐H ☐☐ min	☐☐H ☐☐ min
Bottom Time:	☐☐☐ min	☐☐☐ min	☐☐☐ min
Decompression Completed at:	☐☐H ☐☐ min	☐☐H ☐☐ min	☐☐H ☐☐ min
For surface decompression only: Surface interval:	☐☐☐ min	☐☐☐ min	☐☐☐ min
and time spent in chamber:	☐☐H ☐☐ min	☐☐H ☐☐ min	☐☐H ☐☐ min

Saturation Dives:		
Storage depth:	☐☐☐ feet	☐☐☐ feet
Maximum depth of dive:	☐☐☐ feet	☐☐☐ feet
Time leaving storage depth:	☐☐H ☐☐ min on ☐☐ day	☐☐H ☐☐ min on ☐☐ day
Time returning to storage depth:	☐☐H ☐☐ min on ☐☐ day	☐☐H ☐☐ min on ☐☐ day
Bottom time:	☐☐H ☐☐ min	☐☐H ☐☐ min

Breathing Apparatus used: _____

Breathing Mixture used: _____

Work Description, Equipment and Tools Used: _____

_____

Name of Decompression Schedules used: _____

Note regarding any
Decompression Sickness _____
or other Illness or Injury: _____

Any Other Remarks: _____

_____

Type of Dive	
Scuba	☐
Surface	☐
Wet Bell	☐
Bell Bounce	☐
Saturation	☐
Other	

_____

_____

APPROVED
Name of Diving Contractor: _____

Address of Diving Contractor _____

_____

Name of Diving Supervisor (Print) _____

Signature _____ Date: _____

RECORD OF DIVE

Date of Dive _____ Diver's Signature _____

BOTTOM CONDITION: (X appropriate blocks)
☐ Sand ☐ Shell ☐ Gravel ☐ Hard ☐ Soft

Geographic Location

_____

SEA STATE:
☐ Calm ☐ Fair ☐ Moderate ☐ Heavy ☐ Gale Sea

_____

BOTTOM TEMPERATURE:
☐ Cold (below 55) ☐ Normal (55 to 75) ☐ Warm (above 75)

Vessel or Platform

BOTTOM VISIBILITY:
☐ Poor (0 to 5') ☐ Moderate (5' to 20') ☐ (Good 20 +)

_____

BOTTOM CURRENT:
☐ Weak (0 to 0.5KT) ☐ Moderate (0.5 to 2) ☐ Strong (2+)

_____

Bell Bounce or Surface Dives:	Dive One	Dive Two	Dive Three
Maximum depth of dive:	☐☐☐ feet	☐☐☐ feet	☐☐☐ feet
Time left surface or started pressurization:	☐☐ H ☐☐ min	☐☐ H ☐☐ min	☐☐ H ☐☐ min
Bottom Time:	☐☐ min	☐☐ min	☐☐ min
Decompression Completed at:	☐☐ H ☐☐ min	☐☐ H ☐☐ min	☐☐ H ☐☐ min
For surface decompression only: Surface interval:	☐☐ min	☐☐ min	☐☐ min
and time spent in chamber:	☐☐ H ☐☐ min	☐☐ H ☐☐ min	☐☐ H ☐☐ min

Saturation Dives:		
Storage depth:	☐☐☐ feet	☐☐☐ feet
Maximum depth of dive:	☐☐☐ feet	☐☐☐ feet
Time leaving storage depth:	☐☐ H ☐☐ min on ☐☐ day	☐☐ H ☐☐ min on ☐☐ day
Time returning to storage depth:	☐☐ H ☐☐ min on ☐☐ day	☐☐ H ☐☐ min on ☐☐ day
Bottom time:	☐☐ H ☐☐ min	☐☐ H ☐☐ min

Breathing Apparatus used: _____

Type of Dive	
Scuba	☐
Surface	☐
Wet Bell	☐
Bell Bounce	☐
Saturation	☐
Other	

Breathing Mixture used: _____

Work Description, Equipment and Tools Used:

_____

_____

Name of Decompression Schedules used: _____

Note regarding any
Decompression Sickness
or other Illness or Injury: _____

Any Other Remarks: _____

_____

_____

APPROVED

Name of Diving Contractor: _____

Address of Diving Contractor _____

_____

Name of Diving Supervisor (Print) _____

Signature _____ Date: _____

RECORD OF DIVE

Date of Dive _____ Diver's Signature _____

BOTTOM CONDITION: (X appropriate blocks)
☐ Sand ☐ Shell ☐ Gravel ☐ Hard ☐ Soft

SEA STATE:
☐ Calm ☐ Fair ☐ Moderate ☐ Heavy ☐ Gale Sea

BOTTOM TEMPERATURE:
☐ Cold (below 55) ☐ Normal (55 to 75) ☐ Warm (above 75)

BOTTOM VISIBILITY:
☐ Poor (0 to 5') ☐ Moderate (5' to 20') ☐ (Good 20 +)

BOTTOM CURRENT:
☐ Weak (0 to 0.5KT) ☐ Moderate (0.5 to 2) ☐ Strong (2+)

Geographic Location
_____

_____

Vessel or Platform
_____

_____

Bell Bounce or Surface Dives:

	Dive One	Dive Two	Dive Three
Maximum depth of dive:	☐☐☐ feet	☐☐☐ feet	☐☐☐ feet
Time left surface or started pressurization:	☐☐ H ☐☐ min	☐☐ H ☐☐ min	☐☐ H ☐☐ min
Bottom Time:	☐☐ min	☐☐ min	☐☐ min
Decompression Completed at:	☐☐ H ☐☐ min	☐☐ H ☐☐ min	☐☐ H ☐☐ min
For surface decompression only:			
Surface interval:	☐☐ min	☐☐ min	☐☐ min
and time spent in chamber:	☐☐ H ☐☐ min	☐☐ H ☐☐ min	☐☐ H ☐☐ min

Saturation Dives:

Storage depth:	☐☐☐ feet	☐☐☐ feet
Maximum depth of dive:	☐☐☐ feet	☐☐☐ feet
Time leaving storage depth:	☐☐ H ☐☐ min on ☐☐ day	☐☐ H ☐☐ min on ☐☐ day
Time returning to storage depth:	☐☐ H ☐☐ min on ☐☐ day	☐☐ H ☐☐ min on ☐☐ day
Bottom time:	☐☐ H ☐☐ min	☐☐ H ☐☐ min

Breathing Apparatus used: _____

Breathing Mixture used: _____

Work Description, Equipment and Tools Used: _____

Name of Decompression Schedules used: _____

Note regarding any Decompression Sickness or other Illness or Injury: _____

Any Other Remarks: _____

Type of Dive

Scuba	
Surface	
Wet Bell	
Bell Bounce	
Saturation	

Other _____
_____
_____

APPROVED

Name of Diving Contractor: _____

Address of Diving Contractor _____

Name of Diving Supervisor (Print) _____

Signature _____ Date: _____

RECORD OF DIVE

Date of Dive _____ Diver's Signature _____

BOTTOM CONDITION: (X appropriate blocks)
☐ Sand ☐ Shell ☐ Gravel ☐ Hard ☐ Soft

Geographic Location

_____

SEA STATE:
☐ Calm ☐ Fair ☐ Moderate ☐ Heavy ☐ Gale Sea

_____

BOTTOM TEMPERATURE:
☐ Cold (below 55) ☐ Normal (55 to 75) ☐ Warm (above 75)

Vessel or Platform

BOTTOM VISIBILITY:
☐ Poor (0 to 5') ☐ Moderate (5' to 20') ☐ (Good 20 +)

_____

BOTTOM CURRENT:
☐ Weak (0 to 0.5KT) ☐ Moderate (0.5 to 2) ☐ Strong (2+)

_____

Bell Bounce or Surface Dives:	Dive One	Dive Two	Dive Three
Maximum depth of dive:	☐☐☐ feet	☐☐☐ feet	☐☐☐ feet
Time left surface or started pressurization:	☐☐ H ☐☐ min	☐☐ H ☐☐ min	☐☐ H ☐☐ min
Bottom Time:	☐☐ min	☐☐ min	☐☐ min
Decompression Completed at:	☐☐ H ☐☐ min	☐☐ H ☐☐ min	☐☐ H ☐☐ min
For surface decompression only: Surface interval:	☐☐ min	☐☐ min	☐☐ min
and time spent in chamber:	☐☐ H ☐☐ min	☐☐ H ☐☐ min	☐☐ H ☐☐ min

Saturation Dives:		
Storage depth:	☐☐☐ feet	☐☐☐ feet
Maximum depth of dive:	☐☐☐ feet	☐☐☐ feet
Time leaving storage depth:	☐☐ H ☐☐ min on ☐☐ day	☐☐ H ☐☐ min on ☐☐ day
Time returning to storage depth:	☐☐ H ☐☐ min on ☐☐ day	☐☐ H ☐☐ min on ☐☐ day
Bottom time:	☐☐ H ☐☐ min	☐☐ H ☐☐ min

Breathing Apparatus used: _____

Breathing Mixture used: _____

Work Description, Equipment and Tools Used: _____
_____

Name of Decompression Schedules used: _____

Note regarding any
Decompression Sickness
or other Illness or Injury: _____

Any Other Remarks: _____
_____
_____

Type of Dive	
Scuba	
Surface	
Wet Bell	
Bell Bounce	
Saturation	
Other	

APPROVED
Name of Diving Contractor: _____

Address of Diving Contractor _____
_____

Name of Diving Supervisor (Print) _____

Signature _____ Date: _____

RECORD OF DIVE

Date of Dive _____ Diver's Signature _____

BOTTOM CONDITION: (X appropriate blocks)
☐ Sand ☐ Shell ☐ Gravel ☐ Hard ☐ Soft

Geographic Location

SEA STATE:
☐ Calm ☐ Fair ☐ Moderate ☐ Heavy ☐ Gale Sea

_____

BOTTOM TEMPERATURE:
☐ Cold (below 55) ☐ Normal (55 to 75) ☐ Warm (above 75)

Vessel or Platform

BOTTOM VISIBILITY:
☐ Poor (0 to 5') ☐ Moderate (5' to 20') ☐ (Good 20 +)

_____

BOTTOM CURRENT:
☐ Weak (0 to 0.5KT) ☐ Moderate (0.5 to 2) ☐ Strong (2+)

_____

Bell Bounce or Surface Dives:

	Dive One	Dive Two	Dive Three
Maximum depth of dive:	☐☐☐ feet	☐☐☐ feet	☐☐☐ feet
Time left surface or started pressurization:	☐☐ H ☐☐ min	☐☐ H ☐☐ min	☐☐ H ☐☐ min
Bottom Time:	☐☐☐ min	☐☐☐ min	☐☐☐ min
Decompression Completed at:	☐☐ H ☐☐ min	☐☐ H ☐☐ min	☐☐ H ☐☐ min
For surface decompression only: Surface interval:	☐☐☐ min	☐☐☐ min	☐☐☐ min
and time spent in chamber:	☐☐ H ☐☐ min	☐☐ H ☐☐ min	☐☐ H ☐☐ min

Saturation Dives:

Storage depth:	☐☐☐ feet	☐☐☐ feet
Maximum depth of dive:	☐☐☐ feet	☐☐☐ feet
Time leaving storage depth:	☐☐ H ☐☐ min on ☐☐ day	☐☐ H ☐☐ min on ☐☐ day
Time returning to storage depth:	☐☐ H ☐☐ min on ☐☐ day	☐☐ H ☐☐ min on ☐☐ day
Bottom time:	☐☐ H ☐☐ min	☐☐ H ☐☐ min

Breathing Apparatus used: _____

Breathing Mixture used: _____

Work Description, Equipment and Tools Used: _____
_____

Name of Decompression Schedules used: _____

Note regarding any
Decompression Sickness
or other Illness or Injury: _____
_____
_____

Any Other Remarks: _____
_____
_____

Type of Dive	
Scuba	☐
Surface	☐
Wet Bell	☐
Bell Bounce	☐
Saturation	☐
Other	

APPROVED
Name of Diving Contractor: _____

Address of Diving Contractor _____
_____

Name of Diving Supervisor (Print) _____

Signature _____ Date: _____

RECORD OF DIVE

Date of Dive _____ Diver's Signature _____

BOTTOM CONDITION: (X appropriate blocks)
☐ Sand ☐ Shell ☐ Gravel ☐ Hard ☐ Soft

Geographic Location
_____

SEA STATE:
☐ Calm ☐ Fair ☐ Moderate ☐ Heavy ☐ Gale Sea
_____

BOTTOM TEMPERATURE:
☐ Cold (below 55) ☐ Normal (55 to 75) ☐ Warm (above 75)

Vessel or Platform

BOTTOM VISIBILITY:
☐ Poor (0 to 5') ☐ Moderate (5' to 20') ☐ (Good 20 +)
_____

BOTTOM CURRENT:
☐ Weak (0 to 0.5KT) ☐ Moderate (0.5 to 2) ☐ Strong (2+)
_____

Bell Bounce or Surface Dives:	Dive One	Dive Two	Dive Three
Maximum depth of dive:	☐☐☐ feet	☐☐☐ feet	☐☐ feet
Time left surface or started pressurization:	☐☐ H ☐☐ min	☐☐ H ☐☐ min	☐☐ H ☐☐ min
Bottom Time:	☐☐☐ min	☐☐☐ min	☐☐☐ min
Decompression Completed at:	☐☐ H ☐☐ min	☐☐ H ☐☐ min	☐☐ H ☐☐ min
For surface decompression only: Surface interval:	☐☐☐ min	☐☐☐ min	☐☐☐ min
and time spent in chamber:	☐☐ H ☐☐ min	☐☐ H ☐☐ min	☐☐ H ☐☐ min

Saturation Dives:		
Storage depth:	☐☐☐☐ feet	☐☐☐ feet
Maximum depth of dive:	☐☐☐☐ feet	☐☐☐ feet
Time leaving storage depth:	☐☐ H ☐☐ min on ☐☐ day	☐☐ H ☐☐ min on ☐☐ day
Time returning to storage depth:	☐☐ H ☐☐ min on ☐☐ day	☐☐ H ☐☐ min on ☐☐ day
Bottom time:	☐☐ H ☐☐ min	☐☐ H ☐☐ min

Breathing Apparatus used: _____

Breathing Mixture used: _____

Work Description, Equipment and Tools Used:
_____
_____

Name of Decompression Schedules used: _____

Note regarding any
Decompression Sickness
or other Illness or Injury: _____

Any Other Remarks: _____
_____

Type of Dive	
Scuba	
Surface	
Wet Bell	
Bell Bounce	
Saturation	
Other	

APPROVED

Name of Diving Contractor: _____

Address of Diving Contractor _____
_____

Name of Diving Supervisor (Print) _____

Signature _____ Date: _____

RECORD OF DIVE

Date of Dive _____ Diver's Signature _____

BOTTOM CONDITION: (X appropriate blocks)
☐ Sand ☐ Shell ☐ Gravel ☐ Hard ☐ Soft

SEA STATE:
☐ Calm ☐ Fair ☐ Moderate ☐ Heavy ☐ Gale Sea

BOTTOM TEMPERATURE:
☐ Cold (below 55) ☐ Normal (55 to 75) ☐ Warm (above 75)

BOTTOM VISIBILITY:
☐ Poor (0 to 5') ☐ Moderate (5' to 20') ☐ (Good 20 +)

BOTTOM CURRENT:
☐ Weak (0 to 0.5KT) ☐ Moderate (0.5 to 2) ☐ Strong (2+)

Geographic Location

_____

_____

Vessel or Platform

_____

_____

Bell Bounce or Surface Dives:	Dive One	Dive Two	Dive Three
Maximum depth of dive:	☐☐☐ feet	☐☐☐ feet	☐☐☐ feet
Time left surface or started pressurization:	☐☐ H ☐☐ min	☐☐ H ☐☐ min	☐☐ H ☐☐ min
Bottom Time:	☐☐☐ min	☐☐☐ min	☐☐☐ min
Decompression Completed at:	☐☐ H ☐☐ min	☐☐ H ☐☐ min	☐☐ H ☐☐ min
For surface decompression only: Surface interval:	☐☐☐ min	☐☐☐ min	☐☐☐ min
and time spent in chamber:	☐☐ H ☐☐ min	☐☐ H ☐☐ min	☐☐ H ☐☐ min

Saturation Dives:		
Storage depth:	☐☐☐ feet	☐☐☐ feet
Maximum depth of dive:	☐☐☐ feet	☐☐☐ feet
Time leaving storage depth:	☐☐ H ☐☐ min on ☐☐ day	☐☐ H ☐☐ min on ☐☐ day
Time returning to storage depth:	☐☐ H ☐☐ min on ☐☐ day	☐☐ H ☐☐ min on ☐☐ day
Bottom time:	☐☐ H ☐☐ min	☐☐ H ☐☐ min

Breathing Apparatus used: _____

Breathing Mixture used: _____

Work Description, Equipment and Tools Used: _____

Type of Dive	
Scuba	☐
Surface	☐
Wet Bell	☐
Bell Bounce	☐
Saturation	☐
Other	

_____

Name of Decompression Schedules used: _____

Note regarding any Decompression Sickness or other Illness or Injury: _____

Any Other Remarks: _____

APPROVED
Name of Diving Contractor: _____

Address of Diving Contractor _____

Name of Diving Supervisor (Print) _____

Signature _____ Date: _____

RECORD OF DIVE

Date of Dive _____ Diver's Signature _____

BOTTOM CONDITION: (X appropriate blocks)
☐ Sand ☐ Shell ☐ Gravel ☐ Hard ☐ Soft

Geographic Location
_____

SEA STATE:
☐ Calm ☐ Fair ☐ Moderate ☐ Heavy ☐ Gale Sea

_____

BOTTOM TEMPERATURE:
☐ Cold (below 55) ☐ Normal (55 to 75) ☐ Warm (above 75)

Vessel or Platform

BOTTOM VISIBILITY:
☐ Poor (0 to 5') ☐ Moderate (5' to 20') ☐ (Good 20 +)

_____

BOTTOM CURRENT:
☐ Weak (0 to 0.5KT) ☐ Moderate (0.5 to 2) ☐ Strong (2+)

_____

Bell Bounce or Surface Dives:

	Dive One	Dive Two	Dive Three
Maximum depth of dive:	☐☐☐ feet	☐☐☐ feet	☐☐☐ feet
Time left surface or started pressurization:	☐☐ H ☐☐ min	☐☐ H ☐☐ min	☐☐ H ☐☐ min
Bottom Time:	☐☐ min	☐☐ min	☐☐ min
Decompression Completed at:	☐☐ H ☐☐ min	☐☐ H ☐☐ min	☐☐ H ☐☐ min
For surface decompression only: Surface interval:	☐☐ min	☐☐ min	☐☐ min
and time spent in chamber:	☐☐ H ☐☐ min	☐☐ H ☐☐ min	☐☐ H ☐☐ min

Saturation Dives:

Storage depth:	☐☐☐☐ feet	☐☐☐ feet
Maximum depth of dive:	☐☐☐☐ feet	☐☐☐ feet
Time leaving storage depth:	☐☐ H ☐☐ min on ☐☐ day	☐☐ H ☐☐ min on ☐☐ day
Time returning to storage depth:	☐☐ H ☐☐ min on ☐☐ day	☐☐ H ☐☐ min on ☐☐ day
Bottom time:	☐☐ H ☐☐ min	☐☐ H ☐☐ min

Breathing Apparatus used: _____

_____

Breathing Mixture used: _____

Work Description, Equipment and Tools Used:
_____
_____

Name of Decompression Schedules used: _____

Note regarding any
Decompression Sickness _____
or other Illness or Injury: _____

Any Other Remarks: _____
_____
_____

Type of Dive	
Scuba	
Surface	
Wet Bell	
Bell Bounce	
Saturation	
Other	

_____
_____

APPROVED

Name of Diving Contractor: _____

Address of Diving Contractor _____
_____

Name of Diving Supervisor (Print) _____

Signature _____ Date: _____

RECORD OF DIVE

Date of Dive _____ Diver's Signature _____

BOTTOM CONDITION: (X appropriate blocks)
□ Sand □ Shell □ Gravel □ Hard □ Soft

Geographic Location
_____

SEA STATE:
□ Calm □ Fair □ Moderate □ Heavy □ Gale Sea
_____

BOTTOM TEMPERATURE:
□ Cold (below 55) □ Normal (55 to 75) □ Warm (above 75)

Vessel or Platform

BOTTOM VISIBILITY:
□ Poor (0 to 5') □ Moderate (5' to 20') □ (Good 20 +)
_____

BOTTOM CURRENT:
□ Weak (0 to 0.5KT) □ Moderate (0.5 to 2) □ Strong (2+)
_____

Bell Bounce or Surface Dives:

	Dive One	Dive Two	Dive Three
Maximum depth of dive:	☐☐☐ feet	☐☐☐ feet	☐☐☐ feet
Time left surface or started pressurization:	☐☐ H ☐☐ min	☐☐ H ☐☐ min	☐☐ H ☐☐ min
Bottom Time:	☐☐ min	☐☐ min	☐☐ min
Decompression Completed at:	☐☐ H ☐☐ min	☐☐ H ☐☐ min	☐☐ H ☐☐ min
For surface decompression only: Surface interval:	☐☐ min	☐☐ min	☐☐ min
and time spent in chamber:	☐☐ H ☐☐ min	☐☐ H ☐☐ min	☐☐ H ☐☐ min

Saturation Dives:

Storage depth:	☐☐☐ feet		☐☐☐ feet
Maximum depth of dive:	☐☐☐ feet		☐☐☐ feet
Time leaving storage depth:	☐☐ H ☐☐ min on ☐☐ day		☐☐ H ☐☐ min on ☐☐ day
Time returning to storage depth:	☐☐ H ☐☐ min on ☐☐ day		☐☐ H ☐☐ min on ☐☐ day
Bottom time:	☐☐ H ☐☐ min		☐☐ H ☐☐ min

Breathing Apparatus used: _____

Breathing Mixture used: _____

Work Description, Equipment and Tools Used: _____
_____

Name of Decompression Schedules used: _____

Note regarding any Decompression Sickness or other Illness or Injury: _____

Any Other Remarks: _____
_____

Type of Dive	
Scuba	☐
Surface	☐
Wet Bell	☐
Bell Bounce	☐
Saturation	☐
Other	
_____	
_____	

APPROVED

Name of Diving Contractor: _____

Address of Diving Contractor _____
_____

Name of Diving Supervisor (Print) _____

Signature _____ Date: _____

RECORD OF DIVE

Date of Dive _____ Diver's Signature _____

BOTTOM CONDITION: (X appropriate blocks)
□ Sand   □ Shell   □ Gravel   □ Hard   □ Soft

SEA STATE:
□ Calm   □ Fair   □ Moderate   □ Heavy   □ Gale Sea

BOTTOM TEMPERATURE:
□ Cold (below 55)   □ Normal (55 to 75)   □ Warm (above 75)

BOTTOM VISIBILITY:
□ Poor (0 to 5')   □ Moderate (5' to 20')   □ (Good 20 +)

BOTTOM CURRENT:
□ Weak (0 to 0.5KT)   □ Moderate (0.5 to 2)   □ Strong (2+)

Geographic Location
_____

_____

Vessel or Platform
_____

_____

Bell Bounce or Surface Dives:	Dive One	Dive Two	Dive Three
Maximum depth of dive:	☐☐☐ feet	☐☐☐ feet	☐☐☐ feet
Time left surface or started pressurization:	☐☐ H ☐☐ min	☐☐ H ☐☐ min	☐☐ H ☐☐ min
Bottom Time:	☐☐☐ min	☐☐☐ min	☐☐☐ min
Decompression Completed at:	☐☐ H ☐☐ min	☐☐ H ☐☐ min	☐☐ H ☐☐ min
For surface decompression only: Surface interval:	☐☐ min	☐☐ min	☐☐ min
and time spent in chamber:	☐☐ H ☐☐ min	☐☐ H ☐☐ min	☐☐ H ☐☐ min

Saturation Dives:		
Storage depth:	☐☐☐ feet	☐☐☐ feet
Maximum depth of dive:	☐☐☐ feet	☐☐☐ feet
Time leaving storage depth:	☐☐ H ☐☐ min on ☐☐ day	☐☐ H ☐☐ min on ☐☐ day
Time returning to storage depth:	☐☐ H ☐☐ min on ☐☐ day	☐☐ H ☐☐ min on ☐☐ day
Bottom time:	☐☐ H ☐☐ min	☐☐ H ☐☐ min

Breathing Apparatus used: _____

Breathing Mixture used: _____

Work Description, Equipment and Tools Used: _____

Name of Decompression Schedules used: _____

Note regarding any Decompression Sickness or other Illness or Injury: _____

Any Other Remarks: _____

Type of Dive	
Scuba	
Surface	
Wet Bell	
Bell Bounce	
Saturation	
Other	

APPROVED

Name of Diving Contractor: _____

Address of Diving Contractor _____

Name of Diving Supervisor (Print) _____

Signature _____ Date: _____

RECORD OF DIVE

Date of Dive _____ Diver's Signature _____

BOTTOM CONDITION: (X appropriate blocks)   Geographic Location
☐ Sand ☐ Shell ☐ Gravel ☐ Hard ☐ Soft

SEA STATE:
☐ Calm ☐ Fair ☐ Moderate ☐ Heavy ☐ Gale Sea _____

BOTTOM TEMPERATURE:
☐ Cold (below 55) ☐ Normal (55 to 75) ☐ Warm (above 75)   Vessel or Platform

BOTTOM VISIBILITY:
☐ Poor (0 to 5') ☐ Moderate (5' to 20') ☐ (Good 20 +) _____

BOTTOM CURRENT:
☐ Weak (0 to 0.5KT) ☐ Moderate (0.5 to 2) ☐ Strong (2+)

Bell Bounce or Surface Dives:	Dive One	Dive Two	Dive Three
Maximum depth of dive:	☐☐☐ feet	☐☐ feet	☐☐ feet
Time left surface or started pressurization:	☐☐ H ☐☐ min	☐☐ H ☐☐ min	☐☐ H ☐☐ min
Bottom Time:	☐☐ min	☐☐ min	☐☐ min
Decompression Completed at:	☐☐ H ☐☐ min	☐☐ H ☐☐ min	☐☐ H ☐☐ min
For surface decompression only: Surface interval:	☐☐ min	☐☐ min	☐☐ min
and time spent in chamber:	☐☐ H ☐☐ min	☐☐ H ☐☐ min	☐☐ H ☐☐ min

Saturation Dives:		
Storage depth:	☐☐☐ feet	☐☐☐ feet
Maximum depth of dive:	☐☐☐ feet	☐☐☐ feet
Time leaving storage depth:	☐☐ H ☐☐ min on ☐☐ day	☐☐ H ☐☐ min on ☐☐ day
Time returning to storage depth:	☐☐ H ☐☐ min on ☐☐ day	☐☐ H ☐☐ min on ☐☐ day
Bottom time:	☐☐ H ☐☐ min	☐☐ H ☐☐ min

Breathing Apparatus used: _____

Breathing Mixture used: _____

Work Description, Equipment and Tools Used:
_____
_____
_____

Name of Decompression Schedules used: _____

Note regarding any
Decompression Sickness _____
or other Illness or Injury: _____

Any Other Remarks: _____
_____
_____

Type of Dive	
Scuba	☐
Surface	☐
Wet Bell	☐
Bell Bounce	☐
Saturation	☐
Other	

APPROVED
Name of Diving Contractor: _____

Address of Diving Contractor _____
_____

Name of Diving Supervisor (Print) _____

Signature _____ Date: _____

RECORD OF DIVE

Date of Dive _____ Diver's Signature _____

BOTTOM CONDITION: (X appropriate blocks)
□ Sand □ Shell □ Gravel □ Hard □ Soft

SEA STATE:
□ Calm □ Fair □ Moderate □ Heavy □ Gale Sea

BOTTOM TEMPERATURE:
□ Cold (below 55) □ Normal (55 to 75) □ Warm (above 75)

BOTTOM VISIBILITY:
□ Poor (0 to 5') □ Moderate (5' to 20') □ (Good 20 +)

BOTTOM CURRENT:
□ Weak (0 to 0.5KT) □ Moderate (0.5 to 2) □ Strong (2+)

Geographic Location
_____

_____

Vessel or Platform
_____

_____

Bell Bounce or Surface Dives:	Dive One	Dive Two	Dive Three
Maximum depth of dive:	☐☐☐ feet	☐☐☐ feet	☐☐☐ feet
Time left surface or started pressurization:	☐☐ H ☐☐ min	☐☐ H ☐☐ min	☐☐ H ☐☐ min
Bottom Time:	☐☐ min	☐☐ min	☐☐ min
Decompression Completed at:	☐☐ H ☐☐ min	☐☐ H ☐☐ min	☐☐ H ☐☐ min
For surface decompression only: Surface interval:	☐☐ min	☐☐ min	☐☐ min
and time spent in chamber:	☐☐ H ☐☐ min	☐☐ H ☐☐ min	☐☐ H ☐☐ min

Saturation Dives:		
Storage depth:	☐☐☐ feet	☐☐☐ feet
Maximum depth of dive:	☐☐☐ feet	☐☐☐ feet
Time leaving storage depth:	☐☐ H ☐☐ min on ☐☐ day	☐☐ H ☐☐ min on ☐☐ day
Time returning to storage depth:	☐☐ H ☐☐ min on ☐☐ day	☐☐ H ☐☐ min on ☐☐ day
Bottom time:	☐☐ H ☐☐ min	☐☐ H ☐☐ min

Breathing Apparatus used: _____

Breathing Mixture used: _____

Work Description, Equipment and Tools Used: _____

_____

Name of Decompression Schedules used: _____

Note regarding any
Decompression Sickness _____
or other Illness or Injury: _____

Any Other Remarks: _____

Type of Dive	
Scuba	
Surface	
Wet Bell	
Bell Bounce	
Saturation	
Other	

_____

_____

APPROVED
Name of Diving Contractor: _____

Address of Diving Contractor _____

_____

Name of Diving Supervisor (Print) _____

Signature _____ Date: _____

RECORD OF DIVE

Date of Dive _____ Diver's Signature _____

BOTTOM CONDITION: (X appropriate blocks)
☐ Sand ☐ Shell ☐ Gravel ☐ Hard ☐ Soft

SEA STATE:
☐ Calm ☐ Fair ☐ Moderate ☐ Heavy ☐ Gale Sea

BOTTOM TEMPERATURE:
☐ Cold (below 55) ☐ Normal (55 to 75) ☐ Warm (above 75)

BOTTOM VISIBILITY:
☐ Poor (0 to 5') ☐ Moderate (5' to 20') ☐ (Good 20 +)

BOTTOM CURRENT:
☐ Weak (0 to 0.5KT) ☐ Moderate (0.5 to 2) ☐ Strong (2+)

Geographic Location
_____

Vessel or Platform
_____

Bell Bounce or Surface Dives:	Dive One	Dive Two	Dive Three
Maximum depth of dive:	☐☐☐ feet	☐☐☐ feet	☐☐☐ feet
Time left surface or started pressurization:	☐☐ H ☐☐ min	☐☐ H ☐☐ min	☐☐ H ☐☐ min
Bottom Time:	☐☐ min	☐☐ min	☐☐ min
Decompression Completed at:	☐☐ H ☐☐ min	☐☐ H ☐☐ min	☐☐ H ☐☐ min
For surface decompression only: Surface interval:	☐☐ min	☐☐ min	☐☐ min
and time spent in chamber:	☐☐ H ☐☐ min	☐☐ H ☐☐ min	☐☐ H ☐☐ min

Saturation Dives:		
Storage depth:	☐☐☐ feet	☐☐☐ feet
Maximum depth of dive:	☐☐☐ feet	☐☐☐ feet
Time leaving storage depth:	☐☐ H ☐☐ min on ☐☐ day	☐☐ H ☐☐ min on ☐☐ day
Time returning to storage depth:	☐☐ H ☐☐ min on ☐☐ day	☐☐ H ☐☐ min on ☐☐ day
Bottom time:	☐☐ H ☐☐ min	☐☐ H ☐☐ min

Breathing Apparatus used: _____

Breathing Mixture used: _____

Work Description, Equipment and Tools Used: _____
_____

Name of Decompression Schedules used: _____

Note regarding any
Decompression Sickness
or other Illness or Injury: _____

Any Other Remarks: _____
_____
_____

Type of Dive

Scuba	☐
Surface	☐
Wet Bell	☐
Bell Bounce	☐
Saturation	☐
Other	

_____
_____

APPROVED
Name of Diving Contractor: _____

Address of Diving Contractor _____
_____

Name of Diving Supervisor (Print) _____

Signature _____ Date: _____

RECORD OF DIVE

Date of Dive _____ Diver's Signature _____

BOTTOM CONDITION: (X appropriate blocks)
☐ Sand ☐ Shell ☐ Gravel ☐ Hard ☐ Soft

Geographic Location
_____

SEA STATE:
☐ Calm ☐ Fair ☐ Moderate ☐ Heavy ☐ Gale Sea

_____

BOTTOM TEMPERATURE:
☐ Cold (below 55) ☐ Normal (55 to 75) ☐ Warm (above 75)

Vessel or Platform

BOTTOM VISIBILITY:
☐ Poor (0 to 5') ☐ Moderate (5' to 20') ☐ (Good 20 +)

_____

BOTTOM CURRENT:
☐ Weak (0 to 0.5KT) ☐ Moderate (0.5 to 2) ☐ Strong (2+)

_____

Bell Bounce or Surface Dives:	Dive One	Dive Two	Dive Three
Maximum depth of dive:	☐☐☐ feet	☐☐☐ feet	☐☐☐ feet
Time left surface or started pressurization:	☐☐ H ☐☐ min	☐☐ H ☐☐ min	☐☐ H ☐☐ min
Bottom Time:	☐☐ min	☐☐ min	☐☐ min
Decompression Completed at:	☐☐ H ☐☐ min	☐☐ H ☐☐ min	☐☐ H ☐☐ min
For surface decompression only: Surface interval:	☐☐ min	☐☐ min	☐☐ min
and time spent in chamber:	☐☐ H ☐☐ min	☐☐ H ☐☐ min	☐☐ H ☐☐ min

Saturation Dives:		
Storage depth:	☐☐☐ feet	☐☐☐ feet
Maximum depth of dive:	☐☐☐ feet	☐☐☐ feet
Time leaving storage depth:	☐☐ H ☐☐ min on ☐☐ day	☐☐ H ☐☐ min on ☐☐ day
Time returning to storage depth:	☐☐ H ☐☐ min on ☐☐ day	☐☐ H ☐☐ min on ☐☐ day
Bottom time:	☐☐ H ☐☐ min	☐☐ H ☐☐ min

Breathing Apparatus used: _____

Breathing Mixture used: _____

Work Description, Equipment and Tools Used: _____

Type of Dive	
Scuba	☐
Surface	☐
Wet Bell	☐
Bell Bounce	☐
Saturation	☐
Other	

Name of Decompression Schedules used: _____

Note regarding any Decompression Sickness or other Illness or Injury: _____

Any Other Remarks: _____

APPROVED
Name of Diving Contractor: _____

Address of Diving Contractor _____

Name of Diving Supervisor (Print) _____

Signature _____ Date: _____

RECORD OF DIVE

Date of Dive _____ Diver's Signature _____

BOTTOM CONDITION: (X appropriate blocks)　　　　Geographic Location
☐ Sand ☐ Shell ☐ Gravel ☐ Hard ☐ Soft
SEA STATE:　　　　　　　　　　　　　　　　　_____
☐ Calm ☐ Fair ☐ Moderate ☐ Heavy ☐ Gale Sea
BOTTOM TEMPERATURE:
☐ Cold (below 55) ☐ Normal (55 to 75) ☐ Warm (above 75)　　Vessel or Platform
BOTTOM VISIBILITY:
☐ Poor (0 to 5') ☐ Moderate (5' to 20') ☐ (Good 20 +)　　_____
BOTTOM CURRENT:
☐ Weak (0 to 0.5KT) ☐ Moderate (0.5 to 2) ☐ Strong (2+)　_____

Bell Bounce or Surface Dives:	Dive One	Dive Two	Dive Three
Maximum depth of dive:	☐☐☐ feet	☐☐☐ feet	☐☐☐ feet
Time left surface or started pressurization:	☐☐ H ☐☐ min	☐☐ H ☐☐ min	☐☐ H ☐☐ min
Bottom Time:	☐☐☐ min	☐☐☐ min	☐☐☐ min
Decompression Completed at:	☐☐ H ☐☐ min	☐☐ H ☐☐ min	☐☐ H ☐☐ min
For surface decompression only:			
Surface interval:	☐☐☐ min	☐☐☐ min	☐☐☐ min
and time spent in chamber:	☐☐ H ☐☐ min	☐☐ H ☐☐ min	☐☐ H ☐☐ min

Saturation Dives:		
Storage depth:	☐☐☐☐ feet	☐☐☐☐ feet
Maximum depth of dive:	☐☐☐☐ feet	☐☐☐☐ feet
Time leaving storage depth:	☐☐ H ☐☐ min on ☐☐ day	☐☐ H ☐☐ min on ☐☐ day
Time returning to storage depth:	☐☐ H ☐☐ min on ☐☐ day	☐☐ H ☐☐ min on ☐☐ day
Bottom time:	☐☐ H ☐☐ min	☐☐ H ☐☐ min

Breathing Apparatus used: _____

Breathing Mixture used: _____

Work Description, Equipment and Tools Used: _____

_____

Name of Decompression Schedules used: _____

Note regarding any　　　　_____
Decompression Sickness　　_____
or other Illness or Injury:　　_____

Any Other Remarks: _____

_____

Type of Dive	
Scuba	☐
Surface	☐
Wet Bell	☐
Bell Bounce	☐
Saturation	☐
Other	

APPROVED
Name of Diving Contractor: _____

Address of Diving Contractor _____

Name of Diving Supervisor (Print) _____

Signature _____ Date: _____

RECORD OF DIVE

Date of Dive _____ Diver's Signature _____

BOTTOM CONDITION: (X appropriate blocks)
☐ Sand ☐ Shell ☐ Gravel ☐ Hard ☐ Soft

Geographic Location
_____

SEA STATE:
☐ Calm ☐ Fair ☐ Moderate ☐ Heavy ☐ Gale Sea

_____

BOTTOM TEMPERATURE:
☐ Cold (below 55) ☐ Normal (55 to 75) ☐ Warm (above 75)

Vessel or Platform

BOTTOM VISIBILITY:
☐ Poor (0 to 5') ☐ Moderate (5' to 20') ☐ (Good 20 +)

_____

BOTTOM CURRENT:
☐ Weak (0 to 0.5KT) ☐ Moderate (0.5 to 2) ☐ Strong (2+)

_____

Bell Bounce or Surface Dives:	Dive One	Dive Two	Dive Three
Maximum depth of dive:	☐☐☐ feet	☐☐☐ feet	☐☐☐ feet
Time left surface or started pressurization:	☐☐ H ☐☐ min	☐☐ H ☐☐ min	☐☐ H ☐☐ min
Bottom Time:	☐☐ min	☐☐ min	☐☐ min
Decompression Completed at:	☐☐ H ☐☐ min	☐☐ H ☐☐ min	☐☐ H ☐☐ min
For surface decompression only: Surface interval:	☐☐ min	☐☐ min	☐☐ min
and time spent in chamber:	☐☐ H ☐☐ min	☐☐ H ☐☐ min	☐☐ H ☐☐ min

Saturation Dives:		
Storage depth:	☐☐☐ feet	☐☐☐ feet
Maximum depth of dive:	☐☐☐ feet	☐☐☐ feet
Time leaving storage depth:	☐☐ H ☐☐ min on ☐☐ day	☐☐ H ☐☐ min on ☐☐ day
Time returning to storage depth:	☐☐ H ☐☐ min on ☐☐ day	☐☐ H ☐☐ min on ☐☐ day
Bottom time:	☐☐ H ☐☐ min	☐☐ H ☐☐ min

Breathing Apparatus used: _____

Breathing Mixture used: _____

Work Description, Equipment and Tools Used: _____
_____

Name of Decompression Schedules used: _____

Note regarding any
Decompression Sickness _____
or other Illness or Injury: _____

Any Other Remarks: _____
_____

Type of Dive	
Scuba	☐
Surface	☐
Wet Bell	☐
Bell Bounce	☐
Saturation	☐
Other	
_____	
_____	

APPROVED
Name of Diving Contractor: _____

Address of Diving Contractor _____
_____

Name of Diving Supervisor (Print) _____

Signature _____ Date: _____

RECORD OF DIVE

Date of Dive _____ Diver's Signature _____

BOTTOM CONDITION: (X appropriate blocks)
☐ Sand ☐ Shell ☐ Gravel ☐ Hard ☐ Soft

Geographic Location
_____

SEA STATE:
☐ Calm ☐ Fair ☐ Moderate ☐ Heavy ☐ Gale Sea
_____

BOTTOM TEMPERATURE:
☐ Cold (below 55) ☐ Normal (55 to 75) ☐ Warm (above 75)

Vessel or Platform

BOTTOM VISIBILITY:
☐ Poor (0 to 5') ☐ Moderate (5' to 20') ☐ (Good 20 +)
_____

BOTTOM CURRENT:
☐ Weak (0 to 0.5KT) ☐ Moderate (0.5 to 2) ☐ Strong (2+)
_____

Bell Bounce or Surface Dives:	Dive One	Dive Two	Dive Three
Maximum depth of dive:	☐☐ feet	☐☐ feet	☐☐ feet
Time left surface or started pressurization:	☐☐ H ☐☐ min	☐☐ H ☐☐ min	☐☐ H ☐☐ min
Bottom Time:	☐☐ min	☐☐ min	☐☐ min
Decompression Completed at:	☐☐ H ☐☐ min	☐☐ H ☐☐ min	☐☐ H ☐☐ min
For surface decompression only: Surface interval:	☐☐ min	☐☐ min	☐☐ min
and time spent in chamber:	☐☐ H ☐☐ min	☐☐ H ☐☐ min	☐☐ H ☐☐ min

Saturation Dives:		
Storage depth:	☐☐☐ feet	☐☐☐ feet
Maximum depth of dive:	☐☐☐ feet	☐☐☐ feet
Time leaving storage depth:	☐☐ H ☐☐ min on ☐☐ day	☐☐ H ☐☐ min on ☐☐ day
Time returning to storage depth:	☐☐ H ☐☐ min on ☐☐ day	☐☐ H ☐☐ min on ☐☐ day
Bottom time:	☐☐ H ☐☐ min	☐☐ H ☐☐ min

Breathing Apparatus used: _____

Breathing Mixture used: _____

Work Description, Equipment and Tools Used:
_____
_____

Type of Dive	
Scuba	☐
Surface	☐
Wet Bell	☐
Bell Bounce	☐
Saturation	☐
Other	

Name of Decompression Schedules used: _____

Note regarding any Decompression Sickness or other Illness or Injury: _____

Any Other Remarks: _____
_____
_____

APPROVED
Name of Diving Contractor: _____

Address of Diving Contractor _____
_____

Name of Diving Supervisor (Print) _____

Signature _____ Date: _____

RECORD OF DIVE

Date of Dive _____ Diver's Signature _____

BOTTOM CONDITION: (X appropriate blocks)
☐ Sand ☐ Shell ☐ Gravel ☐ Hard ☐ Soft

Geographic Location

_____

SEA STATE:
☐ Calm ☐ Fair ☐ Moderate ☐ Heavy ☐ Gale Sea

_____

BOTTOM TEMPERATURE:
☐ Cold (below 55) ☐ Normal (55 to 75) ☐ Warm (above 75)

Vessel or Platform

BOTTOM VISIBILITY:
☐ Poor (0 to 5') ☐ Moderate (5' to 20') ☐ (Good 20 +)

_____

BOTTOM CURRENT:
☐ Weak (0 to 0.5KT) ☐ Moderate (0.5 to 2) ☐ Strong (2+)

_____

Bell Bounce or Surface Dives:	Dive One	Dive Two	Dive Three
Maximum depth of dive:	☐☐☐ feet	☐☐☐ feet	☐☐☐ feet
Time left surface or started pressurization:	☐☐ H ☐☐ min	☐☐ H ☐☐ min	☐☐ H ☐☐ min
Bottom Time:	☐☐☐ min	☐☐☐ min	☐☐☐ min
Decompression Completed at:	☐☐ H ☐☐ min	☐☐ H ☐☐ min	☐☐ H ☐☐ min
For surface decompression only: Surface interval:	☐☐☐ min	☐☐☐ min	☐☐☐ min
and time spent in chamber:	☐☐ H ☐☐ min	☐☐ H ☐☐ min	☐☐ H ☐☐ min

Saturation Dives:		
Storage depth:	☐☐☐ feet	☐☐☐ feet
Maximum depth of dive:	☐☐☐ feet	☐☐☐ feet
Time leaving storage depth:	☐☐ H ☐☐ min on ☐☐ day	☐☐ H ☐☐ min on ☐☐ day
Time returning to storage depth:	☐☐ H ☐☐ min on ☐☐ day	☐☐ H ☐☐ min on ☐☐ day
Bottom time:	☐☐ H ☐☐ min	☐☐ H ☐☐ min

Breathing Apparatus used: _____

Breathing Mixture used: _____

Work Description, Equipment and Tools Used: _____

_____

Type of Dive	
Scuba	
Surface	
Wet Bell	
Bell Bounce	
Saturation	
Other	

Name of Decompression Schedules used: _____

Note regarding any
Decompression Sickness
or other Illness or Injury: _____

Any Other Remarks: _____

_____

APPROVED

Name of Diving Contractor: _____

Address of Diving Contractor _____

Name of Diving Supervisor (Print) _____

Signature _____ Date: _____

RECORD OF DIVE

Date of Dive _____ Diver's Signature _____

BOTTOM CONDITION: (X appropriate blocks)   Geographic Location
☐ Sand   ☐ Shell   ☐ Gravel   ☐ Hard   ☐ Soft

SEA STATE: _____
☐ Calm   ☐ Fair   ☐ Moderate   ☐ Heavy   ☐ Gale Sea

BOTTOM TEMPERATURE:
☐ Cold (below 55)   ☐ Normal (55 to 75)   ☐ Warm (above 75)   Vessel or Platform

BOTTOM VISIBILITY:
☐ Poor (0 to 5')   ☐ Moderate (5' to 20')   ☐ (Good 20 +)   _____

BOTTOM CURRENT:
☐ Weak (0 to 0.5KT)   ☐ Moderate (0.5 to 2)   ☐ Strong (2+)   _____

Bell Bounce or Surface Dives:	Dive One	Dive Two	Dive Three
Maximum depth of dive:	☐☐☐ feet	☐☐☐ feet	☐☐☐ feet
Time left surface or started pressurization:	☐☐ H ☐☐ min	☐☐ H ☐☐ min	☐☐ H ☐☐ min
Bottom Time:	☐☐☐ min	☐☐☐ min	☐☐☐ min
Decompression Completed at:	☐☐ H ☐☐ min	☐☐ H ☐☐ min	☐☐ H ☐☐ min
For surface decompression only: Surface interval:	☐☐☐ min	☐☐☐ min	☐☐☐ min
and time spent in chamber:	☐☐ H ☐☐ min	☐☐ H ☐☐ min	☐☐ H ☐☐ min

Saturation Dives:		
Storage depth:	☐☐☐ feet	☐☐☐ feet
Maximum depth of dive:	☐☐☐ feet	☐☐☐ feet
Time leaving storage depth:	☐☐ H ☐☐ min on ☐☐ day	☐☐ H ☐☐ min on ☐☐ day
Time returning to storage depth:	☐☐ H ☐☐ min on ☐☐ day	☐☐ H ☐☐ min on ☐☐ day
Bottom time:	☐☐ H ☐☐ min	☐☐ H ☐☐ min

Breathing Apparatus used: _____

Breathing Mixture used: _____

Work Description, Equipment and Tools Used: _____
_____

Name of Decompression Schedules used: _____

Note regarding any
Decompression Sickness _____
or other Illness or Injury: _____

Type of Dive	
Scuba	
Surface	
Wet Bell	
Bell Bounce	
Saturation	
Other	

Any Other Remarks: _____
_____
_____

APPROVED
Name of Diving Contractor: _____

Address of Diving Contractor _____
_____

Name of Diving Supervisor (Print) _____

Signature _____ Date: _____

RECORD OF DIVE

Date of Dive _____ Diver's Signature _____

BOTTOM CONDITION: (X appropriate blocks)
☐ Sand ☐ Shell ☐ Gravel ☐ Hard ☐ Soft

SEA STATE:
☐ Calm ☐ Fair ☐ Moderate ☐ Heavy ☐ Gale Sea

BOTTOM TEMPERATURE:
☐ Cold (below 55) ☐ Normal (55 to 75) ☐ Warm (above 75)

BOTTOM VISIBILITY:
☐ Poor (0 to 5') ☐ Moderate (5' to 20') ☐ (Good 20 +)

BOTTOM CURRENT:
☐ Weak (0 to 0.5KT) ☐ Moderate (0.5 to 2) ☐ Strong (2+)

Geographic Location
_____

_____

Vessel or Platform
_____

_____

Bell Bounce or Surface Dives:	Dive One	Dive Two	Dive Three
Maximum depth of dive:	☐☐☐ feet	☐☐☐ feet	☐☐☐ feet
Time left surface or started pressurization:	☐☐ H ☐☐ min	☐☐ H ☐☐ min	☐☐ H ☐☐ min
Bottom Time:	☐☐☐ min	☐☐☐ min	☐☐☐ min
Decompression Completed at:	☐☐ H ☐☐ min	☐☐ H ☐☐ min	☐☐ H ☐☐ min
For surface decompression only: Surface interval:	☐☐☐ min	☐☐☐ min	☐☐☐ min
and time spent in chamber:	☐☐ H ☐☐ min	☐☐ H ☐☐ min	☐☐ H ☐☐ min

Saturation Dives:		
Storage depth:	☐☐☐ feet	☐☐☐ feet
Maximum depth of dive:	☐☐☐ feet	☐☐☐ feet
Time leaving storage depth:	☐☐ H ☐☐ min on ☐☐ day	☐☐ H ☐☐ min on ☐☐ day
Time returning to storage depth:	☐☐ H ☐☐ min on ☐☐ day	☐☐ H ☐☐ min on ☐☐ day
Bottom time:	☐☐ H ☐☐ min	☐☐ H ☐☐ min

Breathing Apparatus used: _____

Breathing Mixture used: _____

Work Description, Equipment and Tools Used: _____

_____

Name of Decompression Schedules used: _____

Note regarding any
Decompression Sickness   _____
or other Illness or Injury: _____

Any Other Remarks: _____

_____

Type of Dive	
Scuba	☐
Surface	☐
Wet Bell	☐
Bell Bounce	☐
Saturation	☐
Other	

_____

_____

APPROVED
Name of Diving Contractor: _____

Address of Diving Contractor _____

_____

Name of Diving Supervisor (Print) _____

Signature _____ Date: _____

RECORD OF DIVE

Date of Dive _____ Diver's Signature _____

BOTTOM CONDITION: (X appropriate blocks)
☐ Sand ☐ Shell ☐ Gravel ☐ Hard ☐ Soft

Geographic Location

SEA STATE:
☐ Calm ☐ Fair ☐ Moderate ☐ Heavy ☐ Gale Sea
_____

BOTTOM TEMPERATURE:
☐ Cold (below 55) ☐ Normal (55 to 75) ☐ Warm (above 75)

Vessel or Platform

BOTTOM VISIBILITY:
☐ Poor (0 to 5′) ☐ Moderate (5′ to 20′) ☐ (Good 20 +)
_____

BOTTOM CURRENT:
☐ Weak (0 to 0.5KT) ☐ Moderate (0.5 to 2) ☐ Strong (2+)
_____

Bell Bounce or Surface Dives:	Dive One	Dive Two	Dive Three
Maximum depth of dive:	☐☐☐ feet	☐☐☐ feet	☐☐☐ feet
Time left surface or started pressurization:	☐☐ H ☐☐ min	☐☐ H ☐☐ min	☐☐ H ☐☐ min
Bottom Time:	☐☐☐ min	☐☐☐ min	☐☐☐ min
Decompression Completed at:	☐☐ H ☐☐ min	☐☐ H ☐☐ min	☐☐ H ☐☐ min
For surface decompression only: Surface interval:	☐☐☐ min	☐☐☐ min	☐☐☐ min
and time spent in chamber:	☐☐ H ☐☐ min	☐☐ H ☐☐ min	☐☐ H ☐☐ min

Saturation Dives:		
Storage depth:	☐☐☐ feet	☐☐☐ feet
Maximum depth of dive:	☐☐☐ feet	☐☐☐ feet
Time leaving storage depth:	☐☐ H ☐☐ min on ☐☐ day	☐☐ H ☐☐ min on ☐☐ day
Time returning to storage depth:	☐☐ H ☐☐ min on ☐☐ day	☐☐ H ☐☐ min on ☐☐ day
Bottom time:	☐☐ H ☐☐ min	☐☐ H ☐☐ min

Breathing Apparatus used: _____

Breathing Mixture used: _____

Work Description, Equipment and Tools Used: _____

_____

Type of Dive	
Scuba	☐
Surface	☐
Wet Bell	☐
Bell Bounce	☐
Saturation	☐
Other	

Name of Decompression Schedules used: _____

Note regarding any
Decompression Sickness _____
or other Illness or Injury: _____

Any Other Remarks: _____

_____
_____

APPROVED
Name of Diving Contractor: _____

Address of Diving Contractor _____

_____

Name of Diving Supervisor (Print) _____

Signature _____ Date: _____

RECORD OF DIVE

Date of Dive _____ Diver's Signature _____

BOTTOM CONDITION: (X appropriate blocks)
☐ Sand ☐ Shell ☐ Gravel ☐ Hard ☐ Soft

Geographic Location
_____

SEA STATE:
☐ Calm ☐ Fair ☐ Moderate ☐ Heavy ☐ Gale Sea

_____

BOTTOM TEMPERATURE:
☐ Cold (below 55) ☐ Normal (55 to 75) ☐ Warm (above 75)

Vessel or Platform

BOTTOM VISIBILITY:
☐ Poor (0 to 5') ☐ Moderate (5' to 20') ☐ (Good 20 +)

_____

BOTTOM CURRENT:
☐ Weak (0 to 0.5KT) ☐ Moderate (0.5 to 2) ☐ Strong (2+)

_____

Bell Bounce or Surface Dives:	Dive One	Dive Two	Dive Three
Maximum depth of dive:	☐☐☐ feet	☐☐☐ feet	☐☐☐ feet
Time left surface or started pressurization:	☐☐ H ☐☐ min	☐☐ H ☐☐ min	☐☐ H ☐☐ min
Bottom Time:	☐☐☐ min	☐☐☐ min	☐☐☐ min
Decompression Completed at:	☐☐ H ☐☐ min	☐☐ H ☐☐ min	☐☐ H ☐☐ min
For surface decompression only: Surface interval:	☐☐☐ min	☐☐☐ min	☐☐☐ min
and time spent in chamber:	☐☐ H ☐☐ min	☐☐ H ☐☐ min	☐☐ H ☐☐ min

Saturation Dives:		
Storage depth:	☐☐☐☐ feet	☐☐☐☐ feet
Maximum depth of dive:	☐☐☐☐ feet	☐☐☐☐ feet
Time leaving storage depth:	☐☐ H ☐☐ min on ☐☐ day	☐☐ H ☐☐ min on ☐☐ day
Time returning to storage depth:	☐☐ H ☐☐ min on ☐☐ day	☐☐ H ☐☐ min on ☐☐ day
Bottom time:	☐☐ H ☐☐ min	☐☐ H ☐☐ min

Breathing Apparatus used: _____

Breathing Mixture used: _____

Work Description, Equipment and Tools Used:
_____
_____

Name of Decompression Schedules used: _____

Note regarding any
Decompression Sickness
or other Illness or Injury: _____

Any Other Remarks: _____
_____
_____

Type of Dive	
Scuba	
Surface	
Wet Bell	
Bell Bounce	
Saturation	
Other	

APPROVED
Name of Diving Contractor: _____

Address of Diving Contractor _____
_____

Name of Diving Supervisor (Print) _____

Signature _____ Date: _____

RECORD OF DIVE

Date of Dive _____ Diver's Signature _____

BOTTOM CONDITION: (X appropriate blocks)
□ Sand □ Shell □ Gravel □ Hard □ Soft

Geographic Location

SEA STATE:
□ Calm □ Fair □ Moderate □ Heavy □ Gale Sea

_____

BOTTOM TEMPERATURE:
□ Cold (below 55) □ Normal (55 to 75) □ Warm (above 75)

Vessel or Platform

BOTTOM VISIBILITY:
□ Poor (0 to 5') □ Moderate (5' to 20') □ (Good 20 +)

_____

BOTTOM CURRENT:
□ Weak (0 to 0.5KT) □ Moderate (0.5 to 2) □ Strong (2+)

_____

Bell Bounce or Surface Dives:

	Dive One	Dive Two	Dive Three
Maximum depth of dive:	[ ][ ] feet	[ ][ ] feet	[ ][ ] feet
Time left surface or started pressurization:	[ ] H [ ] min	[ ] H [ ] min	[ ] H [ ] min
Bottom Time:	[ ] min	[ ] min	[ ] min
Decompression Completed at:	[ ] H [ ] min	[ ] H [ ] min	[ ] H [ ] min
For surface decompression only:			
Surface interval:	[ ] min	[ ] min	[ ] min
and time spent in chamber:	[ ] H [ ] min	[ ] H [ ] min	[ ] H [ ] min

Saturation Dives:

Storage depth:	[ ][ ][ ] feet	[ ][ ][ ] feet
Maximum depth of dive:	[ ][ ][ ] feet	[ ][ ][ ] feet
Time leaving storage depth:	[ ] H [ ] min on [ ] day	[ ] H [ ] min on [ ] day
Time returning to storage depth:	[ ] H [ ] min on [ ] day	[ ] H [ ] min on [ ] day
Bottom time:	[ ] H [ ] min	[ ] H [ ] min

Breathing Apparatus used: _____

Breathing Mixture used: _____

Work Description, Equipment and Tools Used: _____

_____

Name of Decompression Schedules used: _____

Note regarding any
Decompression Sickness _____
or other Illness or Injury: _____

Type of Dive

Scuba	[ ]
Surface	[ ]
Wet Bell	[ ]
Bell Bounce	[ ]
Saturation	[ ]
Other	

_____

_____

Any Other Remarks: _____

_____

_____

APPROVED
Name of Diving Contractor: _____

Address of Diving Contractor _____

_____

Name of Diving Supervisor (Print) _____

Signature _____ Date: _____

RECORD OF DIVE

Date of Dive _____ Diver's Signature _____

BOTTOM CONDITION: (X appropriate blocks)
☐ Sand ☐ Shell ☐ Gravel ☐ Hard ☐ Soft

Geographic Location
_____

SEA STATE:
☐ Calm ☐ Fair ☐ Moderate ☐ Heavy ☐ Gale Sea
_____

BOTTOM TEMPERATURE:
☐ Cold (below 55) ☐ Normal (55 to 75) ☐ Warm (above 75)

Vessel or Platform

BOTTOM VISIBILITY:
☐ Poor (0 to 5') ☐ Moderate (5' to 20') ☐ (Good 20 +)
_____

BOTTOM CURRENT:
☐ Weak (0 to 0.5KT) ☐ Moderate (0.5 to 2) ☐ Strong (2+)
_____

Bell Bounce or Surface Dives:	Dive One	Dive Two	Dive Three
Maximum depth of dive:	☐☐☐ feet	☐☐☐ feet	☐☐☐ feet
Time left surface or started pressurization:	☐☐ H ☐☐ min	☐☐ H ☐☐ min	☐☐ H ☐☐ min
Bottom Time:	☐☐☐ min	☐☐☐ min	☐☐☐ min
Decompression Completed at:	☐☐ H ☐☐ min	☐☐ H ☐☐ min	☐☐ H ☐☐ min
For surface decompression only: Surface interval:	☐☐☐ min	☐☐☐ min	☐☐☐ min
and time spent in chamber:	☐☐ H ☐☐ min	☐☐ H ☐☐ min	☐☐ H ☐☐ min

Saturation Dives:		
Storage depth:	☐☐☐ feet	☐☐☐ feet
Maximum depth of dive:	☐☐☐ feet	☐☐☐ feet
Time leaving storage depth:	☐☐ H ☐☐ min on ☐☐ day	☐☐ H ☐☐ min on ☐☐ day
Time returning to storage depth:	☐☐ H ☐☐ min on ☐☐ day	☐☐ H ☐☐ min on ☐☐ day
Bottom time:	☐☐ H ☐☐ min	☐☐ H ☐☐ min

Breathing Apparatus used: _____

Breathing Mixture used: _____

Work Description, Equipment and Tools Used:
_____

Name of Decompression Schedules used: _____

Type of Dive	
Scuba	☐
Surface	☐
Wet Bell	☐
Bell Bounce	☐
Saturation	☐
Other	____
	____
	____

Note regarding any
Decompression Sickness
or other Illness or Injury: _____

Any Other Remarks: _____
_____
_____

APPROVED
Name of Diving Contractor: _____

Address of Diving Contractor _____
_____

Name of Diving Supervisor (Print) _____

Signature _____ Date: _____

RECORD OF DIVE

Date of Dive _____ Diver's Signature _____

BOTTOM CONDITION: (X appropriate blocks)   Geographic Location
☐ Sand ☐ Shell ☐ Gravel ☐ Hard ☐ Soft

SEA STATE: _____
☐ Calm ☐ Fair ☐ Moderate ☐ Heavy ☐ Gale Sea

BOTTOM TEMPERATURE: _____
☐ Cold (below 55) ☐ Normal (55 to 75) ☐ Warm (above 75)   Vessel or Platform

BOTTOM VISIBILITY:
☐ Poor (0 to 5') ☐ Moderate (5' to 20') ☐ (Good 20 +)   _____

BOTTOM CURRENT:
☐ Weak (0 to 0.5KT) ☐ Moderate (0.5 to 2) ☐ Strong (2+)   _____

Bell Bounce or Surface Dives:	Dive One	Dive Two	Dive Three
Maximum depth of dive:	☐☐☐ feet	☐☐☐ feet	☐☐☐ feet
Time left surface or started pressurization:	☐☐ H ☐☐ min	☐☐ H ☐☐ min	☐☐ H ☐☐ min
Bottom Time:	☐☐☐ min	☐☐☐ min	☐☐☐ min
Decompression Completed at:	☐☐ H ☐☐ min	☐☐ H ☐☐ min	☐☐ H ☐☐ min
For surface decompression only: Surface interval:	☐☐☐ min	☐☐☐ min	☐☐☐ min
and time spent in chamber:	☐☐ H ☐☐ min	☐☐ H ☐☐ min	☐☐ H ☐☐ min

Saturation Dives:		
Storage depth:	☐☐☐ feet	☐☐☐ feet
Maximum depth of dive:	☐☐☐ feet	☐☐☐ feet
Time leaving storage depth:	☐☐ H ☐☐ min on ☐☐ day	☐☐ H ☐☐ min on ☐☐ day
Time returning to storage depth:	☐☐ H ☐☐ min on ☐☐ day	☐☐ H ☐☐ min on ☐☐ day
Bottom time:	☐☐ H ☐☐ min	☐☐ H ☐☐ min

Breathing Apparatus used: _____

Breathing Mixture used: _____

Work Description, Equipment and Tools Used: _____

_____

Name of Decompression Schedules used: _____

Note regarding any   _____
Decompression Sickness   _____
or other Illness or Injury: _____

Any Other Remarks: _____

_____
_____

Type of Dive	
Scuba	☐
Surface	☐
Wet Bell	☐
Bell Bounce	☐
Saturation	☐
Other	

APPROVED
Name of Diving Contractor: _____

Address of Diving Contractor _____

_____

Name of Diving Supervisor (Print) _____

Signature _____ Date: _____

RECORD OF DIVE

Date of Dive _____ Diver's Signature _____

BOTTOM CONDITION: (X appropriate blocks)
☐ Sand ☐ Shell ☐ Gravel ☐ Hard ☐ Soft

Geographic Location

SEA STATE:
☐ Calm ☐ Fair ☐ Moderate ☐ Heavy ☐ Gale Sea

_____

BOTTOM TEMPERATURE:
☐ Cold (below 55) ☐ Normal (55 to 75) ☐ Warm (above 75)

_____

Vessel or Platform

BOTTOM VISIBILITY:
☐ Poor (0 to 5') ☐ Moderate (5' to 20') ☐ (Good 20 +)

_____

BOTTOM CURRENT:
☐ Weak (0 to 0.5KT) ☐ Moderate (0.5 to 2) ☐ Strong (2+)

_____

Bell Bounce or Surface Dives:	Dive One	Dive Two	Dive Three
Maximum depth of dive:	☐☐☐ feet	☐☐☐ feet	☐☐☐ feet
Time left surface or started pressurization:	☐☐ H ☐☐ min	☐☐ H ☐☐ min	☐☐ H ☐☐ min
Bottom Time:	☐☐☐ min	☐☐☐ min	☐☐☐ min
Decompression Completed at:	☐☐ H ☐☐ min	☐☐ H ☐☐ min	☐☐ H ☐☐ min
For surface decompression only: Surface interval:	☐☐☐ min	☐☐☐ min	☐☐☐ min
and time spent in chamber:	☐☐ H ☐☐ min	☐☐ H ☐☐ min	☐☐ H ☐☐ min

Saturation Dives:		
Storage depth:	☐☐☐☐ feet	☐☐☐ feet
Maximum depth of dive:	☐☐☐☐ feet	☐☐☐ feet
Time leaving storage depth:	☐☐ H ☐☐ min on ☐☐ day	☐☐ H ☐☐ min on ☐☐ day
Time returning to storage depth:	☐☐ H ☐☐ min on ☐☐ day	☐☐ H ☐☐ min on ☐☐ day
Bottom time:	☐☐ H ☐☐ min	☐☐ H ☐☐ min

Breathing Apparatus used: _____

_____

Breathing Mixture used: _____

Work Description, Equipment and Tools Used:

_____

_____

Name of Decompression Schedules used: _____

Note regarding any
Decompression Sickness   _____
or other Illness or Injury: _____
                               _____

Any Other Remarks: _____

_____

_____

Type of Dive	
Scuba	
Surface	
Wet Bell	
Bell Bounce	
Saturation	
Other	

_____

_____

APPROVED
Name of Diving Contractor: _____

Address of Diving Contractor _____

_____

Name of Diving Supervisor (Print) _____

Signature _____ Date: _____

RECORD OF DIVE

Date of Dive _____ Diver's Signature _____

BOTTOM CONDITION: (X appropriate blocks)
☐ Sand ☐ Shell ☐ Gravel ☐ Hard ☐ Soft

SEA STATE:
☐ Calm ☐ Fair ☐ Moderate ☐ Heavy ☐ Gale Sea

BOTTOM TEMPERATURE:
☐ Cold (below 55) ☐ Normal (55 to 75) ☐ Warm (above 75)

BOTTOM VISIBILITY:
☐ Poor (0 to 5') ☐ Moderate (5' to 20') ☐ (Good 20 +)

BOTTOM CURRENT:
☐ Weak (0 to 0.5KT) ☐ Moderate (0.5 to 2) ☐ Strong (2+)

Geographic Location

_____

Vessel or Platform

_____

_____

Bell Bounce or Surface Dives:	Dive One	Dive Two	Dive Three
Maximum depth of dive:	☐☐☐ feet	☐☐☐ feet	☐☐☐ feet
Time left surface or started pressurization:	☐☐ H ☐☐ min	☐☐ H ☐☐ min	☐☐ H ☐☐ min
Bottom Time:	☐☐ min	☐☐ min	☐☐ min
Decompression Completed at:	☐☐ H ☐☐ min	☐☐ H ☐☐ min	☐☐ H ☐☐ min
For surface decompression only:			
Surface interval:	☐☐ min	☐☐ min	☐☐ min
and time spent in chamber:	☐☐ H ☐☐ min	☐☐ H ☐☐ min	☐☐ H ☐☐ min

Saturation Dives:		
Storage depth:	☐☐☐ feet	☐☐☐ feet
Maximum depth of dive:	☐☐☐ feet	☐☐☐ feet
Time leaving storage depth:	☐☐ H ☐☐ min on ☐☐ day	☐☐ H ☐☐ min on ☐☐ day
Time returning to storage depth:	☐☐ H ☐☐ min on ☐☐ day	☐☐ H ☐☐ min on ☐☐ day
Bottom time:	☐☐ H ☐☐ min	☐☐ H ☐☐ min

Breathing Apparatus used: _____

_____

Breathing Mixture used: _____

_____

Work Description, Equipment and Tools Used:

_____

_____

Name of Decompression Schedules used: _____

Note regarding any
Decompression Sickness
or other Illness or Injury: _____
_____
_____

Any Other Remarks: _____

_____

_____

Type of Dive	
Scuba	
Surface	
Wet Bell	
Bell Bounce	
Saturation	
Other	

Other
_____
_____
_____

APPROVED
Name of Diving Contractor: _____

Address of Diving Contractor _____

_____

Name of Diving Supervisor (Print) _____

Signature _____ Date: _____

RECORD OF DIVE

Date of Dive _____ Diver's Signature _____

BOTTOM CONDITION: (X appropriate blocks)
☐ Sand ☐ Shell ☐ Gravel ☐ Hard ☐ Soft

Geographic Location

SEA STATE:
☐ Calm ☐ Fair ☐ Moderate ☐ Heavy ☐ Gale Sea

_____

BOTTOM TEMPERATURE:
☐ Cold (below 55) ☐ Normal (55 to 75) ☐ Warm (above 75)

Vessel or Platform

BOTTOM VISIBILITY:
☐ Poor (0 to 5') ☐ Moderate (5' to 20') ☐ (Good 20 +)

_____

BOTTOM CURRENT:
☐ Weak (0 to 0.5KT) ☐ Moderate (0.5 to 2) ☐ Strong (2+)

_____

Bell Bounce or Surface Dives:	Dive One	Dive Two	Dive Three
Maximum depth of dive:	☐☐☐ feet	☐☐☐ feet	☐☐☐ feet
Time left surface or started pressurization:	☐☐ H ☐☐ min	☐☐ H ☐☐ min	☐☐ H ☐☐ min
Bottom Time:	☐☐ min	☐☐ min	☐☐ min
Decompression Completed at:	☐☐ H ☐☐ min	☐☐ H ☐☐ min	☐☐ H ☐☐ min
For surface decompression only: Surface interval:	☐☐ min	☐☐ min	☐☐ min
and time spent in chamber:	☐☐ H ☐☐ min	☐☐ H ☐☐ min	☐☐ H ☐☐ min

Saturation Dives:		
Storage depth:	☐☐☐ feet	☐☐☐ feet
Maximum depth of dive:	☐☐☐ feet	☐☐☐ feet
Time leaving storage depth:	☐☐ H ☐☐ min on ☐☐ day	☐☐ H ☐☐ min on ☐☐ day
Time returning to storage depth:	☐☐ H ☐☐ min on ☐☐ day	☐☐ H ☐☐ min on ☐☐ day
Bottom time:	☐☐ H ☐☐ min	☐☐ H ☐☐ min

Breathing Apparatus used: _____

_____

Breathing Mixture used: _____

_____

Work Description, Equipment and Tools Used:

_____

_____

Name of Decompression Schedules used: _____

Note regarding any
Decompression Sickness
or other Illness or Injury: _____

Any Other Remarks: _____

_____

_____

Type of Dive	
Scuba	☐
Surface	☐
Wet Bell	☐
Bell Bounce	☐
Saturation	☐
Other	

_____

_____

APPROVED

Name of Diving Contractor: _____

Address of Diving Contractor _____

_____

Name of Diving Supervisor (Print) _____

Signature _____ Date: _____

RECORD OF DIVE

Date of Dive _____ Diver's Signature _____

BOTTOM CONDITION: (X appropriate blocks)
☐ Sand ☐ Shell ☐ Gravel ☐ Hard ☐ Soft

Geographic Location

_____

SEA STATE:
☐ Calm ☐ Fair ☐ Moderate ☐ Heavy ☐ Gale Sea

_____

BOTTOM TEMPERATURE:
☐ Cold (below 55) ☐ Normal (55 to 75) ☐ Warm (above 75)

Vessel or Platform

BOTTOM VISIBILITY:
☐ Poor (0 to 5') ☐ Moderate (5' to 20') ☐ (Good 20 +)

_____

BOTTOM CURRENT:
☐ Weak (0 to 0.5KT) ☐ Moderate (0.5 to 2) ☐ Strong (2+)

_____

Bell Bounce or Surface Dives:

	Dive One	Dive Two	Dive Three
Maximum depth of dive:	☐☐☐ feet	☐☐☐ feet	☐☐☐ feet
Time left surface or started pressurization:	☐☐ H ☐☐ min	☐☐ H ☐☐ min	☐☐ H ☐☐ min
Bottom Time:	☐☐☐ min	☐☐☐ min	☐☐☐ min
Decompression Completed at:	☐☐ H ☐☐ min	☐☐ H ☐☐ min	☐☐ H ☐☐ min
For surface decompression only: Surface interval:	☐☐☐ min	☐☐☐ min	☐☐☐ min
and time spent in chamber:	☐☐ H ☐☐ min	☐☐ H ☐☐ min	☐☐ H ☐☐ min

Saturation Dives:

Storage depth:	☐☐☐ feet	☐☐☐ feet
Maximum depth of dive:	☐☐☐ feet	☐☐☐ feet
Time leaving storage depth:	☐☐ H ☐☐ min on ☐☐ day	☐☐ H ☐☐ min on ☐☐ day
Time returning to storage depth:	☐☐ H ☐☐ min on ☐☐ day	☐☐ H ☐☐ min on ☐☐ day
Bottom time:	☐☐ H ☐☐ min	☐☐ H ☐☐ min

Breathing Apparatus used: _____

Breathing Mixture used: _____

Work Description, Equipment and Tools Used: _____

Name of Decompression Schedules used: _____

Note regarding any Decompression Sickness or other Illness or Injury: _____

Any Other Remarks: _____

Type of Dive	
Scuba	
Surface	
Wet Bell	
Bell Bounce	
Saturation	
Other	

APPROVED

Name of Diving Contractor: _____

Address of Diving Contractor _____

Name of Diving Supervisor (Print) _____

Signature _____ Date: _____

RECORD OF DIVE

Date of Dive _____ Diver's Signature _____

BOTTOM CONDITION: (X appropriate blocks)
☐ Sand ☐ Shell ☐ Gravel ☐ Hard ☐ Soft

Geographic Location
_____

SEA STATE:
☐ Calm ☐ Fair ☐ Moderate ☐ Heavy ☐ Gale Sea

_____

BOTTOM TEMPERATURE:
☐ Cold (below 55) ☐ Normal (55 to 75) ☐ Warm (above 75)

Vessel or Platform

BOTTOM VISIBILITY:
☐ Poor (0 to 5') ☐ Moderate (5' to 20') ☐ (Good 20 +)

_____

BOTTOM CURRENT:
☐ Weak (0 to 0.5KT) ☐ Moderate (0.5 to 2) ☐ Strong (2+)

_____

Bell Bounce or Surface Dives:	Dive One	Dive Two	Dive Three
Maximum depth of dive:	☐☐☐ feet	☐☐☐ feet	☐☐☐ feet
Time left surface or started pressurization:	☐☐ H ☐☐ min	☐☐ H ☐☐ min	☐☐ H ☐☐ min
Bottom Time:	☐☐☐ min	☐☐☐ min	☐☐☐ min
Decompression Completed at:	☐☐ H ☐☐ min	☐☐ H ☐☐ min	☐☐ H ☐☐ min
For surface decompression only: Surface interval:	☐☐☐ min	☐☐☐ min	☐☐☐ min
and time spent in chamber:	☐☐ H ☐☐ min	☐☐ H ☐☐ min	☐☐ H ☐☐ min

Saturation Dives:			
Storage depth:	☐☐☐☐ feet		☐☐☐☐ feet
Maximum depth of dive:	☐☐☐☐ feet		☐☐☐☐ feet
Time leaving storage depth:	☐☐ H ☐☐ min on ☐☐ day		☐☐ H ☐☐ min on ☐☐ day
Time returning to storage depth:	☐☐ H ☐☐ min on ☐☐ day		☐☐ H ☐☐ min on ☐☐ day
Bottom time:	☐☐ H ☐☐ min		☐☐ H ☐☐ min

Breathing Apparatus used: _____
_____

Breathing Mixture used: _____

Work Description, Equipment and Tools Used:
_____
_____

Name of Decompression Schedules used: _____

Note regarding any
Decompression Sickness _____
or other Illness or Injury: _____

Any Other Remarks: _____
_____
_____

Type of Dive	
Scuba	☐
Surface	☐
Wet Bell	☐
Bell Bounce	☐
Saturation	☐
Other	
_____	
_____	

APPROVED
Name of Diving Contractor: _____

Address of Diving Contractor _____
_____

Name of Diving Supervisor (Print) _____

Signature _____ Date: _____

RECORD OF DIVE

Date of Dive _____ Diver's Signature _____

BOTTOM CONDITION: (X appropriate blocks)
☐ Sand ☐ Shell ☐ Gravel ☐ Hard ☐ Soft

SEA STATE:
☐ Calm ☐ Fair ☐ Moderate ☐ Heavy ☐ Gale Sea

BOTTOM TEMPERATURE:
☐ Cold (below 55) ☐ Normal (55 to 75) ☐ Warm (above 75)

BOTTOM VISIBILITY:
☐ Poor (0 to 5') ☐ Moderate (5' to 20') ☐ (Good 20 +)

BOTTOM CURRENT:
☐ Weak (0 to 0.5KT) ☐ Moderate (0.5 to 2) ☐ Strong (2+)

Geographic Location
_____

_____

Vessel or Platform
_____

_____

Bell Bounce or Surface Dives:	Dive One	Dive Two	Dive Three
Maximum depth of dive:	☐☐☐ feet	☐☐ feet	☐☐☐ feet
Time left surface or started pressurization:	☐☐ H ☐☐ min	☐☐ H ☐☐ min	☐☐ H ☐☐ min
Bottom Time:	☐☐☐ min	☐☐☐ min	☐☐☐ min
Decompression Completed at:	☐☐ H ☐☐ min	☐☐ H ☐☐ min	☐☐ H ☐☐ min
For surface decompression only:			
Surface interval:	☐☐ min	☐☐ min	☐☐ min
and time spent in chamber:	☐☐ H ☐☐ min	☐☐ H ☐☐ min	☐☐ H ☐☐ min

Saturation Dives:		
Storage depth:	☐☐☐ feet	☐☐☐ feet
Maximum depth of dive:	☐☐☐ feet	☐☐☐ feet
Time leaving storage depth:	☐☐ H ☐☐ min on ☐☐ day	☐☐ H ☐☐ min on ☐☐ day
Time returning to storage depth:	☐☐ H ☐☐ min on ☐☐ day	☐☐ H ☐☐ min on ☐☐ day
Bottom time:	☐☐ H ☐☐ min	☐☐ H ☐☐ min

Breathing Apparatus used: _____

Breathing Mixture used: _____

Work Description, Equipment and Tools Used: _____

Name of Decompression Schedules used: _____

Note regarding any
Decompression Sickness _____
or other Illness or Injury:

Any Other Remarks: _____

Type of Dive	
Scuba	
Surface	
Wet Bell	
Bell Bounce	
Saturation	
Other	

_____

_____

APPROVED

Name of Diving Contractor: _____

Address of Diving Contractor _____

_____

Name of Diving Supervisor (Print) _____

Signature _____ Date: _____

RECORD OF DIVE

Date of Dive _____ Diver's Signature _____

BOTTOM CONDITION: (X appropriate blocks)
☐ Sand ☐ Shell ☐ Gravel ☐ Hard ☐ Soft

Geographic Location _____

SEA STATE:
☐ Calm ☐ Fair ☐ Moderate ☐ Heavy ☐ Gale Sea

_____

BOTTOM TEMPERATURE:
☐ Cold (below 55) ☐ Normal (55 to 75) ☐ Warm (above 75)

Vessel or Platform

BOTTOM VISIBILITY:
☐ Poor (0 to 5') ☐ Moderate (5' to 20') ☐ (Good 20 +)

_____

BOTTOM CURRENT:
☐ Weak (0 to 0.5KT) ☐ Moderate (0.5 to 2) ☐ Strong (2+)

_____

Bell Bounce or Surface Dives:	Dive One	Dive Two	Dive Three
Maximum depth of dive:	☐☐☐ feet	☐☐☐ feet	☐☐☐ feet
Time left surface or started pressurization:	☐☐ H ☐☐ min	☐☐ H ☐☐ min	☐☐ H ☐☐ min
Bottom Time:	☐☐☐ min	☐☐☐ min	☐☐☐ min
Decompression Completed at:	☐☐ H ☐☐ min	☐☐ H ☐☐ min	☐☐ H ☐☐ min
For surface decompression only: Surface interval:	☐☐☐ min	☐☐☐ min	☐☐☐ min
and time spent in chamber:	☐☐ H ☐☐ min	☐☐ H ☐☐ min	☐☐ H ☐☐ min

Saturation Dives:		
Storage depth:	☐☐☐ feet	☐☐☐ feet
Maximum depth of dive:	☐☐☐ feet	☐☐☐ feet
Time leaving storage depth:	☐☐ H ☐☐ min on ☐☐ day	☐☐ H ☐☐ min on ☐☐ day
Time returning to storage depth:	☐☐ H ☐☐ min on ☐☐ day	☐☐ H ☐☐ min on ☐☐ day
Bottom time:	☐☐ H ☐☐ min	☐☐ H ☐☐ min

Breathing Apparatus used: _____

Breathing Mixture used: _____

Work Description, Equipment and Tools Used: _____

Type of Dive	
Scuba	☐
Surface	☐
Wet Bell	☐
Bell Bounce	☐
Saturation	☐
Other	

Name of Decompression Schedules used: _____

Note regarding any Decompression Sickness or other Illness or Injury: _____

Any Other Remarks: _____

APPROVED
Name of Diving Contractor: _____

Address of Diving Contractor _____

Name of Diving Supervisor (Print) _____

Signature _____ Date: _____

RECORD OF DIVE

Date of Dive _____ Diver's Signature _____

BOTTOM CONDITION: (X appropriate blocks)
☐ Sand ☐ Shell ☐ Gravel ☐ Hard ☐ Soft

SEA STATE:
☐ Calm ☐ Fair ☐ Moderate ☐ Heavy ☐ Gale Sea

BOTTOM TEMPERATURE:
☐ Cold (below 55) ☐ Normal (55 to 75) ☐ Warm (above 75)

BOTTOM VISIBILITY:
☐ Poor (0 to 5') ☐ Moderate (5' to 20') ☐ (Good 20 +)

BOTTOM CURRENT:
☐ Weak (0 to 0.5KT) ☐ Moderate (0.5 to 2) ☐ Strong (2+)

Geographic Location
_____

_____

Vessel or Platform

_____

Bell Bounce or Surface Dives:

	Dive One	Dive Two	Dive Three
Maximum depth of dive:	☐☐☐ feet	☐☐☐ feet	☐☐☐ feet
Time left surface or started pressurization:	☐☐ H ☐☐ min	☐☐ H ☐☐ min	☐☐ H ☐☐ min
Bottom Time:	☐☐☐ min	☐☐☐ min	☐☐☐ min
Decompression Completed at:	☐☐ H ☐☐ min	☐☐ H ☐☐ min	☐☐ H ☐☐ min
For surface decompression only: Surface interval:	☐☐☐ min	☐☐☐ min	☐☐☐ min
and time spent in chamber:	☐☐ H ☐☐ min	☐☐ H ☐☐ min	☐☐ H ☐☐ min

Saturation Dives:

Storage depth:	☐☐☐ feet	☐☐☐ feet
Maximum depth of dive:	☐☐☐ feet	☐☐☐ feet
Time leaving storage depth:	☐☐ H ☐☐ min on ☐☐ day	☐☐ H ☐☐ min on ☐☐ day
Time returning to storage depth:	☐☐ H ☐☐ min on ☐☐ day	☐☐ H ☐☐ min on ☐☐ day
Bottom time:	☐☐ H ☐☐ min	☐☐ H ☐☐ min

Breathing Apparatus used: _____

_____

Breathing Mixture used: _____

_____

Work Description, Equipment and Tools Used:

_____

_____

Name of Decompression Schedules used: _____

Note regarding any   _____
Decompression Sickness   _____
or other Illness or Injury: _____

Any Other Remarks: _____

_____
_____

Type of Dive	
Scuba	
Surface	
Wet Bell	
Bell Bounce	
Saturation	
Other	
	_____
	_____

APPROVED

Name of Diving Contractor: _____

Address of Diving Contractor _____

_____

Name of Diving Supervisor (Print) _____

Signature _____ Date: _____

RECORD OF DIVE

Date of Dive _____ Diver's Signature _____

BOTTOM CONDITION: (X appropriate blocks)   Geographic Location
☐ Sand ☐ Shell ☐ Gravel ☐ Hard ☐ Soft

SEA STATE: _____
☐ Calm ☐ Fair ☐ Moderate ☐ Heavy ☐ Gale Sea

BOTTOM TEMPERATURE: _____
☐ Cold (below 55) ☐ Normal (55 to 75) ☐ Warm (above 75)   Vessel or Platform

BOTTOM VISIBILITY:
☐ Poor (0 to 5') ☐ Moderate (5' to 20') ☐ (Good 20 +)   _____

BOTTOM CURRENT:
☐ Weak (0 to 0.5KT) ☐ Moderate (0.5 to 2) ☐ Strong (2+)   _____

Bell Bounce or Surface Dives:	Dive One	Dive Two	Dive Three
Maximum depth of dive:	☐☐☐ feet	☐☐☐ feet	☐☐☐ feet
Time left surface or started pressurization:	☐☐ H ☐☐ min	☐☐ H ☐☐ min	☐☐ H ☐☐ min
Bottom Time:	☐☐ min	☐☐ min	☐☐ min
Decompression Completed at:	☐☐ H ☐☐ min	☐☐ H ☐☐ min	☐☐ H ☐☐ min
For surface decompression only: Surface interval:	☐☐ min	☐☐ min	☐☐ min
and time spent in chamber:	☐☐ H ☐☐ min	☐☐ H ☐☐ min	☐☐ H ☐☐ min

Saturation Dives:		
Storage depth:	☐☐☐ feet	☐☐☐ feet
Maximum depth of dive:	☐☐☐ feet	☐☐☐ feet
Time leaving storage depth:	☐☐ H ☐☐ min on ☐☐ day	☐☐ H ☐☐ min on ☐☐ day
Time returning to storage depth:	☐☐ H ☐☐ min on ☐☐ day	☐☐ H ☐☐ min on ☐☐ day
Bottom time:	☐☐ H ☐☐ min	☐☐ H ☐☐ min

Breathing Apparatus used: _____

Breathing Mixture used: _____

Work Description, Equipment and Tools Used:
_____
_____

Name of Decompression Schedules used: _____

Note regarding any   _____
Decompression Sickness   _____
or other Illness or Injury: _____

Any Other Remarks: _____
_____
_____

Type of Dive	
Scuba	
Surface	
Wet Bell	
Bell Bounce	
Saturation	
Other	
	_____
	_____

APPROVED
Name of Diving Contractor: _____

Address of Diving Contractor _____
_____

Name of Diving Supervisor (Print) _____

Signature _____ Date: _____

RECORD OF DIVE

Date of Dive _____ Diver's Signature _____

BOTTOM CONDITION: (X appropriate blocks)   Geographic Location
☐ Sand ☐ Shell ☐ Gravel ☐ Hard ☐ Soft

SEA STATE: _____
☐ Calm ☐ Fair ☐ Moderate ☐ Heavy ☐ Gale Sea

BOTTOM TEMPERATURE: _____
☐ Cold (below 55) ☐ Normal (55 to 75) ☐ Warm (above 75)   Vessel or Platform

BOTTOM VISIBILITY:
☐ Poor (0 to 5') ☐ Moderate (5' to 20') ☐ (Good 20 +)   _____

BOTTOM CURRENT: _____
☐ Weak (0 to 0.5KT) ☐ Moderate (0.5 to 2) ☐ Strong (2+)

Bell Bounce or Surface Dives:	Dive One	Dive Two	Dive Three
Maximum depth of dive:	☐☐☐ feet	☐☐☐ feet	☐☐☐ feet
Time left surface or started pressurization:	☐☐ H ☐☐ min	☐☐ H ☐☐ min	☐☐ H ☐☐ min
Bottom Time:	☐☐☐ min	☐☐☐ min	☐☐☐ min
Decompression Completed at:	☐☐ H ☐☐ min	☐☐ H ☐☐ min	☐☐ H ☐☐ min
For surface decompression only: Surface interval:	☐☐☐ min	☐☐☐ min	☐☐☐ min
and time spent in chamber:	☐☐ H ☐☐ min	☐☐ H ☐☐ min	☐☐ H ☐☐ min

Saturation Dives:		
Storage depth:	☐☐☐ feet	☐☐☐ feet
Maximum depth of dive:	☐☐☐ feet	☐☐☐ feet
Time leaving storage depth:	☐☐ H ☐☐ min on ☐☐ day	☐☐ H ☐☐ min on ☐☐ day
Time returning to storage depth:	☐☐ H ☐☐ min on ☐☐ day	☐☐ H ☐☐ min on ☐☐ day
Bottom time:	☐☐ H ☐☐ min	☐☐ H ☐☐ min

Breathing Apparatus used: _____

Breathing Mixture used: _____

Work Description, Equipment and Tools Used: _____
_____
_____

Name of Decompression Schedules used: _____

Note regarding any   _____
Decompression Sickness   _____
or other Illness or Injury: _____

Any Other Remarks: _____
_____
_____

Type of Dive	
Scuba	
Surface	
Wet Bell	
Bell Bounce	
Saturation	
Other	
	_____
	_____

APPROVED
Name of Diving Contractor: _____

Address of Diving Contractor _____
_____

Name of Diving Supervisor (Print) _____

Signature _____ Date: _____

RECORD OF DIVE

Date of Dive _____ Diver's Signature _____

BOTTOM CONDITION: (X appropriate blocks)
☐ Sand ☐ Shell ☐ Gravel ☐ Hard ☐ Soft

Geographic Location
_____

SEA STATE:
☐ Calm ☐ Fair ☐ Moderate ☐ Heavy ☐ Gale Sea
_____

BOTTOM TEMPERATURE:
☐ Cold (below 55) ☐ Normal (55 to 75) ☐ Warm (above 75)

Vessel or Platform

BOTTOM VISIBILITY:
☐ Poor (0 to 5') ☐ Moderate (5' to 20') ☐ (Good 20 +)
_____

BOTTOM CURRENT:
☐ Weak (0 to 0.5KT) ☐ Moderate (0.5 to 2) ☐ Strong (2+)
_____

Bell Bounce or Surface Dives:	Dive One	Dive Two	Dive Three
Maximum depth of dive:	☐☐☐ feet	☐☐☐ feet	☐☐☐ feet
Time left surface or started pressurization:	☐☐ H ☐☐ min	☐☐ H ☐☐ min	☐☐ H ☐☐ min
Bottom Time:	☐☐☐ min	☐☐☐ min	☐☐☐ min
Decompression Completed at:	☐☐ H ☐☐ min	☐☐ H ☐☐ min	☐☐ H ☐☐ min
For surface decompression only: Surface interval:	☐☐☐ min	☐☐☐ min	☐☐☐ min
and time spent in chamber:	☐☐ H ☐☐ min	☐☐ H ☐☐ min	☐☐ H ☐☐ min

Saturation Dives:		
Storage depth:	☐☐☐ feet	☐☐☐ feet
Maximum depth of dive:	☐☐☐ feet	☐☐☐ feet
Time leaving storage depth:	☐☐ H ☐☐ min on ☐☐ day	☐☐ H ☐☐ min on ☐☐ day
Time returning to storage depth:	☐☐ H ☐☐ min on ☐☐ day	☐☐ H ☐☐ min on ☐☐ day
Bottom time:	☐☐ H ☐☐ min	☐☐ H ☐☐ min

Breathing Apparatus used: _____

Breathing Mixture used: _____

Work Description, Equipment and Tools Used: _____

_____

Name of Decompression Schedules used: _____

Note regarding any
Decompression Sickness
or other Illness or Injury:

Any Other Remarks: _____

Type of Dive	
Scuba	☐
Surface	☐
Wet Bell	☐
Bell Bounce	☐
Saturation	☐
Other	

APPROVED
Name of Diving Contractor: _____

Address of Diving Contractor _____

Name of Diving Supervisor (Print) _____

Signature _____ Date: _____

RECORD OF DIVE

Date of Dive _____ Diver's Signature _____

BOTTOM CONDITION: (X appropriate blocks)
☐ Sand ☐ Shell ☐ Gravel ☐ Hard ☐ Soft

Geographic Location

SEA STATE:
☐ Calm ☐ Fair ☐ Moderate ☐ Heavy ☐ Gale Sea

_____

BOTTOM TEMPERATURE:
☐ Cold (below 55) ☐ Normal (55 to 75) ☐ Warm (above 75)

Vessel or Platform

BOTTOM VISIBILITY:
☐ Poor (0 to 5′) ☐ Moderate (5′ to 20′) ☐ (Good 20 +)

_____

BOTTOM CURRENT:
☐ Weak (0 to 0.5KT) ☐ Moderate (0.5 to 2) ☐ Strong (2+)

_____

Bell Bounce or Surface Dives:

	Dive One	Dive Two	Dive Three
Maximum depth of dive:	☐☐☐ feet	☐☐☐ feet	☐☐☐ feet
Time left surface or started pressurization:	☐☐ H ☐☐ min	☐☐ H ☐☐ min	☐☐ H ☐☐ min
Bottom Time:	☐☐☐ min	☐☐☐ min	☐☐☐ min
Decompression Completed at:	☐☐ H ☐☐ min	☐☐ H ☐☐ min	☐☐ H ☐☐ min
For surface decompression only: Surface interval:	☐☐☐ min	☐☐☐ min	☐☐☐ min
and time spent in chamber:	☐☐ H ☐☐ min	☐☐ H ☐☐ min	☐☐ H ☐☐ min

Saturation Dives:

Storage depth:	☐☐☐☐ feet	☐☐☐☐ feet
Maximum depth of dive:	☐☐☐☐ feet	☐☐☐☐ feet
Time leaving storage depth:	☐☐ H ☐☐ min on ☐☐ day	☐☐ H ☐☐ min on ☐☐ day
Time returning to storage depth:	☐☐ H ☐☐ min on ☐☐ day	☐☐ H ☐☐ min on ☐☐ day
Bottom time:	☐☐ H ☐☐ min	☐☐ H ☐☐ min

Breathing Apparatus used: _____

Breathing Mixture used: _____

Work Description, Equipment and Tools Used: _____

_____

Name of Decompression Schedules used: _____

Note regarding any
Decompression Sickness
or other Illness or Injury: _____

Any Other Remarks: _____

_____

Type of Dive	
Scuba	☐
Surface	☐
Wet Bell	☐
Bell Bounce	☐
Saturation	☐
Other	

_____

_____

APPROVED

Name of Diving Contractor: _____

Address of Diving Contractor _____

_____

Name of Diving Supervisor (Print) _____

Signature _____ Date: _____

RECORD OF DIVE

Date of Dive _____ Diver's Signature _____

BOTTOM CONDITION: (X appropriate blocks)   Geographic Location
☐ Sand ☐ Shell ☐ Gravel ☐ Hard ☐ Soft
SEA STATE: _____
☐ Calm ☐ Fair ☐ Moderate ☐ Heavy ☐ Gale Sea
BOTTOM TEMPERATURE:
☐ Cold (below 55) ☐ Normal (55 to 75) ☐ Warm (above 75)   Vessel or Platform
BOTTOM VISIBILITY:
☐ Poor (0 to 5') ☐ Moderate (5' to 20') ☐ (Good 20 +)   _____
BOTTOM CURRENT:
☐ Weak (0 to 0.5KT) ☐ Moderate (0.5 to 2) ☐ Strong (2+)

Bell Bounce or Surface Dives:	Dive One	Dive Two	Dive Three
Maximum depth of dive:	☐☐☐ feet	☐☐☐ feet	☐☐☐ feet
Time left surface or started pressurization:	☐☐ H ☐☐ min	☐☐ H ☐☐ min	☐☐ H ☐☐ min
Bottom Time:	☐☐ min	☐☐ min	☐☐ min
Decompression Completed at:	☐☐ H ☐☐ min	☐☐ H ☐☐ min	☐☐ H ☐☐ min
For surface decompression only: Surface interval:	☐☐ min	☐☐ min	☐☐ min
and time spent in chamber:	☐☐ H ☐☐ min	☐☐ H ☐☐ min	☐☐ H ☐☐ min

Saturation Dives:		
Storage depth:	☐☐☐ feet	☐☐☐ feet
Maximum depth of dive:	☐☐☐ feet	☐☐☐ feet
Time leaving storage depth:	☐☐ H ☐☐ min on ☐☐ day	☐☐ H ☐☐ min on ☐☐ day
Time returning to storage depth:	☐☐ H ☐☐ min on ☐☐ day	☐☐ H ☐☐ min on ☐☐ day
Bottom time:	☐☐ H ☐☐ min	☐☐ H ☐☐ min

Breathing Apparatus used: _____

Breathing Mixture used: _____

Type of Dive	
Scuba	☐
Surface	☐
Wet Bell	☐
Bell Bounce	☐
Saturation	☐

Work Description, Equipment and Tools Used: _____
_____
_____

Other
_____
_____

Name of Decompression Schedules used: _____

Note regarding any   _____
Decompression Sickness _____
or other Illness or Injury: _____

Any Other Remarks: _____
_____
_____

APPROVED
Name of Diving Contractor: _____

Address of Diving Contractor _____
_____

Name of Diving Supervisor (Print) _____

Signature _____ Date: _____

RECORD OF DIVE

Date of Dive _____ Diver's Signature _____

BOTTOM CONDITION: (X appropriate blocks)
☐ Sand ☐ Shell ☐ Gravel ☐ Hard ☐ Soft

Geographic Location
_____

SEA STATE:
☐ Calm ☐ Fair ☐ Moderate ☐ Heavy ☐ Gale Sea
_____

BOTTOM TEMPERATURE:
☐ Cold (below 55) ☐ Normal (55 to 75) ☐ Warm (above 75)

Vessel or Platform

BOTTOM VISIBILITY:
☐ Poor (0 to 5') ☐ Moderate (5' to 20') ☐ (Good 20 +)
_____

BOTTOM CURRENT:
☐ Weak (0 to 0.5KT) ☐ Moderate (0.5 to 2) ☐ Strong (2+)
_____

Bell Bounce or Surface Dives:

	Dive One	Dive Two	Dive Three
Maximum depth of dive:	☐☐☐ feet	☐☐☐ feet	☐☐☐ feet
Time left surface or started pressurization:	☐☐ H ☐☐ min	☐☐ H ☐☐ min	☐☐ H ☐☐ min
Bottom Time:	☐☐ min	☐☐ min	☐☐ min
Decompression Completed at:	☐☐ H ☐☐ min	☐☐ H ☐☐ min	☐☐ H ☐☐ min
For surface decompression only:			
Surface interval:	☐☐ min	☐☐ min	☐☐ min
and time spent in chamber:	☐☐ H ☐☐ min	☐☐ H ☐☐ min	☐☐ H ☐☐ min

Saturation Dives:

Storage depth:	☐☐☐ feet	☐☐☐ feet
Maximum depth of dive:	☐☐☐ feet	☐☐☐ feet
Time leaving storage depth:	☐☐ H ☐☐ min on ☐☐ day	☐☐ H ☐☐ min on ☐☐ day
Time returning to storage depth:	☐☐ H ☐☐ min on ☐☐ day	☐☐ H ☐☐ min on ☐☐ day
Bottom time:	☐☐ H ☐☐ min	☐☐ H ☐☐ min

Breathing Apparatus used: _____

Breathing Mixture used: _____

Work Description, Equipment and Tools Used: _____
_____

Name of Decompression Schedules used: _____

Note regarding any
Decompression Sickness
or other Illness or Injury: _____

Any Other Remarks: _____
_____
_____

Type of Dive	
Scuba	
Surface	
Wet Bell	
Bell Bounce	
Saturation	
Other	

APPROVED

Name of Diving Contractor: _____

Address of Diving Contractor _____
_____

Name of Diving Supervisor (Print) _____

Signature _____ Date: _____

RECORD OF DIVE

Date of Dive _____ Diver's Signature _____

BOTTOM CONDITION: (X appropriate blocks)   Geographic Location
□ Sand □ Shell □ Gravel □ Hard □ Soft   _____

SEA STATE:
□ Calm □ Fair □ Moderate □ Heavy □ Gale Sea   _____

BOTTOM TEMPERATURE:
□ Cold (below 55) □ Normal (55 to 75) □ Warm (above 75)   Vessel or Platform

BOTTOM VISIBILITY: _____
□ Poor (0 to 5') □ Moderate (5' to 20') □ (Good 20 +)

BOTTOM CURRENT: _____
□ Weak (0 to 0.5KT) □ Moderate (0.5 to 2) □ Strong (2+)

Bell Bounce or Surface Dives:	Dive One	Dive Two	Dive Three
Maximum depth of dive:	☐☐☐ feet	☐☐☐ feet	☐☐☐ feet
Time left surface or started pressurization:	☐☐ H ☐☐ min	☐☐ H ☐☐ min	☐☐ H ☐☐ min
Bottom Time:	☐☐ min	☐☐ min	☐☐ min
Decompression Completed at:	☐☐ H ☐☐ min	☐☐ H ☐☐ min	☐☐ H ☐☐ min
For surface decompression only: Surface interval:	☐☐ min	☐☐ min	☐☐ min
and time spent in chamber:	☐☐ H ☐☐ min	☐☐ H ☐☐ min	☐☐ H ☐☐ min

Saturation Dives:		
Storage depth:	☐☐☐ feet	☐☐☐ feet
Maximum depth of dive:	☐☐☐ feet	☐☐☐ feet
Time leaving storage depth:	☐☐ H ☐☐ min on ☐☐ day	☐☐ H ☐☐ min on ☐☐ day
Time returning to storage depth:	☐☐ H ☐☐ min on ☐☐ day	☐☐ H ☐☐ min on ☐☐ day
Bottom time:	☐☐ H ☐☐ min	☐☐ H ☐☐ min

Breathing Apparatus used: _____

Breathing Mixture used: _____

Work Description, Equipment and Tools Used: _____
_____
_____

Name of Decompression Schedules used: _____

Note regarding any   _____
Decompression Sickness   _____
or other Illness or Injury: _____

Any Other Remarks: _____
_____
_____

Type of Dive	
Scuba	☐
Surface	☐
Wet Bell	☐
Bell Bounce	☐
Saturation	☐
Other	

APPROVED
Name of Diving Contractor: _____

Address of Diving Contractor _____

Name of Diving Supervisor (Print) _____

Signature _____ Date: _____

RECORD OF DIVE

Date of Dive _____ Diver's Signature _____

BOTTOM CONDITION: (X appropriate blocks)
☐ Sand ☐ Shell ☐ Gravel ☐ Hard ☐ Soft

Geographic Location

SEA STATE:
☐ Calm ☐ Fair ☐ Moderate ☐ Heavy ☐ Gale Sea

_____

BOTTOM TEMPERATURE:
☐ Cold (below 55) ☐ Normal (55 to 75) ☐ Warm (above 75)

Vessel or Platform

BOTTOM VISIBILITY:
☐ Poor (0 to 5') ☐ Moderate (5' to 20') ☐ (Good 20 +)

_____

BOTTOM CURRENT:
☐ Weak (0 to 0.5KT) ☐ Moderate (0.5 to 2) ☐ Strong (2+)

_____

Bell Bounce or Surface Dives:

	Dive One	Dive Two	Dive Three
Maximum depth of dive:	☐☐☐ feet	☐☐☐ feet	☐☐☐ feet
Time left surface or started pressurization:	☐☐ H ☐☐ min	☐☐ H ☐☐ min	☐☐ H ☐☐ min
Bottom Time:	☐☐☐ min	☐☐☐ min	☐☐☐ min
Decompression Completed at:	☐☐ H ☐☐ min	☐☐ H ☐☐ min	☐☐ H ☐☐ min
For surface decompression only: Surface interval:	☐☐☐ min	☐☐☐ min	☐☐☐ min
and time spent in chamber:	☐☐ H ☐☐ min	☐☐ H ☐☐ min	☐☐ H ☐☐ min

Saturation Dives:

Storage depth:	☐☐☐ feet	☐☐☐ feet
Maximum depth of dive:	☐☐☐ feet	☐☐☐ feet
Time leaving storage depth:	☐☐ H ☐☐ min on ☐☐ day	☐☐ H ☐☐ min on ☐☐ day
Time returning to storage depth:	☐☐ H ☐☐ min on ☐☐ day	☐☐ H ☐☐ min on ☐☐ day
Bottom time:	☐☐ H ☐☐ min	☐☐ H ☐☐ min

Breathing Apparatus used: _____

_____

Breathing Mixture used: _____

_____

Work Description, Equipment and Tools Used:

_____

_____

Name of Decompression Schedules used: _____

Note regarding any
Decompression Sickness
or other Illness or Injury:

Any Other Remarks: _____

Type of Dive	
Scuba	☐
Surface	☐
Wet Bell	☐
Bell Bounce	☐
Saturation	☐
Other	

_____

_____

APPROVED

Name of Diving Contractor: _____

Address of Diving Contractor _____

_____

Name of Diving Supervisor (Print) _____

Signature _____ Date: _____

RECORD OF DIVE

Date of Dive _____ Diver's Signature _____

BOTTOM CONDITION: (X appropriate blocks)
☐ Sand ☐ Shell ☐ Gravel ☐ Hard ☐ Soft

Geographic Location
_____

SEA STATE:
☐ Calm ☐ Fair ☐ Moderate ☐ Heavy ☐ Gale Sea
_____

BOTTOM TEMPERATURE:
☐ Cold (below 55) ☐ Normal (55 to 75) ☐ Warm (above 75)

Vessel or Platform

BOTTOM VISIBILITY:
☐ Poor (0 to 5') ☐ Moderate (5' to 20') ☐ (Good 20 +)
_____

BOTTOM CURRENT:
☐ Weak (0 to 0.5KT) ☐ Moderate (0.5 to 2) ☐ Strong (2+)
_____

Bell Bounce or Surface Dives:	Dive One	Dive Two	Dive Three
Maximum depth of dive:	☐☐☐ feet	☐☐☐ feet	☐☐☐ feet
Time left surface or started pressurization:	☐☐ H ☐☐ min	☐☐ H ☐☐ min	☐☐ H ☐☐ min
Bottom Time:	☐☐☐ min	☐☐☐ min	☐☐☐ min
Decompression Completed at:	☐☐ H ☐☐ min	☐☐ H ☐☐ min	☐☐ H ☐☐ min
For surface decompression only: Surface interval:	☐☐☐ min	☐☐☐ min	☐☐☐ min
and time spent in chamber:	☐☐ H ☐☐ min	☐☐ H ☐☐ min	☐☐ H ☐☐ min

Saturation Dives:		
Storage depth:	☐☐☐ feet	☐☐☐ feet
Maximum depth of dive:	☐☐☐ feet	☐☐☐ feet
Time leaving storage depth:	☐☐ H ☐☐ min on ☐☐ day	☐☐ H ☐☐ min on ☐☐ day
Time returning to storage depth:	☐☐ H ☐☐ min on ☐☐ day	☐☐ H ☐☐ min on ☐☐ day
Bottom time:	☐☐ H ☐☐ min	☐☐ H ☐☐ min

Breathing Apparatus used: _____

Breathing Mixture used: _____

Work Description, Equipment and Tools Used: _____

Type of Dive	
Scuba	☐
Surface	☐
Wet Bell	☐
Bell Bounce	☐
Saturation	☐
Other	

Name of Decompression Schedules used: _____

Note regarding any
Decompression Sickness
or other Illness or Injury: _____

Any Other Remarks: _____
_____

APPROVED

Name of Diving Contractor: _____

Address of Diving Contractor _____
_____

Name of Diving Supervisor (Print) _____

Signature _____ Date: _____

RECORD OF DIVE

Date of Dive _____ Diver's Signature _____

BOTTOM CONDITION: (X appropriate blocks)
☐ Sand ☐ Shell ☐ Gravel ☐ Hard ☐ Soft

Geographic Location

SEA STATE:
☐ Calm ☐ Fair ☐ Moderate ☐ Heavy ☐ Gale Sea

_____

BOTTOM TEMPERATURE:
☐ Cold (below 55) ☐ Normal (55 to 75) ☐ Warm (above 75)

Vessel or Platform

BOTTOM VISIBILITY:
☐ Poor (0 to 5') ☐ Moderate (5' to 20') ☐ (Good 20 +)

_____

BOTTOM CURRENT:
☐ Weak (0 to 0.5KT) ☐ Moderate (0.5 to 2) ☐ Strong (2+)

Bell Bounce or Surface Dives:	Dive One	Dive Two	Dive Three
Maximum depth of dive:	☐☐☐ feet	☐☐☐ feet	☐☐☐ feet
Time left surface or started pressurization:	☐☐ H ☐☐ min	☐☐ H ☐☐ min	☐☐ H ☐☐ min
Bottom Time:	☐☐☐ min	☐☐☐ min	☐☐☐ min
Decompression Completed at:	☐☐ H ☐☐ min	☐☐ H ☐☐ min	☐☐ H ☐☐ min
For surface decompression only:			
Surface interval:	☐☐☐ min	☐☐☐ min	☐☐☐ min
and time spent in chamber:	☐☐ H ☐☐ min	☐☐ H ☐☐ min	☐☐ H ☐☐ min

Saturation Dives:

Storage depth:	☐☐☐ feet	☐☐☐ feet
Maximum depth of dive:	☐☐☐ feet	☐☐☐ feet
Time leaving storage depth:	☐☐ H ☐☐ min on ☐☐ day	☐☐ H ☐☐ min on ☐☐ day
Time returning to storage depth:	☐☐ H ☐☐ min on ☐☐ day	☐☐ H ☐☐ min on ☐☐ day
Bottom time:	☐☐ H ☐☐ min	☐☐ H ☐☐ min

Breathing Apparatus used: _____

Breathing Mixture used: _____

Work Description, Equipment and Tools Used: _____

_____

Name of Decompression Schedules used: _____

Note regarding any
Decompression Sickness
or other Illness or Injury: _____

Type of Dive	
Scuba	☐
Surface	☐
Wet Bell	☐
Bell Bounce	☐
Saturation	☐
Other	

Any Other Remarks: _____

_____

APPROVED
Name of Diving Contractor: _____

Address of Diving Contractor _____

_____

Name of Diving Supervisor (Print) _____

Signature _____ Date: _____

RECORD OF DIVE

Date of Dive _____ Diver's Signature _____

BOTTOM CONDITION: (X appropriate blocks)
☐ Sand ☐ Shell ☐ Gravel ☐ Hard ☐ Soft

Geographic Location

_____

SEA STATE:
☐ Calm ☐ Fair ☐ Moderate ☐ Heavy ☐ Gale Sea

_____

BOTTOM TEMPERATURE:
☐ Cold (below 55) ☐ Normal (55 to 75) ☐ Warm (above 75)

Vessel or Platform

BOTTOM VISIBILITY:
☐ Poor (0 to 5') ☐ Moderate (5' to 20') ☐ (Good 20 +)

_____

BOTTOM CURRENT:
☐ Weak (0 to 0.5KT) ☐ Moderate (0.5 to 2) ☐ Strong (2+)

_____

Bell Bounce or Surface Dives:	Dive One	Dive Two	Dive Three
Maximum depth of dive:	☐☐☐ feet	☐☐☐ feet	☐☐☐ feet
Time left surface or started pressurization:	☐☐ H ☐☐ min	☐☐ H ☐☐ min	☐☐ H ☐☐ min
Bottom Time:	☐☐☐ min	☐☐☐ min	☐☐☐ min
Decompression Completed at:	☐☐ H ☐☐ min	☐☐ H ☐☐ min	☐☐ H ☐☐ min
For surface decompression only: Surface interval:	☐☐☐ min	☐☐☐ min	☐☐☐ min
and time spent in chamber:	☐☐ H ☐☐ min	☐☐ H ☐☐ min	☐☐ H ☐☐ min

Saturation Dives:		
Storage depth:	☐☐☐ feet	☐☐☐ feet
Maximum depth of dive:	☐☐☐ feet	☐☐☐ feet
Time leaving storage depth:	☐☐ H ☐☐ min on ☐☐ day	☐☐ H ☐☐ min on ☐☐ day
Time returning to storage depth:	☐☐ H ☐☐ min on ☐☐ day	☐☐ H ☐☐ min on ☐☐ day
Bottom time:	☐☐ H ☐☐ min	☐☐ H ☐☐ min

Breathing Apparatus used: _____

Breathing Mixture used: _____

Work Description, Equipment and Tools Used: _____
_____
_____

Name of Decompression Schedules used: _____

Note regarding any
Decompression Sickness _____
or other Illness or Injury: _____

Any Other Remarks: _____
_____
_____

Type of Dive	
Scuba	☐
Surface	☐
Wet Bell	☐
Bell Bounce	☐
Saturation	☐
Other	

_____
_____

APPROVED
Name of Diving Contractor: _____

Address of Diving Contractor _____
_____

Name of Diving Supervisor (Print) _____

Signature _____ Date: _____

RECORD OF DIVE

Date of Dive _____ Diver's Signature _____

BOTTOM CONDITION: (X appropriate blocks)
☐ Sand ☐ Shell ☐ Gravel ☐ Hard ☐ Soft

Geographic Location
_____

SEA STATE:
☐ Calm ☐ Fair ☐ Moderate ☐ Heavy ☐ Gale Sea

_____

BOTTOM TEMPERATURE:
☐ Cold (below 55) ☐ Normal (55 to 75) ☐ Warm (above 75)

Vessel or Platform

BOTTOM VISIBILITY:
☐ Poor (0 to 5') ☐ Moderate (5' to 20') ☐ (Good 20 +)

_____

BOTTOM CURRENT:
☐ Weak (0 to 0.5KT) ☐ Moderate (0.5 to 2) ☐ Strong (2+)

_____

Bell Bounce or Surface Dives:	Dive One	Dive Two	Dive Three
Maximum depth of dive:	☐☐☐ feet	☐☐☐ feet	☐☐☐ feet
Time left surface or started pressurization:	☐☐ H ☐☐ min	☐☐ H ☐☐ min	☐☐ H ☐☐ min
Bottom Time:	☐☐☐ min	☐☐☐ min	☐☐☐ min
Decompression Completed at:	☐☐ H ☐☐ min	☐☐ H ☐☐ min	☐☐ H ☐☐ min
For surface decompression only: Surface interval:	☐☐☐ min	☐☐☐ min	☐☐☐ min
and time spent in chamber:	☐☐ H ☐☐ min	☐☐ H ☐☐ min	☐☐ H ☐☐ min

Saturation Dives:		
Storage depth:	☐☐☐ feet	☐☐☐ feet
Maximum depth of dive:	☐☐☐ feet	☐☐☐ feet
Time leaving storage depth:	☐☐ H ☐☐ min on ☐☐ day	☐☐ H ☐☐ min on ☐☐ day
Time returning to storage depth:	☐☐ H ☐☐ min on ☐☐ day	☐☐ H ☐☐ min on ☐☐ day
Bottom time:	☐☐ H ☐☐ min	☐☐ H ☐☐ min

Breathing Apparatus used: _____

Breathing Mixture used: _____

Work Description, Equipment and Tools Used: _____
_____
_____

Name of Decompression Schedules used: _____

Note regarding any Decompression Sickness or other Illness or Injury: _____
_____
_____

Any Other Remarks: _____
_____
_____

Type of Dive	
Scuba	☐
Surface	☐
Wet Bell	☐
Bell Bounce	☐
Saturation	☐
Other	

_____
_____

APPROVED

Name of Diving Contractor: _____

Address of Diving Contractor _____
_____

Name of Diving Supervisor (Print) _____

Signature _____ Date: _____

RECORD OF DIVE

Date of Dive _____ Diver's Signature _____

BOTTOM CONDITION: (X appropriate blocks)
☐ Sand ☐ Shell ☐ Gravel ☐ Hard ☐ Soft

Geographic Location
_____

SEA STATE:
☐ Calm ☐ Fair ☐ Moderate ☐ Heavy ☐ Gale Sea

_____

BOTTOM TEMPERATURE:
☐ Cold (below 55) ☐ Normal (55 to 75) ☐ Warm (above 75)

Vessel or Platform

BOTTOM VISIBILITY:
☐ Poor (0 to 5') ☐ Moderate (5' to 20') ☐ (Good 20 +)

_____

BOTTOM CURRENT:
☐ Weak (0 to 0.5KT) ☐ Moderate (0.5 to 2) ☐ Strong (2+)

_____

Bell Bounce or Surface Dives:	Dive One	Dive Two	Dive Three
Maximum depth of dive:	☐☐☐ feet	☐☐☐ feet	☐☐☐ feet
Time left surface or started pressurization:	☐☐ H ☐☐ min	☐☐ H ☐☐ min	☐☐ H ☐☐ min
Bottom Time:	☐☐☐ min	☐☐☐ min	☐☐☐ min
Decompression Completed at:	☐☐ H ☐☐ min	☐☐ H ☐☐ min	☐☐ H ☐☐ min
For surface decompression only: Surface interval:	☐☐☐ min	☐☐☐ min	☐☐☐ min
and time spent in chamber:	☐☐ H ☐☐ min	☐☐ H ☐☐ min	☐☐ H ☐☐ min

Saturation Dives:		
Storage depth:	☐☐☐ feet	☐☐☐ feet
Maximum depth of dive:	☐☐☐ feet	☐☐☐ feet
Time leaving storage depth:	☐☐ H ☐☐ min on ☐☐ day	☐☐ H ☐☐ min on ☐☐ day
Time returning to storage depth:	☐☐ H ☐☐ min on ☐☐ day	☐☐ H ☐☐ min on ☐☐ day
Bottom time:	☐☐ H ☐☐ min	☐☐ H ☐☐ min

Breathing Apparatus used: _____

Breathing Mixture used: _____

Work Description, Equipment and Tools Used: _____

Type of Dive	
Scuba	☐
Surface	☐
Wet Bell	☐
Bell Bounce	☐
Saturation	☐
Other	

Name of Decompression Schedules used: _____

Note regarding any Decompression Sickness or other Illness or Injury: _____

Any Other Remarks: _____

APPROVED
Name of Diving Contractor: _____

Address of Diving Contractor _____

Name of Diving Supervisor (Print) _____

Signature _____ Date: _____

RECORD OF DIVE

Date of Dive _____ Diver's Signature _____

BOTTOM CONDITION: (X appropriate blocks)
☐ Sand ☐ Shell ☐ Gravel ☐ Hard ☐ Soft

Geographic Location
_____

SEA STATE:
☐ Calm ☐ Fair ☐ Moderate ☐ Heavy ☐ Gale Sea
_____

BOTTOM TEMPERATURE:
☐ Cold (below 55) ☐ Normal (55 to 75) ☐ Warm (above 75)

Vessel or Platform

BOTTOM VISIBILITY:
☐ Poor (0 to 5') ☐ Moderate (5' to 20') ☐ (Good 20 +)
_____

BOTTOM CURRENT:
☐ Weak (0 to 0.5KT) ☐ Moderate (0.5 to 2) ☐ Strong (2+)
_____

Bell Bounce or Surface Dives:

	Dive One	Dive Two	Dive Three
Maximum depth of dive:	☐☐☐ feet	☐☐☐ feet	☐☐☐ feet
Time left surface or started pressurization:	☐☐ H ☐☐ min	☐☐ H ☐☐ min	☐☐ H ☐☐ min
Bottom Time:	☐☐☐ min	☐☐☐ min	☐☐☐ min
Decompression Completed at:	☐☐ H ☐☐ min	☐☐ H ☐☐ min	☐☐ H ☐☐ min
For surface decompression only: Surface interval:	☐☐☐ min	☐☐☐ min	☐☐☐ min
and time spent in chamber:	☐☐ H ☐☐ min	☐☐ H ☐☐ min	☐☐ H ☐☐ min

Saturation Dives:

Storage depth:	☐☐☐ feet	☐☐☐ feet
Maximum depth of dive:	☐☐☐ feet	☐☐☐ feet
Time leaving storage depth:	☐☐ H ☐☐ min on ☐☐ day	☐☐ H ☐☐ min on ☐☐ day
Time returning to storage depth:	☐☐ H ☐☐ min on ☐☐ day	☐☐ H ☐☐ min on ☐☐ day
Bottom time:	☐☐ H ☐☐ min	☐☐ H ☐☐ min

Breathing Apparatus used: _____

Breathing Mixture used: _____

Work Description, Equipment and Tools Used:
_____
_____

Name of Decompression Schedules used: _____

Note regarding any
Decompression Sickness
or other Illness or Injury: _____

Any Other Remarks: _____
_____
_____

Type of Dive	
Scuba	☐
Surface	☐
Wet Bell	☐
Bell Bounce	☐
Saturation	☐
Other	

APPROVED
Name of Diving Contractor: _____

Address of Diving Contractor _____
_____

Name of Diving Supervisor (Print) _____

Signature _____ Date: _____

RECORD OF DIVE

Date of Dive _____ Diver's Signature _____

BOTTOM CONDITION: (X appropriate blocks)
☐ Sand ☐ Shell ☐ Gravel ☐ Hard ☐ Soft

SEA STATE:
☐ Calm ☐ Fair ☐ Moderate ☐ Heavy ☐ Gale Sea

BOTTOM TEMPERATURE:
☐ Cold (below 55) ☐ Normal (55 to 75) ☐ Warm (above 75)

BOTTOM VISIBILITY:
☐ Poor (0 to 5') ☐ Moderate (5' to 20') ☐ (Good 20 +)

BOTTOM CURRENT:
☐ Weak (0 to 0.5KT) ☐ Moderate (0.5 to 2) ☐ Strong (2+)

Geographic Location
_____

_____

Vessel or Platform
_____

_____

Bell Bounce or Surface Dives:

	Dive One	Dive Two	Dive Three
Maximum depth of dive:	⬜ feet	⬜ feet	⬜ feet
Time left surface or started pressurization:	⬜ H ⬜ min	⬜ H ⬜ min	⬜ H ⬜ min
Bottom Time:	⬜ min	⬜ min	⬜ min
Decompression Completed at:	⬜ H ⬜ min	⬜ H ⬜ min	⬜ H ⬜ min
For surface decompression only: Surface interval:	⬜ min	⬜ min	⬜ min
and time spent in chamber:	⬜ H ⬜ min	⬜ H ⬜ min	⬜ H ⬜ min

Saturation Dives:

Storage depth:	⬜ feet	⬜ feet
Maximum depth of dive:	⬜ feet	⬜ feet
Time leaving storage depth:	⬜ H ⬜ min on ⬜ day	⬜ H ⬜ min on ⬜ day
Time returning to storage depth:	⬜ H ⬜ min on ⬜ day	⬜ H ⬜ min on ⬜ day
Bottom time:	⬜ H ⬜ min	⬜ H ⬜ min

Breathing Apparatus used: _____

Breathing Mixture used: _____

Work Description, Equipment and Tools Used:
_____
_____

Name of Decompression Schedules used: _____

Note regarding any
Decompression Sickness
or other Illness or Injury: _____

Any Other Remarks: _____
_____
_____

Type of Dive	
Scuba	⬜
Surface	⬜
Wet Bell	⬜
Bell Bounce	⬜
Saturation	⬜
Other	

APPROVED

Name of Diving Contractor: _____

Address of Diving Contractor _____
_____

Name of Diving Supervisor (Print) _____

Signature _____ Date: _____

RECORD OF DIVE

Date of Dive _____ Diver's Signature _____

BOTTOM CONDITION: (X appropriate blocks)
☐ Sand ☐ Shell ☐ Gravel ☐ Hard ☐ Soft

Geographic Location
_____

SEA STATE:
☐ Calm ☐ Fair ☐ Moderate ☐ Heavy ☐ Gale Sea
_____

BOTTOM TEMPERATURE:
☐ Cold (below 55) ☐ Normal (55 to 75) ☐ Warm (above 75)

Vessel or Platform

BOTTOM VISIBILITY:
☐ Poor (0 to 5') ☐ Moderate (5' to 20') ☐ (Good 20 +)
_____

BOTTOM CURRENT:
☐ Weak (0 to 0.5KT) ☐ Moderate (0.5 to 2) ☐ Strong (2+)
_____

Bell Bounce or Surface Dives:	Dive One	Dive Two	Dive Three
Maximum depth of dive:	☐☐☐ feet	☐☐☐ feet	☐☐☐ feet
Time left surface or started pressurization:	☐☐ H ☐☐ min	☐☐ H ☐☐ min	☐☐ H ☐☐ min
Bottom Time:	☐☐☐ min	☐☐☐ min	☐☐☐ min
Decompression Completed at:	☐☐ H ☐☐ min	☐☐ H ☐☐ min	☐☐ H ☐☐ min
For surface decompression only: Surface interval:	☐☐☐ min	☐☐☐ min	☐☐☐ min
and time spent in chamber:	☐☐ H ☐☐ min	☐☐ H ☐☐ min	☐☐ H ☐☐ min

Saturation Dives:		
Storage depth:	☐☐☐ feet	☐☐☐ feet
Maximum depth of dive:	☐☐☐ feet	☐☐☐ feet
Time leaving storage depth:	☐☐ H ☐☐ min on ☐☐ day	☐☐ H ☐☐ min on ☐☐ day
Time returning to storage depth:	☐☐ H ☐☐ min on ☐☐ day	☐☐ H ☐☐ min on ☐☐ day
Bottom time:	☐☐ H ☐☐ min	☐☐ H ☐☐ min

Breathing Apparatus used: _____

Breathing Mixture used: _____

Work Description, Equipment and Tools Used:
_____
_____

Name of Decompression Schedules used: _____

Note regarding any   _____
Decompression Sickness   _____
or other Illness or Injury: _____

Any Other Remarks: _____
_____
_____

Type of Dive

Scuba	☐
Surface	☐
Wet Bell	☐
Bell Bounce	☐
Saturation	☐
Other	

_____
_____

APPROVED

Name of Diving Contractor: _____

Address of Diving Contractor _____
_____

Name of Diving Supervisor (Print) _____

Signature _____ Date: _____

RECORD OF DIVE

Date of Dive _____ Diver's Signature _____

BOTTOM CONDITION: (X appropriate blocks)
□ Sand □ Shell □ Gravel □ Hard □ Soft

Geographic Location

_____

SEA STATE:
□ Calm □ Fair □ Moderate □ Heavy □ Gale Sea

_____

BOTTOM TEMPERATURE:
□ Cold (below 55) □ Normal (55 to 75) □ Warm (above 75)

Vessel or Platform

BOTTOM VISIBILITY:
□ Poor (0 to 5') □ Moderate (5' to 20') □ (Good 20 +)

_____

BOTTOM CURRENT:
□ Weak (0 to 0.5KT) □ Moderate (0.5 to 2) □ Strong (2+)

_____

Bell Bounce or Surface Dives:

	Dive One	Dive Two	Dive Three
Maximum depth of dive:	☐☐☐ feet	☐☐☐ feet	☐☐☐ feet
Time left surface or started pressurization:	☐☐ H ☐☐ min	☐☐ H ☐☐ min	☐☐ H ☐☐ min
Bottom Time:	☐☐☐ min	☐☐☐ min	☐☐☐ min
Decompression Completed at:	☐☐ H ☐☐ min	☐☐ H ☐☐ min	☐☐ H ☐☐ min
For surface decompression only: Surface interval:	☐☐ min	☐☐ min	☐☐ min
and time spent in chamber:	☐☐ H ☐☐ min	☐☐ H ☐☐ min	☐☐ H ☐☐ min

Saturation Dives:

Storage depth:	☐☐☐ feet		☐☐☐ feet
Maximum depth of dive:	☐☐☐ feet		☐☐☐ feet
Time leaving storage depth:	☐☐ H ☐☐ min on ☐☐ day		☐☐ H ☐☐ min on ☐☐ day
Time returning to storage depth:	☐☐ H ☐☐ min on ☐☐ day		☐☐ H ☐☐ min on ☐☐ day
Bottom time:	☐☐ H ☐☐ min		☐☐ H ☐☐ min

Breathing Apparatus used: _____

Breathing Mixture used: _____

Work Description, Equipment and Tools Used: _____

_____

Name of Decompression Schedules used: _____

Note regarding any
Decompression Sickness _____
or other Illness or Injury: _____

Any Other Remarks: _____

_____

_____

Type of Dive	
Scuba	☐
Surface	☐
Wet Bell	☐
Bell Bounce	☐
Saturation	☐
Other	

APPROVED

Name of Diving Contractor: _____

Address of Diving Contractor _____

_____

Name of Diving Supervisor (Print) _____

Signature _____ Date: _____

RECORD OF DIVE

Date of Dive _____ Diver's Signature _____

BOTTOM CONDITION: (X appropriate blocks)
☐ Sand ☐ Shell ☐ Gravel ☐ Hard ☐ Soft

Geographic Location
_____

SEA STATE:
☐ Calm ☐ Fair ☐ Moderate ☐ Heavy ☐ Gale Sea

_____

BOTTOM TEMPERATURE:
☐ Cold (below 55) ☐ Normal (55 to 75) ☐ Warm (above 75)

Vessel or Platform

BOTTOM VISIBILITY:
☐ Poor (0 to 5') ☐ Moderate (5' to 20') ☐ (Good 20 +)

_____

BOTTOM CURRENT:
☐ Weak (0 to 0.5KT) ☐ Moderate (0.5 to 2) ☐ Strong (2+)

_____

Bell Bounce or Surface Dives:	Dive One	Dive Two	Dive Three
Maximum depth of dive:	☐☐☐ feet	☐☐☐ feet	☐☐☐ feet
Time left surface or started pressurization:	☐☐ H ☐☐ min	☐☐ H ☐☐ min	☐☐ H ☐☐ min
Bottom Time:	☐☐ min	☐☐ min	☐☐ min
Decompression Completed at:	☐☐ H ☐☐ min	☐☐ H ☐☐ min	☐☐ H ☐☐ min
For surface decompression only: Surface interval:	☐☐☐ min	☐☐☐ min	☐☐☐ min
and time spent in chamber:	☐☐ H ☐☐ min	☐☐ H ☐☐ min	☐☐ H ☐☐ min

Saturation Dives:		
Storage depth:	☐☐☐ feet	☐☐☐ feet
Maximum depth of dive:	☐☐☐ feet	☐☐☐ feet
Time leaving storage depth:	☐☐ H ☐☐ min on ☐☐ day	☐☐ H ☐☐ min on ☐☐ day
Time returning to storage depth:	☐☐ H ☐☐ min on ☐☐ day	☐☐ H ☐☐ min on ☐☐ day
Bottom time:	☐☐ H ☐☐ min	☐☐ H ☐☐ min

Breathing Apparatus used: _____

Breathing Mixture used: _____

Work Description, Equipment and Tools Used:
_____
_____

Type of Dive	
Scuba	☐
Surface	☐
Wet Bell	☐
Bell Bounce	☐
Saturation	☐
Other	

Name of Decompression Schedules used: _____

Note regarding any
Decompression Sickness _____
or other Illness or Injury: _____

Any Other Remarks: _____
_____
_____

APPROVED
Name of Diving Contractor: _____

Address of Diving Contractor _____
_____

Name of Diving Supervisor (Print) _____

Signature _____ Date: _____

RECORD OF DIVE

Date of Dive _____ Diver's Signature _____

BOTTOM CONDITION: (X appropriate blocks)
☐ Sand ☐ Shell ☐ Gravel ☐ Hard ☐ Soft

Geographic Location
_____

SEA STATE:
☐ Calm ☐ Fair ☐ Moderate ☐ Heavy ☐ Gale Sea

_____

BOTTOM TEMPERATURE:
☐ Cold (below 55) ☐ Normal (55 to 75) ☐ Warm (above 75)

Vessel or Platform

BOTTOM VISIBILITY:
☐ Poor (0 to 5') ☐ Moderate (5' to 20') ☐ (Good 20 +)

_____

BOTTOM CURRENT:
☐ Weak (0 to 0.5KT) ☐ Moderate (0.5 to 2) ☐ Strong (2+)

_____

Bell Bounce or Surface Dives:	Dive One	Dive Two	Dive Three
Maximum depth of dive:	☐☐☐ feet	☐☐☐ feet	☐☐☐ feet
Time left surface or started pressurization:	☐☐ H ☐☐ min	☐☐ H ☐☐ min	☐☐ H ☐☐ min
Bottom Time:	☐☐ min	☐☐ min	☐☐ min
Decompression Completed at:	☐☐ H ☐☐ min	☐☐ H ☐☐ min	☐☐ H ☐☐ min
For surface decompression only: Surface interval:	☐☐ min	☐☐ min	☐☐ min
and time spent in chamber:	☐☐ H ☐☐ min	☐☐ H ☐☐ min	☐☐ H ☐☐ min

Saturation Dives:		
Storage depth:	☐☐☐ feet	☐☐☐ feet
Maximum depth of dive:	☐☐☐ feet	☐☐☐ feet
Time leaving storage depth:	☐☐ H ☐☐ min on ☐☐ day	☐☐ H ☐☐ min on ☐☐ day
Time returning to storage depth:	☐☐ H ☐☐ min on ☐☐ day	☐☐ H ☐☐ min on ☐☐ day
Bottom time:	☐☐ H ☐☐ min	☐☐ H ☐☐ min

Breathing Apparatus used: _____

Breathing Mixture used: _____

Work Description, Equipment and Tools Used:
_____
_____
_____

Name of Decompression Schedules used: _____

Note regarding any
Decompression Sickness _____
or other Illness or Injury: _____

Any Other Remarks: _____
_____
_____

Type of Dive	
Scuba	☐
Surface	☐
Wet Bell	☐
Bell Bounce	☐
Saturation	☐
Other	
_____	
_____	

APPROVED

Name of Diving Contractor: _____

Address of Diving Contractor _____

Name of Diving Supervisor (Print) _____

Signature _____ Date: _____

RECORD OF DIVE

Date of Dive _____ Diver's Signature _____

BOTTOM CONDITION: (X appropriate blocks)
☐ Sand ☐ Shell ☐ Gravel ☐ Hard ☐ Soft

Geographic Location
_____

SEA STATE:
☐ Calm ☐ Fair ☐ Moderate ☐ Heavy ☐ Gale Sea
_____

BOTTOM TEMPERATURE:
☐ Cold (below 55) ☐ Normal (55 to 75) ☐ Warm (above 75)

Vessel or Platform

BOTTOM VISIBILITY:
☐ Poor (0 to 5') ☐ Moderate (5' to 20') ☐ (Good 20 +)
_____

BOTTOM CURRENT:
☐ Weak (0 to 0.5KT) ☐ Moderate (0.5 to 2) ☐ Strong (2+)
_____

Bell Bounce or Surface Dives:	Dive One	Dive Two	Dive Three
Maximum depth of dive:	☐☐☐ feet	☐☐☐ feet	☐☐☐ feet
Time left surface or started pressurization:	☐☐ H ☐☐ min	☐☐ H ☐☐ min	☐☐ H ☐☐ min
Bottom Time:	☐☐ min	☐☐ min	☐☐ min
Decompression Completed at:	☐☐ H ☐☐ min	☐☐ H ☐☐ min	☐☐ H ☐☐ min
For surface decompression only: Surface interval:	☐☐ min	☐☐ min	☐☐ min
and time spent in chamber:	☐☐ H ☐☐ min	☐☐ H ☐☐ min	☐☐ H ☐☐ min

Saturation Dives:		
Storage depth:	☐☐☐ feet	☐☐☐ feet
Maximum depth of dive:	☐☐☐ feet	☐☐☐ feet
Time leaving storage depth:	☐☐ H ☐☐ min on ☐☐ day	☐☐ H ☐☐ min on ☐☐ day
Time returning to storage depth:	☐☐ H ☐☐ min on ☐☐ day	☐☐ H ☐☐ min on ☐☐ day
Bottom time:	☐☐ H ☐☐ min	☐☐ H ☐☐ min

Breathing Apparatus used: _____

Breathing Mixture used: _____

Work Description, Equipment and Tools Used:
_____
_____

Name of Decompression Schedules used: _____

Note regarding any
Decompression Sickness _____
or other Illness or Injury: _____

Any Other Remarks: _____
_____
_____

Type of Dive	
Scuba	☐
Surface	☐
Wet Bell	☐
Bell Bounce	☐
Saturation	☐
Other	

_____
_____

APPROVED
Name of Diving Contractor: _____

Address of Diving Contractor _____
_____

Name of Diving Supervisor (Print) _____

Signature _____ Date: _____

RECORD OF DIVE

Date of Dive _____ Diver's Signature _____

BOTTOM CONDITION: (X appropriate blocks)
☐ Sand ☐ Shell ☐ Gravel ☐ Hard ☐ Soft

Geographic Location
_____

SEA STATE:
☐ Calm ☐ Fair ☐ Moderate ☐ Heavy ☐ Gale Sea

_____

BOTTOM TEMPERATURE:
☐ Cold (below 55) ☐ Normal (55 to 75) ☐ Warm (above 75)

Vessel or Platform

BOTTOM VISIBILITY:
☐ Poor (0 to 5') ☐ Moderate (5' to 20') ☐ (Good 20 +)

_____

BOTTOM CURRENT:
☐ Weak (0 to 0.5KT) ☐ Moderate (0.5 to 2) ☐ Strong (2+)

_____

Bell Bounce or Surface Dives:	Dive One	Dive Two	Dive Three
Maximum depth of dive:	☐☐☐ feet	☐☐☐ feet	☐☐☐ feet
Time left surface or started pressurization:	☐☐ H ☐☐ min	☐☐ H ☐☐ min	☐☐ H ☐☐ min
Bottom Time:	☐☐ min	☐☐ min	☐☐ min
Decompression Completed at:	☐☐ H ☐☐ min	☐☐ H ☐☐ min	☐☐ H ☐☐ min
For surface decompression only: Surface interval:	☐☐ min	☐☐ min	☐☐ min
and time spent in chamber:	☐☐ H ☐☐ min	☐☐ H ☐☐ min	☐☐ H ☐☐ min

Saturation Dives:		
Storage depth:	☐☐☐ feet	☐☐☐ feet
Maximum depth of dive:	☐☐☐ feet	☐☐☐ feet
Time leaving storage depth:	☐☐ H ☐☐ min on ☐☐ day	☐☐ H ☐☐ min on ☐☐ day
Time returning to storage depth:	☐☐ H ☐☐ min on ☐☐ day	☐☐ H ☐☐ min on ☐☐ day
Bottom time:	☐☐ H ☐☐ min	☐☐ H ☐☐ min

Breathing Apparatus used: _____

Breathing Mixture used: _____

Work Description, Equipment and Tools Used: _____

_____

Name of Decompression Schedules used: _____

Note regarding any _____
Decompression Sickness _____
or other Illness or Injury: _____

Any Other Remarks: _____

_____

_____

Type of Dive	
Scuba	
Surface	
Wet Bell	
Bell Bounce	
Saturation	
Other	
_____	
_____	

APPROVED
Name of Diving Contractor: _____

Address of Diving Contractor _____

_____

Name of Diving Supervisor (Print) _____

Signature _____ Date: _____

RECORD OF DIVE

Date of Dive _____ Diver's Signature _____

BOTTOM CONDITION: (X appropriate blocks)
☐ Sand ☐ Shell ☐ Gravel ☐ Hard ☐ Soft

Geographic Location
_____

SEA STATE:
☐ Calm ☐ Fair ☐ Moderate ☐ Heavy ☐ Gale Sea
_____

BOTTOM TEMPERATURE:
☐ Cold (below 55) ☐ Normal (55 to 75) ☐ Warm (above 75)

Vessel or Platform

BOTTOM VISIBILITY:
☐ Poor (0 to 5') ☐ Moderate (5' to 20') ☐ (Good 20 +)
_____

BOTTOM CURRENT:
☐ Weak (0 to 0.5KT) ☐ Moderate (0.5 to 2) ☐ Strong (2+)
_____

Bell Bounce or Surface Dives:

	Dive One	Dive Two	Dive Three
Maximum depth of dive:	☐☐☐ feet	☐☐☐ feet	☐☐☐ feet
Time left surface or started pressurization:	☐☐ H ☐☐ min	☐☐ H ☐☐ min	☐☐ H ☐☐ min
Bottom Time:	☐☐☐ min	☐☐☐ min	☐☐☐ min
Decompression Completed at:	☐☐ H ☐☐ min	☐☐ H ☐☐ min	☐☐ H ☐☐ min
For surface decompression only:			
Surface interval:	☐☐ min	☐☐ min	☐☐ min
and time spent in chamber:	☐☐ H ☐☐ min	☐☐ H ☐☐ min	☐☐ H ☐☐ min

Saturation Dives:

Storage depth:	☐☐☐ feet	☐☐☐ feet
Maximum depth of dive:	☐☐☐ feet	☐☐☐ feet
Time leaving storage depth:	☐☐ H ☐☐ min on ☐☐ day	☐☐ H ☐☐ min on ☐☐ day
Time returning to storage depth:	☐☐ H ☐☐ min on ☐☐ day	☐☐ H ☐☐ min on ☐☐ day
Bottom time:	☐☐ H ☐☐ min	☐☐ H ☐☐ min

Breathing Apparatus used: _____

Breathing Mixture used: _____

Work Description, Equipment and Tools Used: _____

Type of Dive	
Scuba	
Surface	
Wet Bell	
Bell Bounce	
Saturation	
Other	

Name of Decompression Schedules used: _____
_____

Note regarding any Decompression Sickness or other Illness or Injury: _____
_____

Any Other Remarks: _____
_____
_____

APPROVED

Name of Diving Contractor: _____

Address of Diving Contractor _____
_____

Name of Diving Supervisor (Print) _____

Signature _____ Date: _____

RECORD OF DIVE

Date of Dive _____ Diver's Signature _____

BOTTOM CONDITION: (X appropriate blocks)
☐ Sand ☐ Shell ☐ Gravel ☐ Hard ☐ Soft

SEA STATE:
☐ Calm ☐ Fair ☐ Moderate ☐ Heavy ☐ Gale Sea

BOTTOM TEMPERATURE:
☐ Cold (below 55) ☐ Normal (55 to 75) ☐ Warm (above 75)

BOTTOM VISIBILITY:
☐ Poor (0 to 5') ☐ Moderate (5' to 20') ☐ (Good 20 +)

BOTTOM CURRENT:
☐ Weak (0 to 0.5KT) ☐ Moderate (0.5 to 2) ☐ Strong (2+)

Geographic Location
_____

_____

Vessel or Platform
_____

_____

Bell Bounce or Surface Dives:	Dive One	Dive Two	Dive Three
Maximum depth of dive:	☐☐☐ feet	☐☐☐ feet	☐☐☐ feet
Time left surface or started pressurization:	☐☐ H ☐☐ min	☐☐ H ☐☐ min	☐☐ H ☐☐ min
Bottom Time:	☐☐☐ min	☐☐☐ min	☐☐☐ min
Decompression Completed at:	☐☐ H ☐☐ min	☐☐ H ☐☐ min	☐☐ H ☐☐ min
For surface decompression only: Surface interval:	☐☐☐ min	☐☐☐ min	☐☐☐ min
and time spent in chamber:	☐☐ H ☐☐ min	☐☐ H ☐☐ min	☐☐ H ☐☐ min

Saturation Dives:		
Storage depth:	☐☐☐ feet	☐☐☐ feet
Maximum depth of dive:	☐☐☐ feet	☐☐☐ feet
Time leaving storage depth:	☐☐ H ☐☐ min on ☐☐ day	☐☐ H ☐☐ min on ☐☐ day
Time returning to storage depth:	☐☐ H ☐☐ min on ☐☐ day	☐☐ H ☐☐ min on ☐☐ day
Bottom time:	☐☐ H ☐☐ min	☐☐ H ☐☐ min

Breathing Apparatus used: _____

_____

Breathing Mixture used: _____

Work Description, Equipment and Tools Used: _____

_____

Name of Decompression Schedules used: _____

Note regarding any
Decompression Sickness _____
or other Illness or Injury: _____

Any Other Remarks: _____

_____

_____

Type of Dive	
Scuba	☐
Surface	☐
Wet Bell	☐
Bell Bounce	☐
Saturation	☐
Other	

_____

_____

APPROVED
Name of Diving Contractor: _____

Address of Diving Contractor _____

_____

Name of Diving Supervisor (Print) _____

Signature _____ Date: _____

RECORD OF DIVE

Date of Dive _____ Diver's Signature _____

BOTTOM CONDITION: (X appropriate blocks)
☐ Sand ☐ Shell ☐ Gravel ☐ Hard ☐ Soft

SEA STATE:
☐ Calm ☐ Fair ☐ Moderate ☐ Heavy ☐ Gale Sea

BOTTOM TEMPERATURE:
☐ Cold (below 55) ☐ Normal (55 to 75) ☐ Warm (above 75)

BOTTOM VISIBILITY:
☐ Poor (0 to 5') ☐ Moderate (5' to 20') ☐ (Good 20 +)

BOTTOM CURRENT:
☐ Weak (0 to 0.5KT) ☐ Moderate (0.5 to 2) ☐ Strong (2+)

Geographic Location
_____

Vessel or Platform
_____

Bell Bounce or Surface Dives:

	Dive One	Dive Two	Dive Three
Maximum depth of dive:	☐☐☐ feet	☐☐☐ feet	☐☐☐ feet
Time left surface or started pressurization:	☐☐ H ☐☐ min	☐☐ H ☐☐ min	☐☐ H ☐☐ min
Bottom Time:	☐☐☐ min	☐☐☐ min	☐☐☐ min
Decompression Completed at:	☐☐ H ☐☐ min	☐☐ H ☐☐ min	☐☐ H ☐☐ min

For surface decompression only:			
Surface interval:	☐☐☐ min	☐☐☐ min	☐☐☐ min
and time spent in chamber:	☐☐ H ☐☐ min	☐☐ H ☐☐ min	☐☐ H ☐☐ min

Saturation Dives:

Storage depth:	☐☐☐ feet	☐☐☐ feet
Maximum depth of dive:	☐☐☐ feet	☐☐☐ feet
Time leaving storage depth:	☐☐ H ☐☐ min on ☐☐ day	☐☐ H ☐☐ min on ☐☐ day
Time returning to storage depth:	☐☐ H ☐☐ min on ☐☐ day	☐☐ H ☐☐ min on ☐☐ day
Bottom time:	☐☐ H ☐☐ min	☐☐ H ☐☐ min

Breathing Apparatus used: _____

Breathing Mixture used: _____
_____

Work Description, Equipment and Tools Used: _____
_____
_____

Name of Decompression Schedules used: _____

Note regarding any Decompression Sickness or other Illness or Injury: _____
_____
_____
_____

Any Other Remarks: _____
_____
_____
_____

Type of Dive	
Scuba	
Surface	
Wet Bell	
Bell Bounce	
Saturation	
Other	

APPROVED
Name of Diving Contractor: _____

Address of Diving Contractor _____
_____

Name of Diving Supervisor (Print) _____

Signature _____ Date: _____

RECORD OF DIVE

Date of Dive _____ Diver's Signature _____

BOTTOM CONDITION: (X appropriate blocks)   Geographic Location
☐ Sand ☐ Shell ☐ Gravel ☐ Hard ☐ Soft

SEA STATE: _____
☐ Calm ☐ Fair ☐ Moderate ☐ Heavy ☐ Gale Sea

BOTTOM TEMPERATURE: Vessel or Platform
☐ Cold (below 55) ☐ Normal (55 to 75) ☐ Warm (above 75)

BOTTOM VISIBILITY: _____
☐ Poor (0 to 5') ☐ Moderate (5' to 20') ☐ (Good 20 +)

BOTTOM CURRENT: _____
☐ Weak (0 to 0.5KT) ☐ Moderate (0.5 to 2) ☐ Strong (2+)

Bell Bounce or Surface Dives:	Dive One	Dive Two	Dive Three
Maximum depth of dive:	☐☐☐ feet	☐☐☐ feet	☐☐☐ feet
Time left surface or started pressurization:	☐☐ H ☐☐ min	☐☐ H ☐☐ min	☐☐ H ☐☐ min
Bottom Time:	☐☐☐ min	☐☐☐ min	☐☐☐ min
Decompression Completed at:	☐☐ H ☐☐ min	☐☐ H ☐☐ min	☐☐ H ☐☐ min
For surface decompression only: Surface interval:	☐☐☐ min	☐☐☐ min	☐☐☐ min
and time spent in chamber:	☐☐ H ☐☐ min	☐☐ H ☐☐ min	☐☐ H ☐☐ min

Saturation Dives:		
Storage depth:	☐☐☐ feet	☐☐☐ feet
Maximum depth of dive:	☐☐☐ feet	☐☐☐ feet
Time leaving storage depth:	☐☐ H ☐☐ min on ☐☐ day	☐☐ H ☐☐ min on ☐☐ day
Time returning to storage depth:	☐☐ H ☐☐ min on ☐☐ day	☐☐ H ☐☐ min on ☐☐ day
Bottom time:	☐☐ H ☐☐ min	☐☐ H ☐☐ min

Breathing Apparatus used: _____

_____   Type of Dive

Breathing Mixture used: _____ | Scuba | ☐ |
                                                       |---|---|
_____ | Surface | ☐ |
                                                       | Wet Bell | ☐ |
Work Description, Equipment and Tools Used: | Bell Bounce | ☐ |
                                                       | Saturation | ☐ |
_____ | Other |

_____   _____

Name of Decompression Schedules used: _____

Note regarding any   _____
Decompression Sickness   _____
or other Illness or Injury: _____

Any Other Remarks: _____

_____
_____
_____

APPROVED
Name of Diving Contractor: _____

Address of Diving Contractor _____

_____

Name of Diving Supervisor (Print) _____

Signature _____ Date: _____

RECORD OF DIVE

Date of Dive _____ Diver's Signature _____

BOTTOM CONDITION: (X appropriate blocks)
☐ Sand ☐ Shell ☐ Gravel ☐ Hard ☐ Soft

SEA STATE:
☐ Calm ☐ Fair ☐ Moderate ☐ Heavy ☐ Gale Sea

BOTTOM TEMPERATURE:
☐ Cold (below 55) ☐ Normal (55 to 75) ☐ Warm (above 75)

BOTTOM VISIBILITY:
☐ Poor (0 to 5') ☐ Moderate (5' to 20') ☐ (Good 20 +)

BOTTOM CURRENT:
☐ Weak (0 to 0.5KT) ☐ Moderate (0.5 to 2) ☐ Strong (2+)

Geographic Location
_____

_____

Vessel or Platform
_____

_____

Bell Bounce or Surface Dives:

	Dive One	Dive Two	Dive Three
Maximum depth of dive:	☐☐☐ feet	☐☐☐ feet	☐☐☐ feet
Time left surface or started pressurization:	☐☐ H ☐☐ min	☐☐ H ☐☐ min	☐☐ H ☐☐ min
Bottom Time:	☐☐☐ min	☐☐☐ min	☐☐☐ min
Decompression Completed at:	☐☐ H ☐☐ min	☐☐ H ☐☐ min	☐☐ H ☐☐ min
For surface decompression only:			
Surface interval:	☐☐☐ min	☐☐☐ min	☐☐☐ min
and time spent in chamber:	☐☐ H ☐☐ min	☐☐ H ☐☐ min	☐☐ H ☐☐ min

Saturation Dives:

Storage depth:	☐☐☐ feet	☐☐☐ feet
Maximum depth of dive:	☐☐☐ feet	☐☐☐ feet
Time leaving storage depth:	☐☐ H ☐☐ min on ☐☐ day	☐☐ H ☐☐ min on ☐☐ day
Time returning to storage depth:	☐☐ H ☐☐ min on ☐☐ day	☐☐ H ☐☐ min on ☐☐ day
Bottom time:	☐☐ H ☐☐ min	☐☐ H ☐☐ min

Breathing Apparatus used: _____

Breathing Mixture used: _____

Work Description, Equipment and Tools Used: _____
_____

Name of Decompression Schedules used: _____

Note regarding any Decompression Sickness or other Illness or Injury: _____

Any Other Remarks: _____
_____
_____

Type of Dive	
Scuba	
Surface	
Wet Bell	
Bell Bounce	
Saturation	
Other	
_____
_____

APPROVED

Name of Diving Contractor: _____

Address of Diving Contractor _____
_____

Name of Diving Supervisor (Print) _____

Signature _____ Date: _____

RECORD OF DIVE

Date of Dive _____ Diver's Signature _____

BOTTOM CONDITION: (X appropriate blocks)
☐ Sand ☐ Shell ☐ Gravel ☐ Hard ☐ Soft

Geographic Location

_____

SEA STATE:
☐ Calm ☐ Fair ☐ Moderate ☐ Heavy ☐ Gale Sea

_____

BOTTOM TEMPERATURE:
☐ Cold (below 55) ☐ Normal (55 to 75) ☐ Warm (above 75)

Vessel or Platform

BOTTOM VISIBILITY:
☐ Poor (0 to 5') ☐ Moderate (5' to 20') ☐ (Good 20 +)

_____

BOTTOM CURRENT:
☐ Weak (0 to 0.5KT) ☐ Moderate (0.5 to 2) ☐ Strong (2+)

_____

Bell Bounce or Surface Dives:	Dive One	Dive Two	Dive Three
Maximum depth of dive:	☐☐☐ feet	☐☐☐ feet	☐☐☐ feet
Time left surface or started pressurization:	☐☐ H ☐☐ min	☐☐ H ☐☐ min	☐☐ H ☐☐ min
Bottom Time:	☐☐ min	☐☐ min	☐☐ min
Decompression Completed at:	☐☐ H ☐☐ min	☐☐ H ☐☐ min	☐☐ H ☐☐ min
For surface decompression only: Surface interval:	☐☐ min	☐☐ min	☐☐ min
and time spent in chamber:	☐☐ H ☐☐ min	☐☐ H ☐☐ min	☐☐ H ☐☐ min

Saturation Dives:		
Storage depth:	☐☐☐☐ feet	☐☐☐ feet
Maximum depth of dive:	☐☐☐☐ feet	☐☐☐ feet
Time leaving storage depth:	☐☐ H ☐☐ min on ☐☐ day	☐☐ H ☐☐ min on ☐☐ day
Time returning to storage depth:	☐☐ H ☐☐ min on ☐☐ day	☐☐ H ☐☐ min on ☐☐ day
Bottom time:	☐☐ H ☐☐ min	☐☐ H ☐☐ min

Breathing Apparatus used: _____

Breathing Mixture used: _____

Work Description, Equipment and Tools Used: _____

Type of Dive	
Scuba	
Surface	
Wet Bell	
Bell Bounce	
Saturation	
Other	

Name of Decompression Schedules used: _____

Note regarding any Decompression Sickness or other Illness or Injury: _____

Any Other Remarks: _____

APPROVED

Name of Diving Contractor: _____

Address of Diving Contractor _____

Name of Diving Supervisor (Print) _____

Signature _____ Date: _____

RECORD OF DIVE

Date of Dive _____ Diver's Signature _____

BOTTOM CONDITION: (X appropriate blocks)
☐ Sand ☐ Shell ☐ Gravel ☐ Hard ☐ Soft

Geographic Location
_____

SEA STATE:
☐ Calm ☐ Fair ☐ Moderate ☐ Heavy ☐ Gale Sea

BOTTOM TEMPERATURE:
☐ Cold (below 55) ☐ Normal (55 to 75) ☐ Warm (above 75)

Vessel or Platform
_____

BOTTOM VISIBILITY:
☐ Poor (0 to 5') ☐ Moderate (5' to 20') ☐ (Good 20 +)

BOTTOM CURRENT:
☐ Weak (0 to 0.5KT) ☐ Moderate (0.5 to 2) ☐ Strong (2+)

Bell Bounce or Surface Dives:	Dive One	Dive Two	Dive Three
Maximum depth of dive:	☐☐☐ feet	☐☐☐ feet	☐☐☐ feet
Time left surface or started pressurization:	☐☐ H ☐☐ min	☐☐ H ☐☐ min	☐☐ H ☐☐ min
Bottom Time:	☐☐☐ min	☐☐☐ min	☐☐☐ min
Decompression Completed at:	☐☐ H ☐☐ min	☐☐ H ☐☐ min	☐☐ H ☐☐ min
For surface decompression only:			
Surface interval:	☐☐☐ min	☐☐☐ min	☐☐☐ min
and time spent in chamber:	☐☐ H ☐☐ min	☐☐ H ☐☐ min	☐☐ H ☐☐ min

Saturation Dives:		
Storage depth:	☐☐☐ feet	☐☐☐ feet
Maximum depth of dive:	☐☐☐ feet	☐☐☐ feet
Time leaving storage depth:	☐☐ H ☐☐ min on ☐☐ day	☐☐ H ☐☐ min on ☐☐ day
Time returning to storage depth:	☐☐ H ☐☐ min on ☐☐ day	☐☐ H ☐☐ min on ☐☐ day
Bottom time:	☐☐ H ☐☐ min	☐☐ H ☐☐ min

Breathing Apparatus used: _____

Breathing Mixture used: _____
_____

Work Description, Equipment and Tools Used: _____
_____

Name of Decompression Schedules used: _____

Note regarding any
Decompression Sickness
or other Illness or Injury:
_____
_____
_____

Any Other Remarks: _____
_____
_____

Type of Dive	
Scuba	
Surface	
Wet Bell	
Bell Bounce	
Saturation	
Other	

_____
_____

APPROVED

Name of Diving Contractor: _____

Address of Diving Contractor _____
_____

Name of Diving Supervisor (Print) _____

Signature _____ Date: _____

RECORD OF DIVE

Date of Dive _____ Diver's Signature _____

BOTTOM CONDITION: (X appropriate blocks)
☐ Sand ☐ Shell ☐ Gravel ☐ Hard ☐ Soft

SEA STATE:
☐ Calm ☐ Fair ☐ Moderate ☐ Heavy ☐ Gale Sea

BOTTOM TEMPERATURE:
☐ Cold (below 55) ☐ Normal (55 to 75) ☐ Warm (above 75)

BOTTOM VISIBILITY:
☐ Poor (0 to 5') ☐ Moderate (5' to 20') ☐ (Good 20 +)

BOTTOM CURRENT:
☐ Weak (0 to 0.5KT) ☐ Moderate (0.5 to 2) ☐ Strong (2+)

Geographic Location

_____

_____

Vessel or Platform

_____

_____

Bell Bounce or Surface Dives:	Dive One	Dive Two	Dive Three
Maximum depth of dive:	☐☐☐ feet	☐☐☐ feet	☐☐☐ feet
Time left surface or started pressurization:	☐☐ H ☐☐ min	☐☐ H ☐☐ min	☐☐ H ☐☐ min
Bottom Time:	☐☐☐ min	☐☐☐ min	☐☐☐ min
Decompression Completed at:	☐☐ H ☐☐ min	☐☐ H ☐☐ min	☐☐ H ☐☐ min
For surface decompression only: Surface interval:	☐☐ min	☐☐ min	☐☐ min
and time spent in chamber:	☐☐ H ☐☐ min	☐☐ H ☐☐ min	☐☐ H ☐☐ min

Saturation Dives:		
Storage depth:	☐☐☐ feet	☐☐☐ feet
Maximum depth of dive:	☐☐☐ feet	☐☐☐ feet
Time leaving storage depth:	☐☐ H ☐☐ min on ☐☐ day	☐☐ H ☐☐ min on ☐☐ day
Time returning to storage depth:	☐☐ H ☐☐ min on ☐☐ day	☐☐ H ☐☐ min on ☐☐ day
Bottom time:	☐☐ H ☐☐ min	☐☐ H ☐☐ min

Breathing Apparatus used: _____

Breathing Mixture used: _____

Work Description, Equipment and Tools Used: _____

Name of Decompression Schedules used: _____

Note regarding any Decompression Sickness or other Illness or Injury: _____

Any Other Remarks: _____

Type of Dive	
Scuba	
Surface	
Wet Bell	
Bell Bounce	
Saturation	
Other	

_____

_____

APPROVED
Name of Diving Contractor: _____

Address of Diving Contractor _____

Name of Diving Supervisor (Print) _____

Signature _____ Date: _____

RECORD OF DIVE

Date of Dive _____ Diver's Signature _____

BOTTOM CONDITION: (X appropriate blocks)
☐ Sand ☐ Shell ☐ Gravel ☐ Hard ☐ Soft

Geographic Location

SEA STATE:
☐ Calm ☐ Fair ☐ Moderate ☐ Heavy ☐ Gale Sea

_____

BOTTOM TEMPERATURE:
☐ Cold (below 55) ☐ Normal (55 to 75) ☐ Warm (above 75)

Vessel or Platform

BOTTOM VISIBILITY:
☐ Poor (0 to 5') ☐ Moderate (5' to 20') ☐ (Good 20 +)

_____

BOTTOM CURRENT:
☐ Weak (0 to 0.5KT) ☐ Moderate (0.5 to 2) ☐ Strong (2+)

Bell Bounce or Surface Dives:	Dive One	Dive Two	Dive Three
Maximum depth of dive:	☐☐☐ feet	☐☐☐ feet	☐☐☐ feet
Time left surface or started pressurization:	☐☐ H ☐☐ min	☐☐ H ☐☐ min	☐☐ H ☐☐ min
Bottom Time:	☐☐☐ min	☐☐☐ min	☐☐☐ min
Decompression Completed at:	☐☐ H ☐☐ min	☐☐ H ☐☐ min	☐☐ H ☐☐ min
For surface decompression only: Surface interval:	☐☐☐ min	☐☐☐ min	☐☐☐ min
and time spent in chamber:	☐☐ H ☐☐ min	☐☐ H ☐☐ min	☐☐ H ☐☐ min

Saturation Dives:		
Storage depth:	☐☐☐ feet	☐☐☐ feet
Maximum depth of dive:	☐☐☐ feet	☐☐☐ feet
Time leaving storage depth:	☐☐ H ☐☐ min on ☐☐ day	☐☐ H ☐☐ min on ☐☐ day
Time returning to storage depth:	☐☐ H ☐☐ min on ☐☐ day	☐☐ H ☐☐ min on ☐☐ day
Bottom time:	☐☐ H ☐☐ min	☐☐ H ☐☐ min

Breathing Apparatus used: _____

Breathing Mixture used: _____

Work Description, Equipment and Tools Used: _____

Type of Dive	
Scuba	☐
Surface	☐
Wet Bell	☐
Bell Bounce	☐
Saturation	☐
Other	

Name of Decompression Schedules used: _____

Note regarding any
Decompression Sickness
or other Illness or Injury: _____

Any Other Remarks: _____

APPROVED
Name of Diving Contractor: _____

Address of Diving Contractor _____

Name of Diving Supervisor (Print) _____

Signature _____ Date: _____

RECORD OF DIVE

Date of Dive _____ Diver's Signature _____

BOTTOM CONDITION: (X appropriate blocks)
☐ Sand ☐ Shell ☐ Gravel ☐ Hard ☐ Soft

Geographic Location
_____

SEA STATE:
☐ Calm ☐ Fair ☐ Moderate ☐ Heavy ☐ Gale Sea
_____

BOTTOM TEMPERATURE:
☐ Cold (below 55) ☐ Normal (55 to 75) ☐ Warm (above 75)

Vessel or Platform

BOTTOM VISIBILITY:
☐ Poor (0 to 5') ☐ Moderate (5' to 20') ☐ (Good 20 +)
_____

BOTTOM CURRENT:
☐ Weak (0 to 0.5KT) ☐ Moderate (0.5 to 2) ☐ Strong (2+)
_____

Bell Bounce or Surface Dives:

	Dive One	Dive Two	Dive Three
Maximum depth of dive:	☐☐☐ feet	☐☐☐ feet	☐☐☐ feet
Time left surface or started pressurization:	☐☐ H ☐☐ min	☐☐ H ☐☐ min	☐☐ H ☐☐ min
Bottom Time:	☐☐☐ min	☐☐☐ min	☐☐☐ min
Decompression Completed at:	☐☐ H ☐☐ min	☐☐ H ☐☐ min	☐☐ H ☐☐ min
For surface decompression only: Surface interval:	☐☐☐ min	☐☐☐ min	☐☐☐ min
and time spent in chamber:	☐☐ H ☐☐ min	☐☐ H ☐☐ min	☐☐ H ☐☐ min

Saturation Dives:

Storage depth:	☐☐☐ feet	☐☐☐ feet
Maximum depth of dive:	☐☐☐ feet	☐☐☐ feet
Time leaving storage depth:	☐☐ H ☐☐ min on ☐☐ day	☐☐ H ☐☐ min on ☐☐ day
Time returning to storage depth:	☐☐ H ☐☐ min on ☐☐ day	☐☐ H ☐☐ min on ☐☐ day
Bottom time:	☐☐ H ☐☐ min	☐☐ H ☐☐ min

Breathing Apparatus used: _____

Breathing Mixture used: _____

Work Description, Equipment and Tools Used:
_____
_____

Name of Decompression Schedules used: _____

Note regarding any
Decompression Sickness
or other Illness or Injury: _____

Any Other Remarks: _____
_____
_____

Type of Dive

Scuba	☐
Surface	☐
Wet Bell	☐
Bell Bounce	☐
Saturation	☐
Other	

_____
_____

APPROVED
Name of Diving Contractor: _____

Address of Diving Contractor _____
_____

Name of Diving Supervisor (Print) _____

Signature _____ Date: _____

RECORD OF DIVE

Date of Dive _____ Diver's Signature _____

BOTTOM CONDITION: (X appropriate blocks)
□ Sand □ Shell □ Gravel □ Hard □ Soft

SEA STATE:
□ Calm □ Fair □ Moderate □ Heavy □ Gale Sea

BOTTOM TEMPERATURE:
□ Cold (below 55) □ Normal (55 to 75) □ Warm (above 75)

BOTTOM VISIBILITY:
□ Poor (0 to 5') □ Moderate (5' to 20') □ (Good 20 +)

BOTTOM CURRENT:
□ Weak (0 to 0.5KT) □ Moderate (0.5 to 2) □ Strong (2+)

Geographic Location
_____
_____

Vessel or Platform
_____
_____

Bell Bounce or Surface Dives:	Dive One	Dive Two	Dive Three
Maximum depth of dive:	□□□ feet	□□□ feet	□□□ feet
Time left surface or started pressurization:	□□ H □□ min	□□ H □□ min	□□ H □□ min
Bottom Time:	□□ min	□□ min	□□ min
Decompression Completed at:	□□ H □□ min	□□ H □□ min	□□ H □□ min
For surface decompression only: Surface interval:	□□ min	□□ min	□□ min
and time spent in chamber:	□□ H □□ min	□□ H □□ min	□□ H □□ min

Saturation Dives:		
Storage depth:	□□□□ feet	□□□□ feet
Maximum depth of dive:	□□□□ feet	□□□□ feet
Time leaving storage depth:	□□ H □□ min on □□ day	□□ H □□ min on □□ day
Time returning to storage depth:	□□ H □□ min on □□ day	□□ H □□ min on □□ day
Bottom time:	□□ H □□ min	□□ H □□ min

Breathing Apparatus used: _____

Breathing Mixture used: _____

Work Description, Equipment and Tools Used: _____
_____

Name of Decompression Schedules used: _____

Note regarding any Decompression Sickness or other Illness or Injury: _____
_____
_____

Any Other Remarks: _____
_____
_____

Type of Dive	
Scuba	□
Surface	□
Wet Bell	□
Bell Bounce	□
Saturation	□
Other	

_____
_____

APPROVED

Name of Diving Contractor: _____

Address of Diving Contractor _____
_____

Name of Diving Supervisor (Print) _____

Signature _____ Date: _____

RECORD OF DIVE

Date of Dive _____ Diver's Signature _____

BOTTOM CONDITION: (X appropriate blocks)   Geographic Location
☐ Sand ☐ Shell ☐ Gravel ☐ Hard ☐ Soft
SEA STATE: _____
☐ Calm ☐ Fair ☐ Moderate ☐ Heavy ☐ Gale Sea
BOTTOM TEMPERATURE: _____
☐ Cold (below 55) ☐ Normal (55 to 75) ☐ Warm (above 75)   Vessel or Platform
BOTTOM VISIBILITY:
☐ Poor (0 to 5') ☐ Moderate (5' to 20') ☐ (Good 20 +)   _____
BOTTOM CURRENT:
☐ Weak (0 to 0.5KT) ☐ Moderate (0.5 to 2) ☐ Strong (2+)   _____

Bell Bounce or Surface Dives:	Dive One	Dive Two	Dive Three
Maximum depth of dive:	☐☐☐ feet	☐☐☐ feet	☐☐☐ feet
Time left surface or started pressurization:	☐☐ H ☐☐ min	☐☐ H ☐☐ min	☐☐ H ☐☐ min
Bottom Time:	☐☐☐ min	☐☐☐ min	☐☐☐ min
Decompression Completed at:	☐☐ H ☐☐ min	☐☐ H ☐☐ min	☐☐ H ☐☐ min
For surface decompression only: Surface interval:	☐☐☐ min	☐☐☐ min	☐☐☐ min
and time spent in chamber:	☐☐ H ☐☐ min	☐☐ H ☐☐ min	☐☐ H ☐☐ min

Saturation Dives:		
Storage depth:	☐☐☐ feet	☐☐☐ feet
Maximum depth of dive:	☐☐☐ feet	☐☐☐ feet
Time leaving storage depth:	☐☐ H ☐☐ min on ☐☐ day	☐☐ H ☐☐ min on ☐☐ day
Time returning to storage depth:	☐☐ H ☐☐ min on ☐☐ day	☐☐ H ☐☐ min on ☐☐ day
Bottom time:	☐☐ H ☐☐ min	☐☐ H ☐☐ min

Breathing Apparatus used: _____

Breathing Mixture used: _____

Work Description, Equipment and Tools Used: _____
_____

Name of Decompression Schedules used: _____

Note regarding any   _____
Decompression Sickness   _____
or other Illness or Injury: _____

Any Other Remarks: _____
_____

Type of Dive
Scuba
Surface
Wet Bell
Bell Bounce
Saturation
Other
____
____

APPROVED
Name of Diving Contractor: _____

Address of Diving Contractor _____
_____

Name of Diving Supervisor (Print) _____

Signature _____ Date: _____

RECORD OF DIVE

Date of Dive _____ Diver's Signature _____

BOTTOM CONDITION: (X appropriate blocks)   Geographic Location
☐ Sand ☐ Shell ☐ Gravel ☐ Hard ☐ Soft   _____
SEA STATE:
☐ Calm ☐ Fair ☐ Moderate ☐ Heavy ☐ Gale Sea   _____
BOTTOM TEMPERATURE:
☐ Cold (below 55) ☐ Normal (55 to 75) ☐ Warm (above 75)   Vessel or Platform
BOTTOM VISIBILITY:
☐ Poor (0 to 5') ☐ Moderate (5' to 20') ☐ (Good 20 +)   _____
BOTTOM CURRENT:
☐ Weak (0 to 0.5KT) ☐ Moderate (0.5 to 2) ☐ Strong (2+)   _____

Bell Bounce or Surface Dives:	Dive One	Dive Two	Dive Three
Maximum depth of dive:	☐☐☐ feet	☐☐☐ feet	☐☐☐ feet
Time left surface or started pressurization:	☐☐ H ☐☐ min	☐☐ H ☐☐ min	☐☐ H ☐☐ min
Bottom Time:	☐☐ min	☐☐ min	☐☐ min
Decompression Completed at:	☐☐ H ☐☐ min	☐☐ H ☐☐ min	☐☐ H ☐☐ min
For surface decompression only: Surface interval:	☐☐ min	☐☐ min	☐☐ min
and time spent in chamber:	☐☐ H ☐☐ min	☐☐ H ☐☐ min	☐☐ H ☐☐ min

Saturation Dives:		
Storage depth:	☐☐☐ feet	☐☐☐ feet
Maximum depth of dive:	☐☐☐ feet	☐☐☐ feet
Time leaving storage depth:	☐☐ H ☐☐ min on ☐☐ day	☐☐ H ☐☐ min on ☐☐ day
Time returning to storage depth:	☐☐ H ☐☐ min on ☐☐ day	☐☐ H ☐☐ min on ☐☐ day
Bottom time:	☐☐ H ☐☐ min	☐☐ H ☐☐ min

Breathing Apparatus used: _____

Breathing Mixture used: _____

Work Description, Equipment and Tools Used: _____

_____

Name of Decompression Schedules used: _____

Note regarding any   _____
Decompression Sickness   _____
or other Illness or Injury: _____

Any Other Remarks: _____

Type of Dive	
Scuba	
Surface	
Wet Bell	
Bell Bounce	
Saturation	
Other	

APPROVED
Name of Diving Contractor: _____

Address of Diving Contractor _____

Name of Diving Supervisor (Print) _____

Signature _____ Date: _____

RECORD OF DIVE

Date of Dive _____ Diver's Signature _____

BOTTOM CONDITION: (X appropriate blocks)
☐ Sand ☐ Shell ☐ Gravel ☐ Hard ☐ Soft

Geographic Location
_____

SEA STATE:
☐ Calm ☐ Fair ☐ Moderate ☐ Heavy ☐ Gale Sea

_____

BOTTOM TEMPERATURE:
☐ Cold (below 55) ☐ Normal (55 to 75) ☐ Warm (above 75)

Vessel or Platform

BOTTOM VISIBILITY:
☐ Poor (0 to 5') ☐ Moderate (5' to 20') ☐ (Good 20 +)

_____

BOTTOM CURRENT:
☐ Weak (0 to 0.5KT) ☐ Moderate (0.5 to 2) ☐ Strong (2+)

_____

Bell Bounce or Surface Dives:	Dive One	Dive Two	Dive Three
Maximum depth of dive:	☐☐☐ feet	☐☐☐ feet	☐☐☐ feet
Time left surface or started pressurization:	☐☐ H ☐☐ min	☐☐ H ☐☐ min	☐☐ H ☐☐ min
Bottom Time:	☐☐ min	☐☐ min	☐☐ min
Decompression Completed at:	☐☐ H ☐☐ min	☐☐ H ☐☐ min	☐☐ H ☐☐ min
For surface decompression only: Surface interval:	☐☐ min	☐☐ min	☐☐ min
and time spent in chamber:	☐☐ H ☐☐ min	☐☐ H ☐☐ min	☐☐ H ☐☐ min

Saturation Dives:		
Storage depth:	☐☐☐ feet	☐☐☐ feet
Maximum depth of dive:	☐☐☐ feet	☐☐☐ feet
Time leaving storage depth:	☐☐ H ☐☐ min on ☐☐ day	☐☐ H ☐☐ min on ☐☐ day
Time returning to storage depth:	☐☐ H ☐☐ min on ☐☐ day	☐☐ H ☐☐ min on ☐☐ day
Bottom time:	☐☐ H ☐☐ min	☐☐ H ☐☐ min

Breathing Apparatus used: _____

Breathing Mixture used: _____

Work Description, Equipment and Tools Used: _____

Name of Decompression Schedules used: _____

Note regarding any _____
Decompression Sickness _____
or other Illness or Injury: _____

Any Other Remarks: _____

Type of Dive	
Scuba	☐
Surface	☐
Wet Bell	☐
Bell Bounce	☐
Saturation	☐
Other	

APPROVED
Name of Diving Contractor: _____

Address of Diving Contractor _____

Name of Diving Supervisor (Print) _____

Signature _____ Date: _____

RECORD OF DIVE

Date of Dive _____ Diver's Signature _____

BOTTOM CONDITION: (X appropriate blocks)   Geographic Location
☐ Sand ☐ Shell ☐ Gravel ☐ Hard ☐ Soft   _____

SEA STATE:
☐ Calm ☐ Fair ☐ Moderate ☐ Heavy ☐ Gale Sea   _____

BOTTOM TEMPERATURE:
☐ Cold (below 55) ☐ Normal (55 to 75) ☐ Warm (above 75)   Vessel or Platform

BOTTOM VISIBILITY:
☐ Poor (0 to 5') ☐ Moderate (5' to 20') ☐ (Good 20 +)   _____

BOTTOM CURRENT:
☐ Weak (0 to 0.5KT) ☐ Moderate (0.5 to 2) ☐ Strong (2+)   _____

Bell Bounce or Surface Dives:	Dive One	Dive Two	Dive Three
Maximum depth of dive:	☐☐☐ feet	☐☐☐ feet	☐☐☐ feet
Time left surface or started pressurization:	☐☐ H ☐☐ min	☐☐ H ☐☐ min	☐☐ H ☐☐ min
Bottom Time:	☐☐ min	☐☐ min	☐☐ min
Decompression Completed at:	☐☐ H ☐☐ min	☐☐ H ☐☐ min	☐☐ H ☐☐ min
For surface decompression only: Surface interval:	☐☐ min	☐☐ min	☐☐ min
and time spent in chamber:	☐☐ H ☐☐ min	☐☐ H ☐☐ min	☐☐ H ☐☐ min

Saturation Dives:		
Storage depth:	☐☐☐ feet	☐☐☐ feet
Maximum depth of dive:	☐☐☐ feet	☐☐☐ feet
Time leaving storage depth:	☐☐ H ☐☐ min on ☐☐ day	☐☐ H ☐☐ min on ☐☐ day
Time returning to storage depth:	☐☐ H ☐☐ min on ☐☐ day	☐☐ H ☐☐ min on ☐☐ day
Bottom time:	☐☐ H ☐☐ min	☐☐ H ☐☐ min

Breathing Apparatus used: _____

Breathing Mixture used: _____

Work Description, Equipment and Tools Used: _____

Name of Decompression Schedules used: _____

Note regarding any
Decompression Sickness   _____
or other Illness or Injury: _____

Any Other Remarks: _____

Type of Dive	
Scuba	
Surface	
Wet Bell	
Bell Bounce	
Saturation	
Other	

APPROVED
Name of Diving Contractor: _____

Address of Diving Contractor _____

Name of Diving Supervisor (Print) _____

Signature _____ Date: _____

RECORD OF DIVE

Date of Dive _____ Diver's Signature _____

BOTTOM CONDITION: (X appropriate blocks)   Geographic Location
☐ Sand ☐ Shell ☐ Gravel ☐ Hard ☐ Soft

SEA STATE: _____
☐ Calm ☐ Fair ☐ Moderate ☐ Heavy ☐ Gale Sea

BOTTOM TEMPERATURE: _____
☐ Cold (below 55) ☐ Normal (55 to 75) ☐ Warm (above 75)   Vessel or Platform

BOTTOM VISIBILITY:
☐ Poor (0 to 5') ☐ Moderate (5' to 20') ☐ (Good 20 +)   _____

BOTTOM CURRENT:
☐ Weak (0 to 0.5KT) ☐ Moderate (0.5 to 2) ☐ Strong (2+)   _____

Bell Bounce or Surface Dives:	Dive One	Dive Two	Dive Three
Maximum depth of dive:	☐☐☐ feet	☐☐☐ feet	☐☐☐ feet
Time left surface or started pressurization:	☐☐ H ☐☐ min	☐☐ H ☐☐ min	☐☐ H ☐☐ min
Bottom Time:	☐☐ min	☐☐ min	☐☐ min
Decompression Completed at:	☐☐ H ☐☐ min	☐☐ H ☐☐ min	☐☐ H ☐☐ min
For surface decompression only: Surface interval:	☐☐ min	☐☐ min	☐☐ min
and time spent in chamber:	☐☐ H ☐☐ min	☐☐ H ☐☐ min	☐☐ H ☐☐ min

Saturation Dives:		
Storage depth:	☐☐☐ feet	☐☐☐ feet
Maximum depth of dive:	☐☐☐ feet	☐☐☐ feet
Time leaving storage depth:	☐☐ H ☐☐ min on ☐☐ day	☐☐ H ☐☐ min on ☐☐ day
Time returning to storage depth:	☐☐ H ☐☐ min on ☐☐ day	☐☐ H ☐☐ min on ☐☐ day
Bottom time:	☐☐ H ☐☐ min	☐☐ H ☐☐ min

Breathing Apparatus used: _____

Breathing Mixture used: _____

Work Description, Equipment and Tools Used: _____

Name of Decompression Schedules used: _____

Note regarding any   _____
Decompression Sickness   _____
or other Illness or Injury: _____

Any Other Remarks: _____

Type of Dive

Scuba	☐
Surface	☐
Wet Bell	☐
Bell Bounce	☐
Saturation	☐
Other	

_____

_____

APPROVED

Name of Diving Contractor: _____

Address of Diving Contractor _____

Name of Diving Supervisor (Print) _____

Signature _____ Date: _____

RECORD OF DIVE

Date of Dive _____ Diver's Signature _____

BOTTOM CONDITION: (X appropriate blocks)
☐ Sand ☐ Shell ☐ Gravel ☐ Hard ☐ Soft

SEA STATE:
☐ Calm ☐ Fair ☐ Moderate ☐ Heavy ☐ Gale Sea

BOTTOM TEMPERATURE:
☐ Cold (below 55) ☐ Normal (55 to 75) ☐ Warm (above 75)

BOTTOM VISIBILITY:
☐ Poor (0 to 5') ☐ Moderate (5' to 20') ☐ (Good 20 +)

BOTTOM CURRENT:
☐ Weak (0 to 0.5KT) ☐ Moderate (0.5 to 2) ☐ Strong (2+)

Geographic Location
_____

_____

Vessel or Platform
_____

_____

Bell Bounce or Surface Dives:	Dive One	Dive Two	Dive Three
Maximum depth of dive:	☐☐☐ feet	☐☐☐ feet	☐☐☐ feet
Time left surface or started pressurization:	☐☐ H ☐☐ min	☐☐ H ☐☐ min	☐☐ H ☐☐ min
Bottom Time:	☐☐ min	☐☐ min	☐☐ min
Decompression Completed at:	☐☐ H ☐☐ min	☐☐ H ☐☐ min	☐☐ H ☐☐ min
For surface decompression only: Surface interval:	☐☐ min	☐☐ min	☐☐ min
and time spent in chamber:	☐☐ H ☐☐ min	☐☐ H ☐☐ min	☐☐ H ☐☐ min

Saturation Dives:		
Storage depth:	☐☐☐ feet	☐☐☐ feet
Maximum depth of dive:	☐☐☐ feet	☐☐☐ feet
Time leaving storage depth:	☐☐ H ☐☐ min on ☐☐ day	☐☐ H ☐☐ min on ☐☐ day
Time returning to storage depth:	☐☐ H ☐☐ min on ☐☐ day	☐☐ H ☐☐ min on ☐☐ day
Bottom time:	☐☐ H ☐☐ min	☐☐ H ☐☐ min

Breathing Apparatus used: _____

Breathing Mixture used: _____

Work Description, Equipment and Tools Used: _____

Name of Decompression Schedules used: _____

Note regarding any
Decompression Sickness
or other Illness or Injury: _____

Any Other Remarks: _____

Type of Dive

Scuba	
Surface	
Wet Bell	
Bell Bounce	
Saturation	

Other
_____

_____

APPROVED

Name of Diving Contractor: _____

Address of Diving Contractor _____

Name of Diving Supervisor (Print) _____

Signature _____ Date: _____

RECORD OF DIVE

Date of Dive _____ Diver's Signature _____

BOTTOM CONDITION: (X appropriate blocks)   Geographic Location
☐ Sand ☐ Shell ☐ Gravel ☐ Hard ☐ Soft   _____

SEA STATE:
☐ Calm ☐ Fair ☐ Moderate ☐ Heavy ☐ Gale Sea   _____

BOTTOM TEMPERATURE:
☐ Cold (below 55) ☐ Normal (55 to 75) ☐ Warm (above 75)   Vessel or Platform

BOTTOM VISIBILITY:
☐ Poor (0 to 5') ☐ Moderate (5' to 20') ☐ (Good 20 +)   _____

BOTTOM CURRENT:
☐ Weak (0 to 0.5KT) ☐ Moderate (0.5 to 2) ☐ Strong (2+)   _____

Bell Bounce or Surface Dives:	Dive One	Dive Two	Dive Three
Maximum depth of dive:	☐☐☐ feet	☐☐☐ feet	☐☐☐ feet
Time left surface or started pressurization:	☐☐ H ☐☐ min	☐☐ H ☐☐ min	☐☐ H ☐☐ min
Bottom Time:	☐☐☐ min	☐☐☐ min	☐☐☐ min
Decompression Completed at:	☐☐ H ☐☐ min	☐☐ H ☐☐ min	☐☐ H ☐☐ min
For surface decompression only: Surface interval:	☐☐☐ min	☐☐☐ min	☐☐☐ min
and time spent in chamber:	☐☐ H ☐☐ min	☐☐ H ☐☐ min	☐☐ H ☐☐ min

Saturation Dives:		
Storage depth:	☐☐☐☐ feet	☐☐☐☐ feet
Maximum depth of dive:	☐☐☐☐ feet	☐☐☐☐ feet
Time leaving storage depth:	☐☐ H ☐☐ min on ☐☐ day	☐☐ H ☐☐ min on ☐☐ day
Time returning to storage depth:	☐☐ H ☐☐ min on ☐☐ day	☐☐ H ☐☐ min on ☐☐ day
Bottom time:	☐☐ H ☐☐ min	☐☐ H ☐☐ min

Breathing Apparatus used: _____

Breathing Mixture used: _____

Work Description, Equipment and Tools Used: _____

Type of Dive	
Scuba	☐
Surface	☐
Wet Bell	☐
Bell Bounce	☐
Saturation	☐
Other	

Name of Decompression Schedules used: _____

Note regarding any
Decompression Sickness
or other Illness or Injury: _____

Any Other Remarks: _____
_____
_____

APPROVED
Name of Diving Contractor: _____
Address of Diving Contractor _____
_____

Name of Diving Supervisor (Print) _____
Signature _____ Date: _____

RECORD OF DIVE

Date of Dive _____ Diver's Signature _____

BOTTOM CONDITION: (X appropriate blocks)
☐ Sand ☐ Shell ☐ Gravel ☐ Hard ☐ Soft

Geographic Location
_____

SEA STATE:
☐ Calm ☐ Fair ☐ Moderate ☐ Heavy ☐ Gale Sea

_____

BOTTOM TEMPERATURE:
☐ Cold (below 55) ☐ Normal (55 to 75) ☐ Warm (above 75)

Vessel or Platform

BOTTOM VISIBILITY:
☐ Poor (0 to 5') ☐ Moderate (5' to 20') ☐ (Good 20 +)

_____

BOTTOM CURRENT:
☐ Weak (0 to 0.5KT) ☐ Moderate (0.5 to 2) ☐ Strong (2+)

_____

Bell Bounce or Surface Dives:

	Dive One	Dive Two	Dive Three
Maximum depth of dive:	☐☐☐ feet	☐☐☐ feet	☐☐☐ feet
Time left surface or started pressurization:	☐☐ H ☐☐ min	☐☐ H ☐☐ min	☐☐ H ☐☐ min
Bottom Time:	☐☐ min	☐☐ min	☐☐ min
Decompression Completed at:	☐☐ H ☐☐ min	☐☐ H ☐☐ min	☐☐ H ☐☐ min
For surface decompression only: Surface interval:	☐☐ min	☐☐ min	☐☐ min
and time spent in chamber:	☐☐ H ☐☐ min	☐☐ H ☐☐ min	☐☐ H ☐☐ min

Saturation Dives:

Storage depth:	☐☐☐ feet		☐☐☐ feet
Maximum depth of dive:	☐☐☐ feet		☐☐☐ feet
Time leaving storage depth:	☐☐ H ☐☐ min on ☐☐ day		☐☐ H ☐☐ min on ☐☐ day
Time returning to storage depth:	☐☐ H ☐☐ min on ☐☐ day		☐☐ H ☐☐ min on ☐☐ day
Bottom time:	☐☐ H ☐☐ min		☐☐ H ☐☐ min

Breathing Apparatus used: _____

Breathing Mixture used: _____

Work Description, Equipment and Tools Used: _____

Name of Decompression Schedules used: _____

Note regarding any
Decompression Sickness _____
or other Illness or Injury: _____

Any Other Remarks: _____

Type of Dive	
Scuba	☐
Surface	☐
Wet Bell	☐
Bell Bounce	☐
Saturation	☐
Other	

APPROVED

Name of Diving Contractor: _____

Address of Diving Contractor _____

Name of Diving Supervisor (Print) _____

Signature _____ Date: _____

RECORD OF DIVE

Date of Dive _____ Diver's Signature _____

BOTTOM CONDITION: (X appropriate blocks)
☐ Sand ☐ Shell ☐ Gravel ☐ Hard ☐ Soft

Geographic Location
_____

SEA STATE:
☐ Calm ☐ Fair ☐ Moderate ☐ Heavy ☐ Gale Sea

_____

BOTTOM TEMPERATURE:
☐ Cold (below 55) ☐ Normal (55 to 75) ☐ Warm (above 75)

Vessel or Platform

BOTTOM VISIBILITY:
☐ Poor (0 to 5') ☐ Moderate (5' to 20') ☐ (Good 20 +)

_____

BOTTOM CURRENT:
☐ Weak (0 to 0.5KT) ☐ Moderate (0.5 to 2) ☐ Strong (2+)

_____

Bell Bounce or Surface Dives:	Dive One	Dive Two	Dive Three
Maximum depth of dive:	☐☐☐ feet	☐☐☐ feet	☐☐☐ feet
Time left surface or started pressurization:	☐☐ H ☐☐ min	☐☐ H ☐☐ min	☐☐ H ☐☐ min
Bottom Time:	☐☐ min	☐☐ min	☐☐ min
Decompression Completed at:	☐☐ H ☐☐ min	☐☐ H ☐☐ min	☐☐ H ☐☐ min
For surface decompression only: Surface interval:	☐☐ min	☐☐ min	☐☐ min
and time spent in chamber:	☐☐ H ☐☐ min	☐☐ H ☐☐ min	☐☐ H ☐☐ min

Saturation Dives:		
Storage depth:	☐☐☐ feet	☐☐☐ feet
Maximum depth of dive:	☐☐☐ feet	☐☐☐ feet
Time leaving storage depth:	☐☐ H ☐☐ min on ☐☐ day	☐☐ H ☐☐ min on ☐☐ day
Time returning to storage depth:	☐☐ H ☐☐ min on ☐☐ day	☐☐ H ☐☐ min on ☐☐ day
Bottom time:	☐☐ H ☐☐ min	☐☐ H ☐☐ min

Breathing Apparatus used: _____
_____

Breathing Mixture used: _____
_____

Work Description, Equipment and Tools Used:
_____
_____

Name of Decompression Schedules used: _____

Note regarding any   _____
Decompression Sickness   _____
or other Illness or Injury: _____

Any Other Remarks: _____
_____
_____

Type of Dive	
Scuba	☐
Surface	☐
Wet Bell	☐
Bell Bounce	☐
Saturation	☐
Other	
_____	
_____	

APPROVED
Name of Diving Contractor: _____

Address of Diving Contractor _____
_____

Name of Diving Supervisor (Print) _____

Signature _____ Date: _____

RECORD OF DIVE

Date of Dive _____ Diver's Signature _____

BOTTOM CONDITION: (X appropriate blocks)
☐ Sand ☐ Shell ☐ Gravel ☐ Hard ☐ Soft

SEA STATE:
☐ Calm ☐ Fair ☐ Moderate ☐ Heavy ☐ Gale Sea

BOTTOM TEMPERATURE:
☐ Cold (below 55) ☐ Normal (55 to 75) ☐ Warm (above 75)

BOTTOM VISIBILITY:
☐ Poor (0 to 5') ☐ Moderate (5' to 20') ☐ (Good 20 +)

BOTTOM CURRENT:
☐ Weak (0 to 0.5KT) ☐ Moderate (0.5 to 2) ☐ Strong (2+)

Geographic Location
_____

_____

Vessel or Platform
_____

_____

Bell Bounce or Surface Dives:

	Dive One	Dive Two	Dive Three
Maximum depth of dive:	☐☐☐ feet	☐☐☐ feet	☐☐☐ feet
Time left surface or started pressurization:	☐☐ H ☐☐ min	☐☐ H ☐☐ min	☐☐ H ☐☐ min
Bottom Time:	☐☐☐ min	☐☐☐ min	☐☐☐ min
Decompression Completed at:	☐☐ H ☐☐ min	☐☐ H ☐☐ min	☐☐ H ☐☐ min
For surface decompression only: Surface interval:	☐☐ min	☐☐ min	☐☐ min
and time spent in chamber:	☐☐ H ☐☐ min	☐☐ H ☐☐ min	☐☐ H ☐☐ min

Saturation Dives:

Storage depth:	☐☐☐ feet	☐☐☐ feet
Maximum depth of dive:	☐☐☐ feet	☐☐☐ feet
Time leaving storage depth:	☐☐ H ☐☐ min on ☐☐ day	☐☐ H ☐☐ min on ☐☐ day
Time returning to storage depth:	☐☐ H ☐☐ min on ☐☐ day	☐☐ H ☐☐ min on ☐☐ day
Bottom time:	☐☐ H ☐☐ min	☐☐ H ☐☐ min

Breathing Apparatus used: _____

_____

Breathing Mixture used: _____

_____

Work Description, Equipment and Tools Used:

_____

_____

Name of Decompression Schedules used: _____

Note regarding any
Decompression Sickness
or other Illness or Injury:

Any Other Remarks: _____

Type of Dive	
Scuba	
Surface	
Wet Bell	
Bell Bounce	
Saturation	
Other	

_____

_____

APPROVED

Name of Diving Contractor: _____

Address of Diving Contractor _____

_____

Name of Diving Supervisor (Print) _____

Signature _____ Date: _____

RECORD OF DIVE

Date of Dive _____ Diver's Signature _____

BOTTOM CONDITION: (X appropriate blocks)
☐ Sand ☐ Shell ☐ Gravel ☐ Hard ☐ Soft

SEA STATE:
☐ Calm ☐ Fair ☐ Moderate ☐ Heavy ☐ Gale Sea

BOTTOM TEMPERATURE:
☐ Cold (below 55) ☐ Normal (55 to 75) ☐ Warm (above 75)

BOTTOM VISIBILITY:
☐ Poor (0 to 5') ☐ Moderate (5' to 20') ☐ (Good 20 +)

BOTTOM CURRENT:
☐ Weak (0 to 0.5KT) ☐ Moderate (0.5 to 2) ☐ Strong (2+)

Geographic Location
_____

Vessel or Platform
_____

Bell Bounce or Surface Dives:	Dive One	Dive Two	Dive Three
Maximum depth of dive:	☐☐☐ feet	☐☐☐ feet	☐☐ feet
Time left surface or started pressurization:	☐☐ H ☐☐ min	☐☐ H ☐☐ min	☐☐ H ☐ min
Bottom Time:	☐☐☐ min	☐☐☐ min	☐☐☐ min
Decompression Completed at:	☐☐ H ☐☐ min	☐☐ H ☐☐ min	☐☐ H ☐☐ min

For surface decompression only:			
Surface interval:	☐☐☐ min	☐☐☐ min	☐☐☐ min
and time spent in chamber:	☐☐ H ☐☐ min	☐☐ H ☐☐ min	☐☐ H ☐☐ min

Saturation Dives:

Storage depth:	☐☐☐☐ feet	☐☐☐☐ feet
Maximum depth of dive:	☐☐☐☐ feet	☐☐☐☐ feet
Time leaving storage depth:	☐☐ H ☐☐ min on ☐☐ day	☐☐ H ☐☐ min on ☐☐ day
Time returning to storage depth:	☐☐ H ☐☐ min on ☐☐ day	☐☐ H ☐☐ min on ☐☐ day
Bottom time:	☐☐ H ☐☐ min	☐☐ H ☐☐ min

Breathing Apparatus used: _____

Breathing Mixture used: _____

Work Description, Equipment and Tools Used:
_____
_____

Name of Decompression Schedules used: _____

Note regarding any Decompression Sickness or other Illness or Injury: _____

Any Other Remarks: _____
_____
_____

Type of Dive	
Scuba	
Surface	
Wet Bell	
Bell Bounce	
Saturation	
Other	

_____
_____

APPROVED
Name of Diving Contractor: _____

Address of Diving Contractor _____
_____

Name of Diving Supervisor (Print) _____

Signature _____ Date: _____

RECORD OF DIVE

Date of Dive _____ Diver's Signature _____

BOTTOM CONDITION: (X appropriate blocks)   Geographic Location
☐ Sand ☐ Shell ☐ Gravel ☐ Hard ☐ Soft
SEA STATE: _____
☐ Calm ☐ Fair ☐ Moderate ☐ Heavy ☐ Gale Sea
BOTTOM TEMPERATURE: _____
☐ Cold (below 55) ☐ Normal (55 to 75) ☐ Warm (above 75)   Vessel or Platform
BOTTOM VISIBILITY:
☐ Poor (0 to 5') ☐ Moderate (5' to 20') ☐ (Good 20 +)   _____
BOTTOM CURRENT:
☐ Weak (0 to 0.5KT) ☐ Moderate (0.5 to 2) ☐ Strong (2+) _____

Bell Bounce or Surface Dives:	Dive One	Dive Two	Dive Three
Maximum depth of dive:	☐☐☐ feet	☐☐☐ feet	☐☐☐ feet
Time left surface or started pressurization:	☐☐ H ☐☐ min	☐☐ H ☐☐ min	☐☐ H ☐☐ min
Bottom Time:	☐☐ min	☐☐ min	☐☐ min
Decompression Completed at:	☐☐ H ☐☐ min	☐☐ H ☐☐ min	☐☐ H ☐☐ min
For surface decompression only: Surface interval:	☐☐ min	☐☐ min	☐☐ min
and time spent in chamber:	☐☐ H ☐☐ min	☐☐ H ☐☐ min	☐☐ H ☐☐ min

Saturation Dives:		
Storage depth:	☐☐☐ feet	☐☐☐ feet
Maximum depth of dive:	☐☐☐ feet	☐☐☐ feet
Time leaving storage depth:	☐☐ H ☐☐ min on ☐☐ day	☐☐ H ☐☐ min on ☐☐ day
Time returning to storage depth:	☐☐ H ☐☐ min on ☐☐ day	☐☐ H ☐☐ min on ☐☐ day
Bottom time:	☐☐ H ☐☐ min	☐☐ H ☐☐ min

Breathing Apparatus used: _____

Breathing Mixture used: _____

Work Description, Equipment and Tools Used: _____

Name of Decompression Schedules used: _____

Note regarding any   _____
Decompression Sickness   _____
or other Illness or Injury: _____

Any Other Remarks: _____

Type of Dive

Scuba	☐
Surface	☐
Wet Bell	☐
Bell Bounce	☐
Saturation	☐
Other	

APPROVED
Name of Diving Contractor: _____

Address of Diving Contractor _____

Name of Diving Supervisor (Print) _____

Signature _____ Date: _____

RECORD OF DIVE

Date of Dive _____ Diver's Signature _____

BOTTOM CONDITION: (X appropriate blocks)
☐ Sand ☐ Shell ☐ Gravel ☐ Hard ☐ Soft

Geographic Location

SEA STATE:
☐ Calm ☐ Fair ☐ Moderate ☐ Heavy ☐ Gale Sea

_____

BOTTOM TEMPERATURE:
☐ Cold (below 55) ☐ Normal (55 to 75) ☐ Warm (above 75)

Vessel or Platform

BOTTOM VISIBILITY:
☐ Poor (0 to 5') ☐ Moderate (5' to 20') ☐ (Good 20 +)

_____

BOTTOM CURRENT:
☐ Weak (0 to 0.5KT) ☐ Moderate (0.5 to 2) ☐ Strong (2+)

_____

Bell Bounce or Surface Dives:

	Dive One	Dive Two	Dive Three
Maximum depth of dive:	☐☐☐ feet	☐☐☐ feet	☐☐☐ feet
Time left surface or started pressurization:	☐☐ H ☐☐ min	☐☐ H ☐☐ min	☐☐ H ☐☐ min
Bottom Time:	☐☐☐ min	☐☐☐ min	☐☐☐ min
Decompression Completed at:	☐☐ H ☐☐ min	☐☐ H ☐☐ min	☐☐ H ☐☐ min
For surface decompression only: Surface interval:	☐☐☐ min	☐☐☐ min	☐☐☐ min
and time spent in chamber:	☐☐ H ☐☐ min	☐☐ H ☐☐ min	☐☐ H ☐☐ min

Saturation Dives:

Storage depth:	☐☐☐☐ feet	☐☐☐☐ feet
Maximum depth of dive:	☐☐☐☐ feet	☐☐☐☐ feet
Time leaving storage depth:	☐☐ H ☐☐ min on ☐☐ day	☐☐ H ☐☐ min on ☐☐ day
Time returning to storage depth:	☐☐ H ☐☐ min on ☐☐ day	☐☐ H ☐☐ min on ☐☐ day
Bottom time:	☐☐ H ☐☐ min	☐☐ H ☐☐ min

Breathing Apparatus used: _____

_____

Type of Dive

Breathing Mixture used: _____

Type of Dive	
Scuba	☐
Surface	☐
Wet Bell	☐
Bell Bounce	☐
Saturation	☐
Other	

Work Description, Equipment and Tools Used:

_____

_____

_____

Name of Decompression Schedules used: _____

Note regarding any
Decompression Sickness
or other Illness or Injury:

_____

_____

_____

Any Other Remarks: _____

_____

_____

APPROVED

Name of Diving Contractor: _____

Address of Diving Contractor _____

_____

Name of Diving Supervisor (Print) _____

Signature _____ Date: _____

RECORD OF DIVE

Date of Dive _____ Diver's Signature _____

BOTTOM CONDITION: (X appropriate blocks)
□ Sand □ Shell □ Gravel □ Hard □ Soft

Geographic Location

_____

SEA STATE:
□ Calm □ Fair □ Moderate □ Heavy □ Gale Sea

BOTTOM TEMPERATURE:
□ Cold (below 55) □ Normal (55 to 75) □ Warm (above 75)

Vessel or Platform

BOTTOM VISIBILITY:
□ Poor (0 to 5') □ Moderate (5' to 20') □ (Good 20 +)

_____

BOTTOM CURRENT:
□ Weak (0 to 0.5KT) □ Moderate (0.5 to 2) □ Strong (2+)

Bell Bounce or Surface Dives:	Dive One	Dive Two	Dive Three
Maximum depth of dive:	☐☐☐ feet	☐☐☐ feet	☐☐☐ feet
Time left surface or started pressurization:	☐ H ☐☐ min	☐☐ H ☐ min	☐☐ H ☐ min
Bottom Time:	☐☐ min	☐☐ min	☐☐ min
Decompression Completed at:	☐☐ H ☐☐ min	☐☐ H ☐☐ min	☐☐ H ☐☐ min
For surface decompression only:			
Surface interval:	☐☐ min	☐☐ min	☐☐ min
and time spent in chamber:	☐ H ☐☐ min	☐☐ H ☐☐ min	☐ H ☐☐ min

Saturation Dives:			
Storage depth:	☐☐☐ feet		☐☐☐ feet
Maximum depth of dive:	☐☐☐ feet		☐☐☐ feet
Time leaving storage depth:	☐☐ H ☐☐ min on ☐☐ day		☐☐ H ☐☐ min on ☐☐ day
Time returning to storage depth:	☐☐ H ☐☐ min on ☐☐ day		☐☐ H ☐☐ min on ☐☐ day
Bottom time:	☐☐ H ☐☐ min		☐☐ H ☐☐ min

Breathing Apparatus used: _____

_____

Breathing Mixture used: _____

_____

Work Description, Equipment and Tools Used:

_____

_____

Name of Decompression Schedules used: _____

Note regarding any
Decompression Sickness _____
or other Illness or Injury: _____

Any Other Remarks: _____

_____

_____

Type of Dive	
Scuba	
Surface	
Wet Bell	
Bell Bounce	
Saturation	
Other	

_____

APPROVED
Name of Diving Contractor: _____

Address of Diving Contractor _____

_____

Name of Diving Supervisor (Print) _____

Signature _____ Date: _____

RECORD OF DIVE

Date of Dive _____ Diver's Signature _____

BOTTOM CONDITION: (X appropriate blocks)
☐ Sand ☐ Shell ☐ Gravel ☐ Hard ☐ Soft

Geographic Location
_____

SEA STATE:
☐ Calm ☐ Fair ☐ Moderate ☐ Heavy ☐ Gale Sea
_____

BOTTOM TEMPERATURE:
☐ Cold (below 55) ☐ Normal (55 to 75) ☐ Warm (above 75)

Vessel or Platform
_____

BOTTOM VISIBILITY:
☐ Poor (0 to 5') ☐ Moderate (5' to 20') ☐ (Good 20 +)
_____

BOTTOM CURRENT:
☐ Weak (0 to 0.5KT) ☐ Moderate (0.5 to 2) ☐ Strong (2+)
_____

Bell Bounce or Surface Dives:	Dive One	Dive Two	Dive Three
Maximum depth of dive:	☐☐☐ feet	☐☐☐ feet	☐☐☐ feet
Time left surface or started pressurization:	☐☐ H ☐☐ min	☐☐ H ☐☐ min	☐☐ H ☐☐ min
Bottom Time:	☐☐ min	☐☐ min	☐☐ min
Decompression Completed at:	☐☐ H ☐☐ min	☐☐ H ☐☐ min	☐☐ H ☐☐ min
For surface decompression only: Surface interval:	☐☐ min	☐☐ min	☐☐ min
and time spent in chamber:	☐☐ H ☐☐ min	☐☐ H ☐☐ min	☐☐ H ☐☐ min

Saturation Dives:		
Storage depth:	☐☐☐ feet	☐☐☐ feet
Maximum depth of dive:	☐☐☐ feet	☐☐☐ feet
Time leaving storage depth:	☐☐ H ☐☐ min on ☐☐ day	☐☐ H ☐☐ min on ☐☐ day
Time returning to storage depth:	☐☐ H ☐☐ min on ☐☐ day	☐☐ H ☐☐ min on ☐☐ day
Bottom time:	☐☐ H ☐☐ min	☐☐ H ☐☐ min

Breathing Apparatus used: _____
_____

Breathing Mixture used: _____
_____

Work Description, Equipment and Tools Used: _____
_____
_____

Name of Decompression Schedules used: _____

Note regarding any
Decompression Sickness _____
or other Illness or Injury: _____

Any Other Remarks: _____
_____
_____

Type of Dive	
Scuba	
Surface	
Wet Bell	
Bell Bounce	
Saturation	
Other	

_____
_____

APPROVED
Name of Diving Contractor: _____

Address of Diving Contractor _____
_____

Name of Diving Supervisor (Print) _____

Signature _____ Date: _____

RECORD OF DIVE

Date of Dive _____ Diver's Signature _____

BOTTOM CONDITION: (X appropriate blocks)
☐ Sand ☐ Shell ☐ Gravel ☐ Hard ☐ Soft

SEA STATE:
☐ Calm ☐ Fair ☐ Moderate ☐ Heavy ☐ Gale Sea

BOTTOM TEMPERATURE:
☐ Cold (below 55) ☐ Normal (55 to 75) ☐ Warm (above 75)

BOTTOM VISIBILITY:
☐ Poor (0 to 5') ☐ Moderate (5' to 20') ☐ (Good 20 +)

BOTTOM CURRENT:
☐ Weak (0 to 0.5KT) ☐ Moderate (0.5 to 2) ☐ Strong (2+)

Geographic Location
_____

_____

Vessel or Platform
_____

_____

Bell Bounce or Surface Dives:	Dive One	Dive Two	Dive Three
Maximum depth of dive:	☐☐☐ feet	☐☐☐ feet	☐☐☐ feet
Time left surface or started pressurization:	☐☐ H ☐☐ min	☐☐ H ☐☐ min	☐☐ H ☐☐ min
Bottom Time:	☐☐☐ min	☐☐☐ min	☐☐☐ min
Decompression Completed at:	☐☐ H ☐☐ min	☐☐ H ☐☐ min	☐☐ H ☐☐ min
For surface decompression only:			
Surface interval:	☐☐☐ min	☐☐☐ min	☐☐☐ min
and time spent in chamber:	☐☐ H ☐☐ min	☐☐ H ☐☐ min	☐☐ H ☐☐ min

Saturation Dives:		
Storage depth:	☐☐☐ feet	☐☐☐ feet
Maximum depth of dive:	☐☐☐ feet	☐☐☐ feet
Time leaving storage depth:	☐☐ H ☐☐ min on ☐☐ day	☐☐ H ☐☐ min on ☐☐ day
Time returning to storage depth:	☐☐ H ☐☐ min on ☐☐ day	☐☐ H ☐☐ min on ☐☐ day
Bottom time:	☐☐ H ☐☐ min	☐☐ H ☐☐ min

Breathing Apparatus used: _____

Breathing Mixture used: _____

Work Description, Equipment and Tools Used: _____

Name of Decompression Schedules used: _____

Note regarding any Decompression Sickness or other Illness or Injury: _____

Any Other Remarks: _____

Type of Dive	
Scuba	
Surface	
Wet Bell	
Bell Bounce	
Saturation	
Other	

APPROVED

Name of Diving Contractor: _____

Address of Diving Contractor _____

Name of Diving Supervisor (Print) _____

Signature _____ Date: _____

RECORD OF DIVE

Date of Dive _____ Diver's Signature _____

BOTTOM CONDITION: (X appropriate blocks)
☐ Sand   ☐ Shell   ☐ Gravel   ☐ Hard   ☐ Soft

Geographic Location
_____

SEA STATE:
☐ Calm   ☐ Fair   ☐ Moderate   ☐ Heavy   ☐ Gale Sea

BOTTOM TEMPERATURE:
☐ Cold (below 55)   ☐ Normal (55 to 75)   ☐ Warm (above 75)

Vessel or Platform
_____

BOTTOM VISIBILITY:
☐ Poor (0 to 5')   ☐ Moderate (5' to 20')   ☐ (Good 20 +)

BOTTOM CURRENT:
☐ Weak (0 to 0.5KT)   ☐ Moderate (0.5 to 2)   ☐ Strong (2+)

Bell Bounce or Surface Dives:	Dive One	Dive Two	Dive Three
Maximum depth of dive:	☐☐☐ feet	☐☐☐ feet	☐☐☐ feet
Time left surface or started pressurization:	☐☐ H ☐☐ min	☐☐ H ☐☐ min	☐☐ H ☐☐ min
Bottom Time:	☐☐☐ min	☐☐☐ min	☐☐☐ min
Decompression Completed at:	☐☐ H ☐☐ min	☐☐ H ☐☐ min	☐☐ H ☐☐ min
For surface decompression only: Surface interval:	☐☐ min	☐☐ min	☐☐ min
and time spent in chamber:	☐☐ H ☐☐ min	☐☐ H ☐☐ min	☐☐ H ☐☐ min

Saturation Dives:		
Storage depth:	☐☐☐ feet	☐☐☐ feet
Maximum depth of dive:	☐☐☐ feet	☐☐☐ feet
Time leaving storage depth:	☐☐ H ☐☐ min on ☐☐ day	☐☐ H ☐☐ min on ☐☐ day
Time returning to storage depth:	☐☐ H ☐☐ min on ☐☐ day	☐☐ H ☐☐ min on ☐☐ day
Bottom time:	☐☐ H ☐☐ min	☐☐ H ☐☐ min

Breathing Apparatus used: _____

Breathing Mixture used: _____

Work Description, Equipment and Tools Used: _____

Name of Decompression Schedules used: _____

Note regarding any Decompression Sickness or other Illness or Injury: _____

Any Other Remarks: _____

Type of Dive	
Scuba	☐
Surface	☐
Wet Bell	☐
Bell Bounce	☐
Saturation	☐
Other	

APPROVED
Name of Diving Contractor: _____

Address of Diving Contractor _____

Name of Diving Supervisor (Print) _____

Signature _____ Date: _____

RECORD OF DIVE

Date of Dive _____ Diver's Signature _____

BOTTOM CONDITION: (X appropriate blocks)
☐ Sand ☐ Shell ☐ Gravel ☐ Hard ☐ Soft

Geographic Location

SEA STATE:
☐ Calm ☐ Fair ☐ Moderate ☐ Heavy ☐ Gale Sea

_____

BOTTOM TEMPERATURE:
☐ Cold (below 55) ☐ Normal (55 to 75) ☐ Warm (above 75)

Vessel or Platform

BOTTOM VISIBILITY:
☐ Poor (0 to 5') ☐ Moderate (5' to 20') ☐ (Good 20 +)

_____

BOTTOM CURRENT:
☐ Weak (0 to 0.5KT) ☐ Moderate (0.5 to 2) ☐ Strong (2+)

Bell Bounce or Surface Dives:	Dive One	Dive Two	Dive Three
Maximum depth of dive:	☐☐☐ feet	☐☐☐ feet	☐☐☐ feet
Time left surface or started pressurization:	☐☐ H ☐☐ min	☐☐ H ☐☐ min	☐☐ H ☐☐ min
Bottom Time:	☐☐ min	☐☐ min	☐☐ min
Decompression Completed at:	☐☐ H ☐☐ min	☐☐ H ☐☐ min	☐☐ H ☐☐ min
For surface decompression only: Surface interval:	☐☐ min	☐☐ min	☐☐ min
and time spent in chamber:	☐☐ H ☐☐ min	☐☐ H ☐☐ min	☐☐ H ☐☐ min

Saturation Dives:		
Storage depth:	☐☐☐ feet	☐☐☐ feet
Maximum depth of dive:	☐☐☐ feet	☐☐☐ feet
Time leaving storage depth:	☐☐ H ☐☐ min on ☐☐ day	☐☐ H ☐☐ min on ☐☐ day
Time returning to storage depth:	☐☐ H ☐☐ min on ☐☐ day	☐☐ H ☐☐ min on ☐☐ day
Bottom time:	☐☐ H ☐☐ min	☐☐ H ☐☐ min

Breathing Apparatus used: _____

Breathing Mixture used: _____

Work Description, Equipment and Tools Used:
_____
_____

Name of Decompression Schedules used: _____

Note regarding any
Decompression Sickness   _____
or other Illness or Injury: _____

Any Other Remarks: _____
_____
_____

Type of Dive	
Scuba	
Surface	
Wet Bell	
Bell Bounce	
Saturation	
Other	

APPROVED
Name of Diving Contractor: _____

Address of Diving Contractor _____
_____

Name of Diving Supervisor (Print) _____

Signature _____ Date: _____

RECORD OF DIVE

Date of Dive _____ Diver's Signature _____

BOTTOM CONDITION: (X appropriate blocks)　　　　　　Geographic Location
☐ Sand ☐ Shell ☐ Gravel ☐ Hard ☐ Soft
SEA STATE:　　　　　　　　　　　　　　　　　　　　　_____
☐ Calm ☐ Fair ☐ Moderate ☐ Heavy ☐ Gale Sea
BOTTOM TEMPERATURE:　　　　　　　　　　　　　　　Vessel or Platform
☐ Cold (below 55) ☐ Normal (55 to 75) ☐ Warm (above 75)
BOTTOM VISIBILITY:　　　　　　　　　　　　　　　　　_____
☐ Poor (0 to 5') ☐ Moderate (5' to 20') ☐ (Good 20 +)
BOTTOM CURRENT:　　　　　　　　　　　　　　　　　　_____
☐ Weak (0 to 0.5KT) ☐ Moderate (0.5 to 2) ☐ Strong (2+)

Bell Bounce or Surface Dives:

	Dive One	Dive Two	Dive Three
Maximum depth of dive:	☐☐☐ feet	☐☐☐ feet	☐☐☐ feet
Time left surface or started pressurization:	☐☐ H ☐☐ min	☐☐ H ☐☐ min	☐☐ H ☐☐ min
Bottom Time:	☐☐ min	☐☐ min	☐☐ min
Decompression Completed at:	☐☐ H ☐☐ min	☐☐ H ☐☐ min	☐☐ H ☐☐ min
For surface decompression only: Surface interval:	☐☐ min	☐☐ min	☐☐ min
and time spent in chamber:	☐☐ H ☐☐ min	☐☐ H ☐☐ min	☐☐ H ☐☐ min

Saturation Dives:

Storage depth:	☐☐☐ feet	☐☐☐ feet	
Maximum depth of dive:	☐☐☐ feet	☐☐☐ feet	
Time leaving storage depth:	☐☐ H ☐☐ min on ☐☐ day	☐☐ H ☐☐ min on ☐☐ day	
Time returning to storage depth:	☐☐ H ☐☐ min on ☐☐ day	☐☐ H ☐☐ min on ☐☐ day	
Bottom time:	☐☐ H ☐☐ min	☐☐ H ☐☐ min	

Breathing Apparatus used: _____

Breathing Mixture used: _____

Work Description, Equipment and Tools Used: _____
_____
_____

Name of Decompression Schedules used: _____

Note regarding any　　　_____
Decompression Sickness　_____
or other Illness or Injury:　_____

Any Other Remarks: _____
_____
_____

Type of Dive	
Scuba	
Surface	
Wet Bell	
Bell Bounce	
Saturation	
Other	

APPROVED
Name of Diving Contractor: _____

Address of Diving Contractor _____
_____

Name of Diving Supervisor (Print) _____

Signature _____ Date: _____

RECORD OF DIVE

Date of Dive _____ Diver's Signature _____

BOTTOM CONDITION: (X appropriate blocks)
☐ Sand ☐ Shell ☐ Gravel ☐ Hard ☐ Soft

Geographic Location

SEA STATE:
☐ Calm ☐ Fair ☐ Moderate ☐ Heavy ☐ Gale Sea

_____

BOTTOM TEMPERATURE:
☐ Cold (below 55) ☐ Normal (55 to 75) ☐ Warm (above 75)

Vessel or Platform

BOTTOM VISIBILITY:
☐ Poor (0 to 5') ☐ Moderate (5' to 20') ☐ (Good 20 +)

_____

BOTTOM CURRENT:
☐ Weak (0 to 0.5KT) ☐ Moderate (0.5 to 2) ☐ Strong (2+)

_____

Bell Bounce or Surface Dives:	Dive One	Dive Two	Dive Three
Maximum depth of dive:	☐☐☐ feet	☐☐☐ feet	☐☐☐ feet
Time left surface or started pressurization:	☐☐ H ☐☐ min	☐☐ H ☐☐ min	☐☐ H ☐☐ min
Bottom Time:	☐☐☐ min	☐☐☐ min	☐☐☐ min
Decompression Completed at:	☐☐ H ☐☐ min	☐☐ H ☐☐ min	☐☐ H ☐☐ min
For surface decompression only: Surface interval:	☐☐☐ min	☐☐☐ min	☐☐☐ min
and time spent in chamber:	☐☐ H ☐☐ min	☐☐ H ☐☐ min	☐☐ H ☐☐ min

Saturation Dives:		
Storage depth:	☐☐☐ feet	☐☐☐ feet
Maximum depth of dive:	☐☐☐ feet	☐☐☐ feet
Time leaving storage depth:	☐☐ H ☐☐ min on ☐☐ day	☐☐ H ☐☐ min on ☐☐ day
Time returning to storage depth:	☐☐ H ☐☐ min on ☐☐ day	☐☐ H ☐☐ min on ☐☐ day
Bottom time:	☐☐ H ☐☐ min	☐☐ H ☐☐ min

Breathing Apparatus used: _____

_____

Breathing Mixture used: _____

_____

Work Description, Equipment and Tools Used:

_____

_____

Name of Decompression Schedules used: _____

Note regarding any
Decompression Sickness
or other Illness or Injury:

Any Other Remarks: _____

Type of Dive	
Scuba	☐
Surface	☐
Wet Bell	☐
Bell Bounce	☐
Saturation	☐
Other	

APPROVED

Name of Diving Contractor: _____

Address of Diving Contractor _____

_____

Name of Diving Supervisor (Print) _____

Signature _____ Date: _____

RECORD OF DIVE

Date of Dive _____ Diver's Signature _____

BOTTOM CONDITION: (X appropriate blocks)   Geographic Location
☐ Sand ☐ Shell ☐ Gravel ☐ Hard ☐ Soft

SEA STATE: _____
☐ Calm ☐ Fair ☐ Moderate ☐ Heavy ☐ Gale Sea

BOTTOM TEMPERATURE:
☐ Cold (below 55) ☐ Normal (55 to 75) ☐ Warm (above 75)   Vessel or Platform

BOTTOM VISIBILITY:
☐ Poor (0 to 5') ☐ Moderate (5' to 20') ☐ (Good 20 +)   _____

BOTTOM CURRENT:
☐ Weak (0 to 0.5KT) ☐ Moderate (0.5 to 2) ☐ Strong (2+)   _____

Bell Bounce or Surface Dives:	Dive One	Dive Two	Dive Three
Maximum depth of dive:	☐☐☐ feet	☐☐☐ feet	☐☐☐ feet
Time left surface or started pressurization:	☐☐ H ☐☐ min	☐☐ H ☐☐ min	☐☐ H ☐☐ min
Bottom Time:	☐☐ min	☐☐ min	☐☐ min
Decompression Completed at:	☐☐ H ☐☐ min	☐☐ H ☐☐ min	☐☐ H ☐☐ min
For surface decompression only: Surface interval:	☐☐ min	☐☐ min	☐☐ min
and time spent in chamber:	☐☐ H ☐☐ min	☐☐ H ☐☐ min	☐☐ H ☐☐ min

Saturation Dives:		
Storage depth:	☐☐☐ feet	☐☐☐ feet
Maximum depth of dive:	☐☐☐ feet	☐☐☐ feet
Time leaving storage depth:	☐☐ H ☐☐ min on ☐☐ day	☐☐ H ☐☐ min on ☐☐ day
Time returning to storage depth:	☐☐ H ☐☐ min on ☐☐ day	☐☐ H ☐☐ min on ☐☐ day
Bottom time:	☐☐ H ☐☐ min	☐☐ H ☐☐ min

Breathing Apparatus used: _____

Breathing Mixture used: _____

Work Description, Equipment and Tools Used:
_____
_____

Type of Dive	
Scuba	☐
Surface	☐
Wet Bell	☐
Bell Bounce	☐
Saturation	☐
Other	

Name of Decompression Schedules used: _____

Note regarding any   _____
Decompression Sickness   _____
or other Illness or Injury: _____

Any Other Remarks: _____
_____
_____

APPROVED
Name of Diving Contractor: _____

Address of Diving Contractor _____
_____

Name of Diving Supervisor (Print) _____

Signature _____ Date: _____

RECORD OF DIVE

Date of Dive _____ Diver's Signature _____

BOTTOM CONDITION: (X appropriate blocks)
☐ Sand ☐ Shell ☐ Gravel ☐ Hard ☐ Soft

SEA STATE:
☐ Calm ☐ Fair ☐ Moderate ☐ Heavy ☐ Gale Sea

BOTTOM TEMPERATURE:
☐ Cold (below 55) ☐ Normal (55 to 75) ☐ Warm (above 75)

BOTTOM VISIBILITY:
☐ Poor (0 to 5') ☐ Moderate (5' to 20') ☐ (Good 20 +)

BOTTOM CURRENT:
☐ Weak (0 to 0.5KT) ☐ Moderate (0.5 to 2) ☐ Strong (2+)

Geographic Location

_____

_____

Vessel or Platform

_____

_____

Bell Bounce or Surface Dives:	Dive One	Dive Two	Dive Three
Maximum depth of dive:	☐☐☐ feet	☐☐☐ feet	☐☐☐ feet
Time left surface or started pressurization:	☐☐H ☐☐ min	☐☐H ☐☐ min	☐☐H ☐☐ min
Bottom Time:	☐☐ min	☐☐ min	☐☐ min
Decompression Completed at:	☐☐H ☐☐ min	☐☐H ☐☐ min	☐☐H ☐☐ min
For surface decompression only:			
Surface interval:	☐☐ min	☐☐ min	☐☐ min
and time spent in chamber:	☐☐H ☐☐ min	☐☐H ☐☐ min	☐☐H ☐☐ min

Saturation Dives:		
Storage depth:	☐☐☐ feet	☐☐☐ feet
Maximum depth of dive:	☐☐☐ feet	☐☐☐ feet
Time leaving storage depth:	☐☐H ☐☐ min on ☐☐ day	☐☐H ☐☐ min on ☐☐ day
Time returning to storage depth:	☐☐H ☐☐ min on ☐☐ day	☐☐H ☐☐ min on ☐☐ day
Bottom time:	☐☐H ☐☐ min	☐☐H ☐☐ min

Breathing Apparatus used: _____

Breathing Mixture used: _____

Work Description, Equipment and Tools Used: _____

_____

Name of Decompression Schedules used: _____

Note regarding any
Decompression Sickness   _____
or other Illness or Injury: _____

Any Other Remarks: _____

_____

Type of Dive	
Scuba	
Surface	
Wet Bell	
Bell Bounce	
Saturation	

Other

_____

_____

APPROVED
Name of Diving Contractor: _____

Address of Diving Contractor _____

_____

Name of Diving Supervisor (Print) _____

Signature _____ Date: _____

RECORD OF DIVE

Date of Dive _____ Diver's Signature _____

BOTTOM CONDITION: (X appropriate blocks)
☐ Sand ☐ Shell ☐ Gravel ☐ Hard ☐ Soft

SEA STATE:
☐ Calm ☐ Fair ☐ Moderate ☐ Heavy ☐ Gale Sea

BOTTOM TEMPERATURE:
☐ Cold (below 55) ☐ Normal (55 to 75) ☐ Warm (above 75)

BOTTOM VISIBILITY:
☐ Poor (0 to 5') ☐ Moderate (5' to 20') ☐ (Good 20 +)

BOTTOM CURRENT:
☐ Weak (0 to 0.5KT) ☐ Moderate (0.5 to 2) ☐ Strong (2+)

Geographic Location
_____

Vessel or Platform
_____

Bell Bounce or Surface Dives:	Dive One	Dive Two	Dive Three
Maximum depth of dive:	☐☐☐ feet	☐☐ feet	☐☐☐ feet
Time left surface or started pressurization:	☐☐ H ☐☐ min	☐☐ H ☐☐ min	☐☐ H ☐☐ min
Bottom Time:	☐☐ min	☐☐ min	☐☐ min
Decompression Completed at:	☐☐ H ☐☐ min	☐☐ H ☐☐ min	☐☐ H ☐☐ min
For surface decompression only: Surface interval:	☐☐ min	☐☐ min	☐☐ min
and time spent in chamber:	☐☐ H ☐☐ min	☐☐ H ☐☐ min	☐☐ H ☐☐ min

Saturation Dives:		
Storage depth:	☐☐☐ feet	☐☐☐ feet
Maximum depth of dive:	☐☐☐ feet	☐☐☐ feet
Time leaving storage depth:	☐☐ H ☐☐ min on ☐☐ day	☐☐ H ☐☐ min on ☐☐ day
Time returning to storage depth:	☐☐ H ☐☐ min on ☐☐ day	☐☐ H ☐☐ min on ☐☐ day
Bottom time:	☐☐ H ☐☐ min	☐☐ H ☐☐ min

Breathing Apparatus used: _____

Breathing Mixture used: _____

Work Description, Equipment and Tools Used: _____
_____

Name of Decompression Schedules used: _____

Note regarding any
Decompression Sickness
or other Illness or Injury: _____

Any Other Remarks: _____
_____

Type of Dive	
Scuba	☐
Surface	☐
Wet Bell	☐
Bell Bounce	☐
Saturation	☐
Other	

APPROVED
Name of Diving Contractor: _____

Address of Diving Contractor _____

Name of Diving Supervisor (Print) _____

Signature _____ Date: _____

RECORD OF DIVE

Date of Dive _____ Diver's Signature _____

BOTTOM CONDITION: (X appropriate blocks)   Geographic Location
☐ Sand ☐ Shell ☐ Gravel ☐ Hard ☐ Soft   _____

SEA STATE:
☐ Calm ☐ Fair ☐ Moderate ☐ Heavy ☐ Gale Sea   _____

BOTTOM TEMPERATURE:
☐ Cold (below 55) ☐ Normal (55 to 75) ☐ Warm (above 75)   Vessel or Platform

BOTTOM VISIBILITY:
☐ Poor (0 to 5') ☐ Moderate (5' to 20') ☐ (Good 20 +)   _____

BOTTOM CURRENT:
☐ Weak (0 to 0.5KT) ☐ Moderate (0.5 to 2) ☐ Strong (2+)   _____

Bell Bounce or Surface Dives:	Dive One	Dive Two	Dive Three
Maximum depth of dive:	☐☐☐ feet	☐☐☐ feet	☐☐☐ feet
Time left surface or started pressurization:	☐☐ H ☐☐ min	☐☐ H ☐☐ min	☐☐ H ☐☐ min
Bottom Time:	☐☐☐ min	☐☐☐ min	☐☐☐ min
Decompression Completed at:	☐☐ H ☐☐ min	☐☐ H ☐☐ min	☐☐ H ☐☐ min
For surface decompression only: Surface interval:	☐☐☐ min	☐☐☐ min	☐☐☐ min
and time spent in chamber:	☐☐ H ☐☐ min	☐☐ H ☐☐ min	☐☐ H ☐☐ min

Saturation Dives:		
Storage depth:	☐☐☐ feet	☐☐☐ feet
Maximum depth of dive:	☐☐☐ feet	☐☐☐ feet
Time leaving storage depth:	☐☐ H ☐☐ min on ☐☐ day	☐☐ H ☐☐ min on ☐☐ day
Time returning to storage depth:	☐☐ H ☐☐ min on ☐☐ day	☐☐ H ☐☐ min on ☐☐ day
Bottom time:	☐☐ H ☐☐ min	☐☐ H ☐☐ min

Breathing Apparatus used: _____

Breathing Mixture used: _____

Work Description, Equipment and Tools Used: _____

_____

Name of Decompression Schedules used: _____

Note regarding any   _____
Decompression Sickness   _____
or other Illness or Injury: _____

Any Other Remarks: _____

_____

_____

Type of Dive	
Scuba	☐
Surface	☐
Wet Bell	☐
Bell Bounce	☐
Saturation	☐
Other	_____
	_____
	_____

APPROVED
Name of Diving Contractor: _____

Address of Diving Contractor _____

_____

Name of Diving Supervisor (Print) _____

Signature _____ Date: _____

RECORD OF DIVE

Date of Dive _____ Diver's Signature _____

BOTTOM CONDITION: (X appropriate blocks)   Geographic Location
☐ Sand ☐ Shell ☐ Gravel ☐ Hard ☐ Soft
SEA STATE: _____
☐ Calm ☐ Fair ☐ Moderate ☐ Heavy ☐ Gale Sea
BOTTOM TEMPERATURE: _____
☐ Cold (below 55) ☐ Normal (55 to 75) ☐ Warm (above 75)   Vessel or Platform
BOTTOM VISIBILITY:
☐ Poor (0 to 5') ☐ Moderate (5' to 20') ☐ (Good 20 +)   _____
BOTTOM CURRENT:
☐ Weak (0 to 0.5KT) ☐ Moderate (0.5 to 2) ☐ Strong (2+)   _____

Bell Bounce or Surface Dives:	Dive One	Dive Two	Dive Three
Maximum depth of dive:	☐☐☐ feet	☐☐☐ feet	☐☐☐ feet
Time left surface or started pressurization:	☐☐ H ☐☐ min	☐☐ H ☐☐ min	☐☐ H ☐☐ min
Bottom Time:	☐☐ min	☐☐ min	☐☐ min
Decompression Completed at:	☐☐ H ☐☐ min	☐☐ H ☐☐ min	☐☐ H ☐☐ min
For surface decompression only: Surface interval:	☐☐ min	☐☐ min	☐☐ min
and time spent in chamber:	☐☐ H ☐☐ min	☐☐ H ☐☐ min	☐☐ H ☐☐ min

Saturation Dives:		
Storage depth:	☐☐☐ feet	☐☐☐ feet
Maximum depth of dive:	☐☐☐ feet	☐☐☐ feet
Time leaving storage depth:	☐☐ H ☐☐ min on ☐☐ day	☐☐ H ☐☐ min on ☐☐ day
Time returning to storage depth:	☐☐ H ☐☐ min on ☐☐ day	☐☐ H ☐☐ min on ☐☐ day
Bottom time:	☐☐ H ☐☐ min	☐☐ H ☐☐ min

Breathing Apparatus used: _____

Breathing Mixture used: _____

Work Description, Equipment and Tools Used: _____
_____
_____

Name of Decompression Schedules used: _____

Note regarding any   _____
Decompression Sickness   _____
or other Illness or Injury: _____

Any Other Remarks: _____
_____
_____

Type of Dive	
Scuba	☐
Surface	☐
Wet Bell	☐
Bell Bounce	☐
Saturation	☐
Other	

APPROVED
Name of Diving Contractor: _____

Address of Diving Contractor _____

Name of Diving Supervisor (Print) _____

Signature _____ Date: _____

RECORD OF DIVE

Date of Dive _____ Diver's Signature _____

BOTTOM CONDITION: (X appropriate blocks)
☐ Sand ☐ Shell ☐ Gravel ☐ Hard ☐ Soft

Geographic Location
_____

SEA STATE:
☐ Calm ☐ Fair ☐ Moderate ☐ Heavy ☐ Gale Sea

_____

BOTTOM TEMPERATURE:
☐ Cold (below 55) ☐ Normal (55 to 75) ☐ Warm (above 75)

Vessel or Platform

BOTTOM VISIBILITY:
☐ Poor (0 to 5') ☐ Moderate (5' to 20') ☐ (Good 20 +)

_____

BOTTOM CURRENT:
☐ Weak (0 to 0.5KT) ☐ Moderate (0.5 to 2) ☐ Strong (2+)

_____

Bell Bounce or Surface Dives:	Dive One	Dive Two	Dive Three
Maximum depth of dive:	☐☐☐ feet	☐☐☐ feet	☐☐☐ feet
Time left surface or started pressurization:	☐☐ H ☐☐ min	☐☐ H ☐☐ min	☐☐ H ☐☐ min
Bottom Time:	☐☐ min	☐☐ min	☐☐ min
Decompression Completed at:	☐☐ H ☐☐ min	☐☐ H ☐☐ min	☐☐ H ☐☐ min
For surface decompression only: Surface interval:	☐☐ min	☐☐ min	☐☐ min
and time spent in chamber:	☐☐ H ☐☐ min	☐☐ H ☐☐ min	☐☐ H ☐☐ min

Saturation Dives:		
Storage depth:	☐☐☐ feet	☐☐☐ feet
Maximum depth of dive:	☐☐☐ feet	☐☐☐ feet
Time leaving storage depth:	☐☐ H ☐☐ min on ☐☐ day	☐☐ H ☐☐ min on ☐☐ day
Time returning to storage depth:	☐☐ H ☐☐ min on ☐☐ day	☐☐ H ☐☐ min on ☐☐ day
Bottom time:	☐☐ H ☐☐ min	☐☐ H ☐☐ min

Breathing Apparatus used: _____
_____

Breathing Mixture used: _____
_____

Work Description, Equipment and Tools Used: _____
_____
_____

Name of Decompression Schedules used: _____

Note regarding any
Decompression Sickness _____
or other Illness or Injury: _____

Any Other Remarks: _____
_____
_____

Type of Dive	
Scuba	
Surface	
Wet Bell	
Bell Bounce	
Saturation	
Other	

_____
_____

APPROVED
Name of Diving Contractor: _____

Address of Diving Contractor _____
_____

Name of Diving Supervisor (Print) _____

Signature _____ Date: _____

RECORD OF DIVE

Date of Dive _____ Diver's Signature _____

BOTTOM CONDITION: (X appropriate blocks)   Geographic Location
☐ Sand ☐ Shell ☐ Gravel ☐ Hard ☐ Soft

SEA STATE: _____
☐ Calm ☐ Fair ☐ Moderate ☐ Heavy ☐ Gale Sea

BOTTOM TEMPERATURE:
☐ Cold (below 55) ☐ Normal (55 to 75) ☐ Warm (above 75)   Vessel or Platform

BOTTOM VISIBILITY:
☐ Poor (0 to 5') ☐ Moderate (5' to 20') ☐ (Good 20 +)   _____

BOTTOM CURRENT:
☐ Weak (0 to 0.5KT) ☐ Moderate (0.5 to 2) ☐ Strong (2+)   _____

Bell Bounce or Surface Dives:	Dive One	Dive Two	Dive Three
Maximum depth of dive:	☐☐☐ feet	☐☐☐ feet	☐☐☐ feet
Time left surface or started pressurization:	☐☐ H ☐☐ min	☐☐ H ☐☐ min	☐☐ H ☐☐ min
Bottom Time:	☐☐☐ min	☐☐☐ min	☐☐☐ min
Decompression Completed at:	☐☐ H ☐☐ min	☐☐ H ☐☐ min	☐☐ H ☐☐ min
For surface decompression only: Surface interval:	☐☐☐ min	☐☐☐ min	☐☐☐ min
and time spent in chamber:	☐☐ H ☐☐ min	☐☐ H ☐☐ min	☐☐ H ☐☐ min

Saturation Dives:		
Storage depth:	☐☐☐ feet	☐☐☐ feet
Maximum depth of dive:	☐☐☐ feet	☐☐☐ feet
Time leaving storage depth:	☐☐ H ☐☐ min on ☐☐ day	☐☐ H ☐☐ min on ☐☐ day
Time returning to storage depth:	☐☐ H ☐☐ min on ☐☐ day	☐☐ H ☐☐ min on ☐☐ day
Bottom time:	☐☐ H ☐☐ min	☐☐ H ☐☐ min

Breathing Apparatus used: _____

Breathing Mixture used: _____

Work Description, Equipment and Tools Used:

_____

_____

Type of Dive

Scuba	☐
Surface	☐
Wet Bell	☐
Bell Bounce	☐
Saturation	☐
Other	

Name of Decompression Schedules used: _____

Note regarding any   _____
Decompression Sickness   _____
or other Illness or Injury: _____

Any Other Remarks: _____

_____

_____

APPROVED
Name of Diving Contractor: _____

Address of Diving Contractor _____

_____

Name of Diving Supervisor (Print) _____

Signature _____ Date: _____

RECORD OF DIVE

Date of Dive _____ Diver's Signature _____

BOTTOM CONDITION: (X appropriate blocks)
☐ Sand ☐ Shell ☐ Gravel ☐ Hard ☐ Soft

Geographic Location
_____

SEA STATE:
☐ Calm ☐ Fair ☐ Moderate ☐ Heavy ☐ Gale Sea

_____

BOTTOM TEMPERATURE:
☐ Cold (below 55) ☐ Normal (55 to 75) ☐ Warm (above 75)

Vessel or Platform

BOTTOM VISIBILITY:
☐ Poor (0 to 5') ☐ Moderate (5' to 20') ☐ (Good 20 +)

_____

BOTTOM CURRENT:
☐ Weak (0 to 0.5KT) ☐ Moderate (0.5 to 2) ☐ Strong (2+)

_____

Bell Bounce or Surface Dives:	Dive One	Dive Two	Dive Three
Maximum depth of dive:	☐☐☐ feet	☐☐☐ feet	☐☐☐ feet
Time left surface or started pressurization:	☐☐ H ☐☐ min	☐☐ H ☐☐ min	☐☐ H ☐☐ min
Bottom Time:	☐☐☐ min	☐☐☐ min	☐☐☐ min
Decompression Completed at:	☐☐ H ☐☐ min	☐☐ H ☐☐ min	☐☐ H ☐☐ min
For surface decompression only: Surface interval:	☐☐☐ min	☐☐☐ min	☐☐☐ min
and time spent in chamber:	☐☐ H ☐☐ min	☐☐ H ☐☐ min	☐☐ H ☐☐ min

Saturation Dives:		
Storage depth:	☐☐☐ feet	☐☐☐ feet
Maximum depth of dive:	☐☐☐ feet	☐☐☐ feet
Time leaving storage depth:	☐☐ H ☐☐ min on ☐☐ day	☐☐ H ☐☐ min on ☐☐ day
Time returning to storage depth:	☐☐ H ☐☐ min on ☐☐ day	☐☐ H ☐☐ min on ☐☐ day
Bottom time:	☐☐ H ☐☐ min	☐☐ H ☐☐ min

Breathing Apparatus used: _____

Breathing Mixture used: _____

Work Description, Equipment and Tools Used: _____
_____

Name of Decompression Schedules used: _____

Note regarding any
Decompression Sickness
or other Illness or Injury: _____

Any Other Remarks: _____
_____
_____

Type of Dive	
Scuba	☐
Surface	☐
Wet Bell	☐
Bell Bounce	☐
Saturation	☐
Other	

_____
_____

APPROVED
Name of Diving Contractor: _____

Address of Diving Contractor _____
_____

Name of Diving Supervisor (Print) _____

Signature _____ Date: _____

RECORD OF DIVE

Date of Dive _____ Diver's Signature _____

BOTTOM CONDITION: (X appropriate blocks)
☐ Sand ☐ Shell ☐ Gravel ☐ Hard ☐ Soft

Geographic Location
_____

SEA STATE:
☐ Calm ☐ Fair ☐ Moderate ☐ Heavy ☐ Gale Sea
_____

BOTTOM TEMPERATURE:
☐ Cold (below 55) ☐ Normal (55 to 75) ☐ Warm (above 75)

Vessel or Platform

BOTTOM VISIBILITY:
☐ Poor (0 to 5') ☐ Moderate (5' to 20') ☐ (Good 20 +)
_____

BOTTOM CURRENT:
☐ Weak (0 to 0.5KT) ☐ Moderate (0.5 to 2) ☐ Strong (2+)
_____

Bell Bounce or Surface Dives:	Dive One	Dive Two	Dive Three
Maximum depth of dive:	☐☐☐ feet	☐☐☐ feet	☐☐☐ feet
Time left surface or started pressurization:	☐☐ H ☐☐ min	☐☐ H ☐☐ min	☐☐ H ☐☐ min
Bottom Time:	☐☐☐ min	☐☐☐ min	☐☐☐ min
Decompression Completed at:	☐☐ H ☐☐ min	☐☐ H ☐☐ min	☐☐ H ☐☐ min
For surface decompression only: Surface interval:	☐☐☐ min	☐☐☐ min	☐☐☐ min
and time spent in chamber:	☐☐ H ☐☐ min	☐☐ H ☐☐ min	☐☐ H ☐☐ min

Saturation Dives:		
Storage depth:	☐☐☐ feet	☐☐☐ feet
Maximum depth of dive:	☐☐☐ feet	☐☐☐ feet
Time leaving storage depth:	☐☐ H ☐☐ min on ☐☐ day	☐☐ H ☐☐ min on ☐☐ day
Time returning to storage depth:	☐☐ H ☐☐ min on ☐☐ day	☐☐ H ☐☐ min on ☐☐ day
Bottom time:	☐☐ H ☐☐ min	☐☐ H ☐☐ min

Breathing Apparatus used: _____

Breathing Mixture used: _____

Work Description, Equipment and Tools Used:
_____
_____

Name of Decompression Schedules used: _____

Note regarding any
Decompression Sickness
or other Illness or Injury:
_____
_____
_____

Any Other Remarks: _____
_____
_____

Type of Dive	
Scuba	☐
Surface	☐
Wet Bell	☐
Bell Bounce	☐
Saturation	☐
Other	

_____
_____

APPROVED
Name of Diving Contractor: _____

Address of Diving Contractor _____

_____

Name of Diving Supervisor (Print) _____

Signature _____ Date: _____

RECORD OF DIVE

Date of Dive _____ Diver's Signature _____

BOTTOM CONDITION: (X appropriate blocks)
☐ Sand ☐ Shell ☐ Gravel ☐ Hard ☐ Soft

Geographic Location

SEA STATE:
☐ Calm ☐ Fair ☐ Moderate ☐ Heavy ☐ Gale Sea

_____

BOTTOM TEMPERATURE:
☐ Cold (below 55) ☐ Normal (55 to 75) ☐ Warm (above 75)

Vessel or Platform

BOTTOM VISIBILITY:
☐ Poor (0 to 5') ☐ Moderate (5' to 20') ☐ (Good 20 +)

_____

BOTTOM CURRENT:
☐ Weak (0 to 0.5KT) ☐ Moderate (0.5 to 2) ☐ Strong (2+)

_____

Bell Bounce or Surface Dives:	Dive One	Dive Two	Dive Three
Maximum depth of dive:	☐☐☐ feet	☐☐☐ feet	☐☐☐ feet
Time left surface or started pressurization:	☐☐ H ☐☐ min	☐☐ H ☐☐ min	☐☐ H ☐☐ min
Bottom Time:	☐☐☐ min	☐☐☐ min	☐☐☐ min
Decompression Completed at:	☐☐ H ☐☐ min	☐☐ H ☐☐ min	☐☐ H ☐☐ min
For surface decompression only:			
Surface interval:	☐☐☐ min	☐☐☐ min	☐☐☐ min
and time spent in chamber:	☐☐ H ☐☐ min	☐☐ H ☐☐ min	☐☐ H ☐☐ min

Saturation Dives:		
Storage depth:	☐☐☐ feet	☐☐☐ feet
Maximum depth of dive:	☐☐☐ feet	☐☐☐ feet
Time leaving storage depth:	☐☐ H ☐☐ min on ☐☐ day	☐☐ H ☐☐ min on ☐☐ day
Time returning to storage depth:	☐☐ H ☐☐ min on ☐☐ day	☐☐ H ☐☐ min on ☐☐ day
Bottom time:	☐☐ H ☐☐ min	☐☐ H ☐☐ min

Breathing Apparatus used: _____

Breathing Mixture used: _____

Work Description, Equipment and Tools Used: _____

Name of Decompression Schedules used: _____

Note regarding any
Decompression Sickness
or other Illness or Injury: _____

Any Other Remarks: _____

Type of Dive	
Scuba	☐
Surface	☐
Wet Bell	☐
Bell Bounce	☐
Saturation	☐
Other	

_____

APPROVED

Name of Diving Contractor: _____

Address of Diving Contractor _____

Name of Diving Supervisor (Print) _____

Signature _____ Date: _____

RECORD OF DIVE

Date of Dive _____ Diver's Signature _____

BOTTOM CONDITION: (X appropriate blocks)
☐ Sand ☐ Shell ☐ Gravel ☐ Hard ☐ Soft

SEA STATE:
☐ Calm ☐ Fair ☐ Moderate ☐ Heavy ☐ Gale Sea

BOTTOM TEMPERATURE:
☐ Cold (below 55) ☐ Normal (55 to 75) ☐ Warm (above 75)

BOTTOM VISIBILITY:
☐ Poor (0 to 5') ☐ Moderate (5' to 20') ☐ (Good 20 +)

BOTTOM CURRENT:
☐ Weak (0 to 0.5KT) ☐ Moderate (0.5 to 2) ☐ Strong (2+)

Geographic Location
_____

_____

Vessel or Platform
_____

_____

Bell Bounce or Surface Dives:

	Dive One	Dive Two	Dive Three
Maximum depth of dive:	☐☐☐ feet	☐☐☐ feet	☐☐☐ feet
Time left surface or started pressurization:	☐☐ H ☐☐ min	☐☐ H ☐☐ min	☐☐ H ☐☐ min
Bottom Time:	☐☐☐ min	☐☐☐ min	☐☐☐ min
Decompression Completed at:	☐☐ H ☐☐ min	☐☐ H ☐☐ min	☐☐ H ☐☐ min
For surface decompression only: Surface interval:	☐☐☐ min	☐☐☐ min	☐☐☐ min
and time spent in chamber:	☐☐ H ☐☐ min	☐☐ H ☐☐ min	☐☐ H ☐☐ min

Saturation Dives:

Storage depth:	☐☐☐ feet	☐☐☐ feet
Maximum depth of dive:	☐☐☐ feet	☐☐☐ feet
Time leaving storage depth:	☐☐ H ☐☐ min on ☐☐ day	☐☐ H ☐☐ min on ☐☐ day
Time returning to storage depth:	☐☐ H ☐☐ min on ☐☐ day	☐☐ H ☐☐ min on ☐☐ day
Bottom time:	☐☐ H ☐☐ min	☐☐ H ☐☐ min

Breathing Apparatus used: _____

_____

Breathing Mixture used: _____

Work Description, Equipment and Tools Used: _____

_____

_____

Name of Decompression Schedules used: _____

Note regarding any
Decompression Sickness
or other Illness or Injury: _____

_____

_____

Any Other Remarks: _____

_____

_____

Type of Dive

Scuba	
Surface	
Wet Bell	
Bell Bounce	
Saturation	

Other
_____

_____

APPROVED

Name of Diving Contractor: _____

Address of Diving Contractor _____

_____

Name of Diving Supervisor (Print) _____

Signature _____ Date: _____

RECORD OF DIVE

Date of Dive _____ Diver's Signature _____

BOTTOM CONDITION: (X appropriate blocks)
☐ Sand ☐ Shell ☐ Gravel ☐ Hard ☐ Soft

Geographic Location
_____

SEA STATE:
☐ Calm ☐ Fair ☐ Moderate ☐ Heavy ☐ Gale Sea
_____

BOTTOM TEMPERATURE:
☐ Cold (below 55) ☐ Normal (55 to 75) ☐ Warm (above 75)

Vessel or Platform

BOTTOM VISIBILITY:
☐ Poor (0 to 5') ☐ Moderate (5' to 20') ☐ (Good 20 +)
_____

BOTTOM CURRENT:
☐ Weak (0 to 0.5KT) ☐ Moderate (0.5 to 2) ☐ Strong (2+)
_____

Bell Bounce or Surface Dives:

	Dive One	Dive Two	Dive Three
Maximum depth of dive:	☐☐☐ feet	☐☐☐ feet	☐☐☐ feet
Time left surface or started pressurization:	☐☐ H ☐☐ min	☐☐ H ☐☐ min	☐☐ H ☐☐ min
Bottom Time:	☐☐☐ min	☐☐☐ min	☐☐☐ min
Decompression Completed at:	☐☐ H ☐☐ min	☐☐ H ☐☐ min	☐☐ H ☐☐ min
For surface decompression only: Surface interval:	☐☐☐ min	☐☐☐ min	☐☐☐ min
and time spent in chamber:	☐☐ H ☐☐ min	☐☐ H ☐☐ min	☐☐ H ☐☐ min

Saturation Dives:

Storage depth:	☐☐☐ feet	☐☐☐ feet
Maximum depth of dive:	☐☐☐ feet	☐☐☐ feet
Time leaving storage depth:	☐☐ H ☐☐ min on ☐☐ day	☐☐ H ☐☐ min on ☐☐ day
Time returning to storage depth:	☐☐ H ☐☐ min on ☐☐ day	☐☐ H ☐☐ min on ☐☐ day
Bottom time:	☐☐ H ☐☐ min	☐☐ H ☐☐ min

Breathing Apparatus used: _____

Breathing Mixture used: _____

Work Description, Equipment and Tools Used: _____
_____

Name of Decompression Schedules used: _____

Note regarding any Decompression Sickness or other Illness or Injury: _____
_____
_____

Any Other Remarks: _____
_____
_____

Type of Dive

Scuba	☐
Surface	☐
Wet Bell	☐
Bell Bounce	☐
Saturation	☐

Other
_____
_____

APPROVED

Name of Diving Contractor: _____

Address of Diving Contractor _____
_____

Name of Diving Supervisor (Print) _____

Signature _____ Date: _____

RECORD OF DIVE

Date of Dive _____ Diver's Signature _____

BOTTOM CONDITION: (X appropriate blocks)   Geographic Location
☐ Sand ☐ Shell ☐ Gravel ☐ Hard ☐ Soft
SEA STATE: _____
☐ Calm ☐ Fair ☐ Moderate ☐ Heavy ☐ Gale Sea
BOTTOM TEMPERATURE:
☐ Cold (below 55) ☐ Normal (55 to 75) ☐ Warm (above 75)   Vessel or Platform
BOTTOM VISIBILITY:
☐ Poor (0 to 5′) ☐ Moderate (5′ to 20′) ☐ (Good 20 +)   _____
BOTTOM CURRENT:
☐ Weak (0 to 0.5KT) ☐ Moderate (0.5 to 2) ☐ Strong (2+)   _____

Bell Bounce or Surface Dives:	Dive One	Dive Two	Dive Three
Maximum depth of dive:	☐☐☐ feet	☐☐☐ feet	☐☐☐ feet
Time left surface or started pressurization:	☐☐ H ☐☐ min	☐☐ H ☐☐ min	☐☐ H ☐☐ min
Bottom Time:	☐☐☐ min	☐☐☐ min	☐☐☐ min
Decompression Completed at:	☐☐ H ☐☐ min	☐☐ H ☐☐ min	☐☐ H ☐☐ min
For surface decompression only: Surface interval:	☐☐ min	☐☐ min	☐☐ min
and time spent in chamber:	☐☐ H ☐☐ min	☐☐ H ☐☐ min	☐☐ H ☐☐ min

Saturation Dives:		
Storage depth:	☐☐☐ feet	☐☐☐ feet
Maximum depth of dive:	☐☐☐ feet	☐☐☐ feet
Time leaving storage depth:	☐☐ H ☐☐ min on ☐☐ day	☐☐ H ☐☐ min on ☐☐ day
Time returning to storage depth:	☐☐ H ☐☐ min on ☐☐ day	☐☐ H ☐☐ min on ☐☐ day
Bottom time:	☐☐ H ☐☐ min	☐☐ H ☐☐ min

Breathing Apparatus used: _____

_____

Breathing Mixture used: _____

_____

Work Description, Equipment and Tools Used: _____

_____

_____

Type of Dive	
Scuba	
Surface	
Wet Bell	
Bell Bounce	
Saturation	
Other	

Name of Decompression Schedules used: _____

Note regarding any   _____
Decompression Sickness   _____
or other Illness or Injury: _____

Any Other Remarks: _____

_____

_____

APPROVED
Name of Diving Contractor: _____

Address of Diving Contractor _____

_____

Name of Diving Supervisor (Print) _____

Signature _____ Date: _____

RECORD OF DIVE

Date of Dive _____ Diver's Signature _____

BOTTOM CONDITION: (X appropriate blocks)
☐ Sand ☐ Shell ☐ Gravel ☐ Hard ☐ Soft

Geographic Location

SEA STATE:
☐ Calm ☐ Fair ☐ Moderate ☐ Heavy ☐ Gale Sea

_____

BOTTOM TEMPERATURE:
☐ Cold (below 55) ☐ Normal (55 to 75) ☐ Warm (above 75)

_____

Vessel or Platform

BOTTOM VISIBILITY:
☐ Poor (0 to 5') ☐ Moderate (5' to 20') ☐ (Good 20 +)

_____

BOTTOM CURRENT:
☐ Weak (0 to 0.5KT) ☐ Moderate (0.5 to 2) ☐ Strong (2+)

_____

Bell Bounce or Surface Dives:	Dive One	Dive Two	Dive Three
Maximum depth of dive:	☐☐ feet	☐☐ feet	☐☐ feet
Time left surface or started pressurization:	☐☐ H ☐☐ min	☐☐ H ☐☐ min	☐☐ H ☐☐ min
Bottom Time:	☐☐ min	☐☐ min	☐☐ min
Decompression Completed at:	☐☐ H ☐☐ min	☐☐ H ☐☐ min	☐☐ H ☐☐ min
For surface decompression only:			
Surface interval:	☐☐ min	☐☐ min	☐☐ min
and time spent in chamber:	☐☐ H ☐☐ min	☐☐ H ☐☐ min	☐☐ H ☐☐ min

Saturation Dives:		
Storage depth:	☐☐☐ feet	☐☐☐ feet
Maximum depth of dive:	☐☐☐ feet	☐☐☐ feet
Time leaving storage depth:	☐☐ H ☐☐ min on ☐☐ day	☐☐ H ☐☐ min on ☐☐ day
Time returning to storage depth:	☐☐ H ☐☐ min on ☐☐ day	☐☐ H ☐☐ min on ☐☐ day
Bottom time:	☐☐ H ☐☐ min	☐☐ H ☐☐ min

Breathing Apparatus used: _____

Breathing Mixture used: _____

Work Description, Equipment and Tools Used: _____
_____

Name of Decompression Schedules used: _____

Note regarding any Decompression Sickness or other Illness or Injury: _____

Any Other Remarks: _____
_____
_____

Type of Dive	
Scuba	☐
Surface	☐
Wet Bell	☐
Bell Bounce	☐
Saturation	☐
Other	_____
	_____
	_____

APPROVED

Name of Diving Contractor: _____

Address of Diving Contractor _____
_____

Name of Diving Supervisor (Print) _____

Signature _____ Date: _____

RECORD OF DIVE

Date of Dive _____ Diver's Signature _____

BOTTOM CONDITION: (X appropriate blocks)
☐ Sand ☐ Shell ☐ Gravel ☐ Hard ☐ Soft

Geographic Location
_____

SEA STATE:
☐ Calm ☐ Fair ☐ Moderate ☐ Heavy ☐ Gale Sea

_____

BOTTOM TEMPERATURE:
☐ Cold (below 55) ☐ Normal (55 to 75) ☐ Warm (above 75)

Vessel or Platform

BOTTOM VISIBILITY:
☐ Poor (0 to 5') ☐ Moderate (5' to 20') ☐ (Good 20 +)

_____

BOTTOM CURRENT:
☐ Weak (0 to 0.5KT) ☐ Moderate (0.5 to 2) ☐ Strong (2+)

_____

Bell Bounce or Surface Dives:	Dive One	Dive Two	Dive Three
Maximum depth of dive:	☐☐☐ feet	☐☐☐ feet	☐☐☐ feet
Time left surface or started pressurization:	☐☐ H ☐☐ min	☐☐ H ☐☐ min	☐☐ H ☐☐ min
Bottom Time:	☐☐ min	☐☐ min	☐☐ min
Decompression Completed at:	☐☐ H ☐☐ min	☐☐ H ☐☐ min	☐☐ H ☐☐ min
For surface decompression only: Surface interval:	☐☐ min	☐☐ min	☐☐ min
and time spent in chamber:	☐☐ H ☐☐ min	☐☐ H ☐☐ min	☐☐ H ☐☐ min

Saturation Dives:		
Storage depth:	☐☐☐ feet	☐☐☐ feet
Maximum depth of dive:	☐☐☐ feet	☐☐☐ feet
Time leaving storage depth:	☐☐ H ☐☐ min on ☐☐ day	☐☐ H ☐☐ min on ☐☐ day
Time returning to storage depth:	☐☐ H ☐☐ min on ☐☐ day	☐☐ H ☐☐ min on ☐☐ day
Bottom time:	☐☐ H ☐☐ min	☐☐ H ☐☐ min

Breathing Apparatus used: _____

Breathing Mixture used: _____

Work Description, Equipment and Tools Used:
_____
_____

Name of Decompression Schedules used: _____

Note regarding any
Decompression Sickness
or other Illness or Injury:
_____

Any Other Remarks: _____
_____
_____

Type of Dive	
Scuba	
Surface	
Wet Bell	
Bell Bounce	
Saturation	
Other	

APPROVED
Name of Diving Contractor: _____

Address of Diving Contractor _____
_____

Name of Diving Supervisor (Print) _____

Signature _____ Date: _____

RECORD OF DIVE

Date of Dive _____ Diver's Signature _____

BOTTOM CONDITION: (X appropriate blocks)
☐ Sand ☐ Shell ☐ Gravel ☐ Hard ☐ Soft

Geographic Location

SEA STATE:
☐ Calm ☐ Fair ☐ Moderate ☐ Heavy ☐ Gale Sea

_____

BOTTOM TEMPERATURE:
☐ Cold (below 55) ☐ Normal (55 to 75) ☐ Warm (above 75)

Vessel or Platform

BOTTOM VISIBILITY:
☐ Poor (0 to 5') ☐ Moderate (5' to 20') ☐ (Good 20 +)

_____

BOTTOM CURRENT:
☐ Weak (0 to 0.5KT) ☐ Moderate (0.5 to 2) ☐ Strong (2+)

_____

Bell Bounce or Surface Dives:	Dive One	Dive Two	Dive Three
Maximum depth of dive:	☐☐☐ feet	☐☐☐ feet	☐☐☐ feet
Time left surface or started pressurization:	☐☐ H ☐☐ min	☐☐ H ☐☐ min	☐☐ H ☐☐ min
Bottom Time:	☐☐☐ min	☐☐☐ min	☐☐☐ min
Decompression Completed at:	☐☐ H ☐☐ min	☐☐ H ☐☐ min	☐☐ H ☐☐ min
For surface decompression only: Surface interval:	☐☐☐ min	☐☐☐ min	☐☐☐ min
and time spent in chamber:	☐☐ H ☐☐ min	☐☐ H ☐☐ min	☐☐ H ☐☐ min

Saturation Dives:		
Storage depth:	☐☐☐☐ feet	☐☐☐☐ feet
Maximum depth of dive:	☐☐☐☐ feet	☐☐☐☐ feet
Time leaving storage depth:	☐☐ H ☐☐ min on ☐☐ day	☐☐ H ☐☐ min on ☐☐ day
Time returning to storage depth:	☐☐ H ☐☐ min on ☐☐ day	☐☐ H ☐☐ min on ☐☐ day
Bottom time:	☐☐ H ☐☐ min	☐☐ H ☐☐ min

Breathing Apparatus used: _____

Breathing Mixture used: _____

Work Description, Equipment and Tools Used: _____

_____

Name of Decompression Schedules used: _____

Note regarding any
Decompression Sickness
or other Illness or Injury: _____

Any Other Remarks: _____

_____

Type of Dive	
Scuba	☐
Surface	☐
Wet Bell	☐
Bell Bounce	☐
Saturation	☐
Other	

_____

APPROVED

Name of Diving Contractor: _____

Address of Diving Contractor _____

_____

Name of Diving Supervisor (Print) _____

Signature _____ Date: _____

DIVE SUMMARY SHEET

Year	0-100'	101-165'	166-300'	301-500'	501-1000'	1000+	A	B	C	D

A. Number of Air Dives
B. Number of Gas Dives

C. Number of Saturation Dives
D. Number of Days Worked This Year

- 224 -